DECALOGUE

Writer: Brian Michael Bendis
Artist: Alex Maleev

Colorist: Dave Stewart
Letterers: Virtual Calligraphy's Cory Petit
Editor: Jennifer Lee
Assistant Editor: Cory Sedlmeier
Executive Editor: Axel Alonso
Special thanks to Nathan Cosby

Collection Editor: Jennifer Grünwald
Assistant Editor: Michael Short
Senior Editor, Special Projects: Jeff Youngquist
Director of Sales: David Gabriel
Production: Loretta Krol
Book Designer: Jeof Vita
Creative Director: Tom Marvelli

Editor in Chief: Joe Quesada
Publisher: Dan Buckley

PREVIOUSLY

One of the biggest tabloid newspapers in the city
outed Matt Murdock: Daredevil's Secret Identity
Revealed.

The secret is out.

Matt Murdock is now faced with a continuing
uphill battle of publicly denying his secret life
as Daredevil for fear of disbarment or jail. But
Matt's public struggle makes his alter ego more
popular with the people than ever before.

Then Daredevil does the unthinkable.

Faced with the growing frustration that his fight
with the Kingpin would never end, Daredevil beats
him and declares himself the Kingpin. His new
rule is clean up or get out.

That was a year ago.

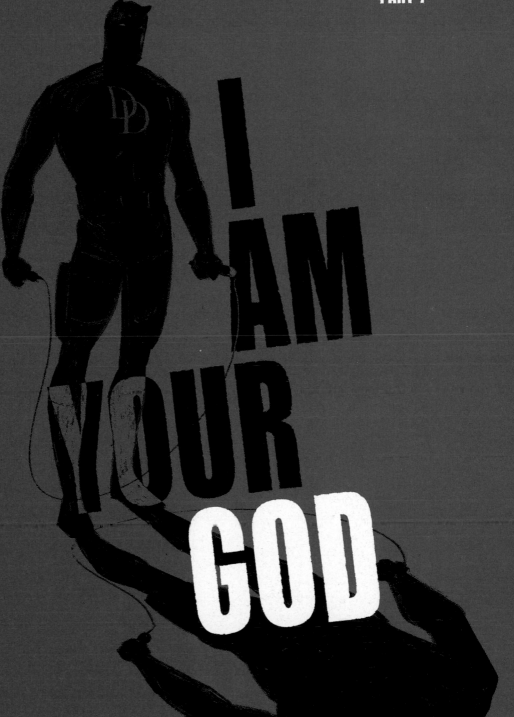

DAREDEVIL

DECALOGUE
PART 1

#71

I AM YOUR GOD

THE DEVIL AMONG US

A conversation support group of Hell's Kitchen to discuss Daredevil and the effect on your daily life.
Join Reverend...
discussion.
Participation urged but not required.

Where:
St. Mary's Church
Basement room 2
7:30 p.m.
Wednesday nights

Light refreshments.

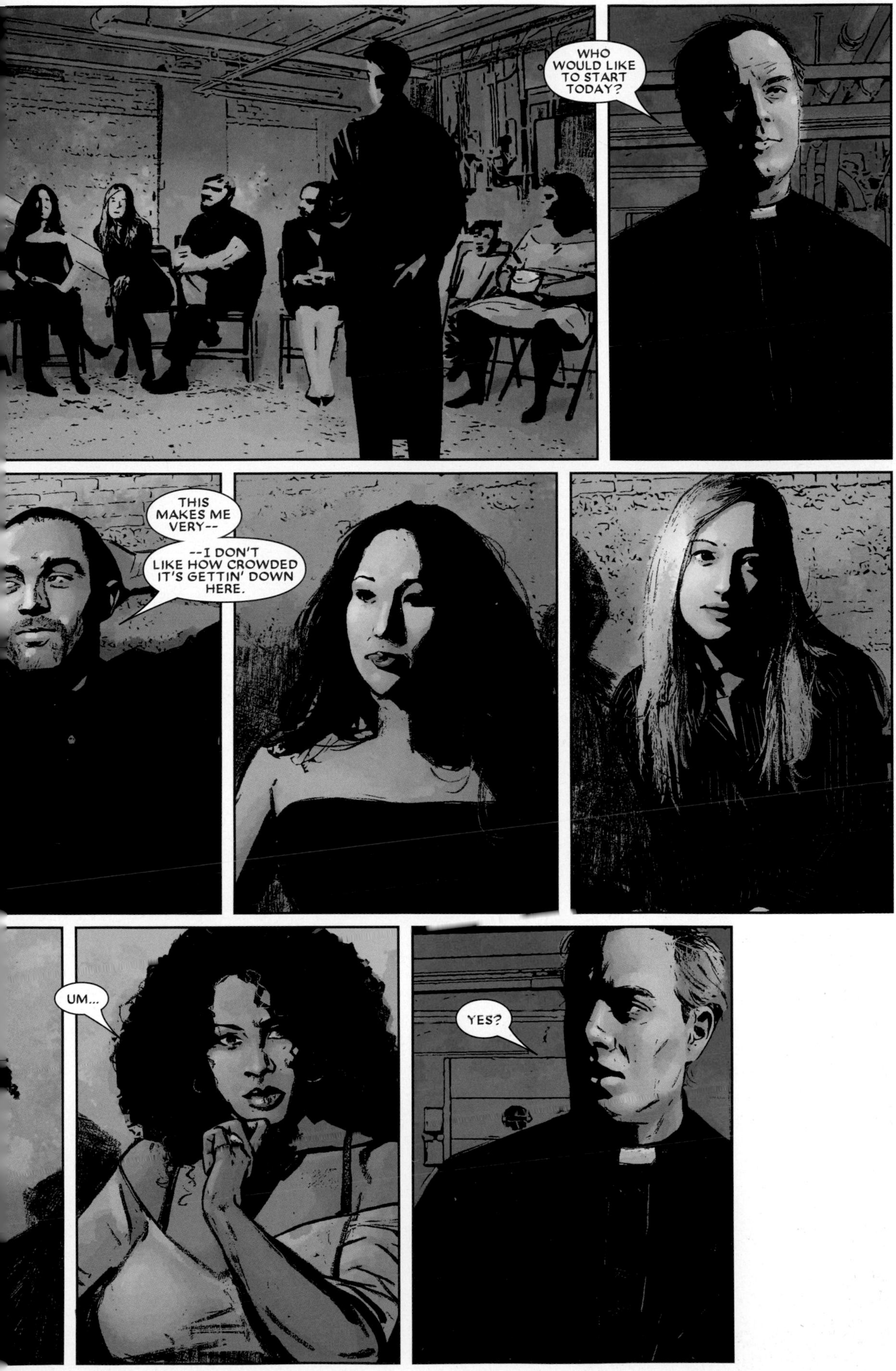
WHO WOULD LIKE TO START TODAY?
THIS MAKES ME VERY--
--I DON'T LIKE HOW CROWDED IT'S GETTIN' DOWN HERE.
UM...
YES?

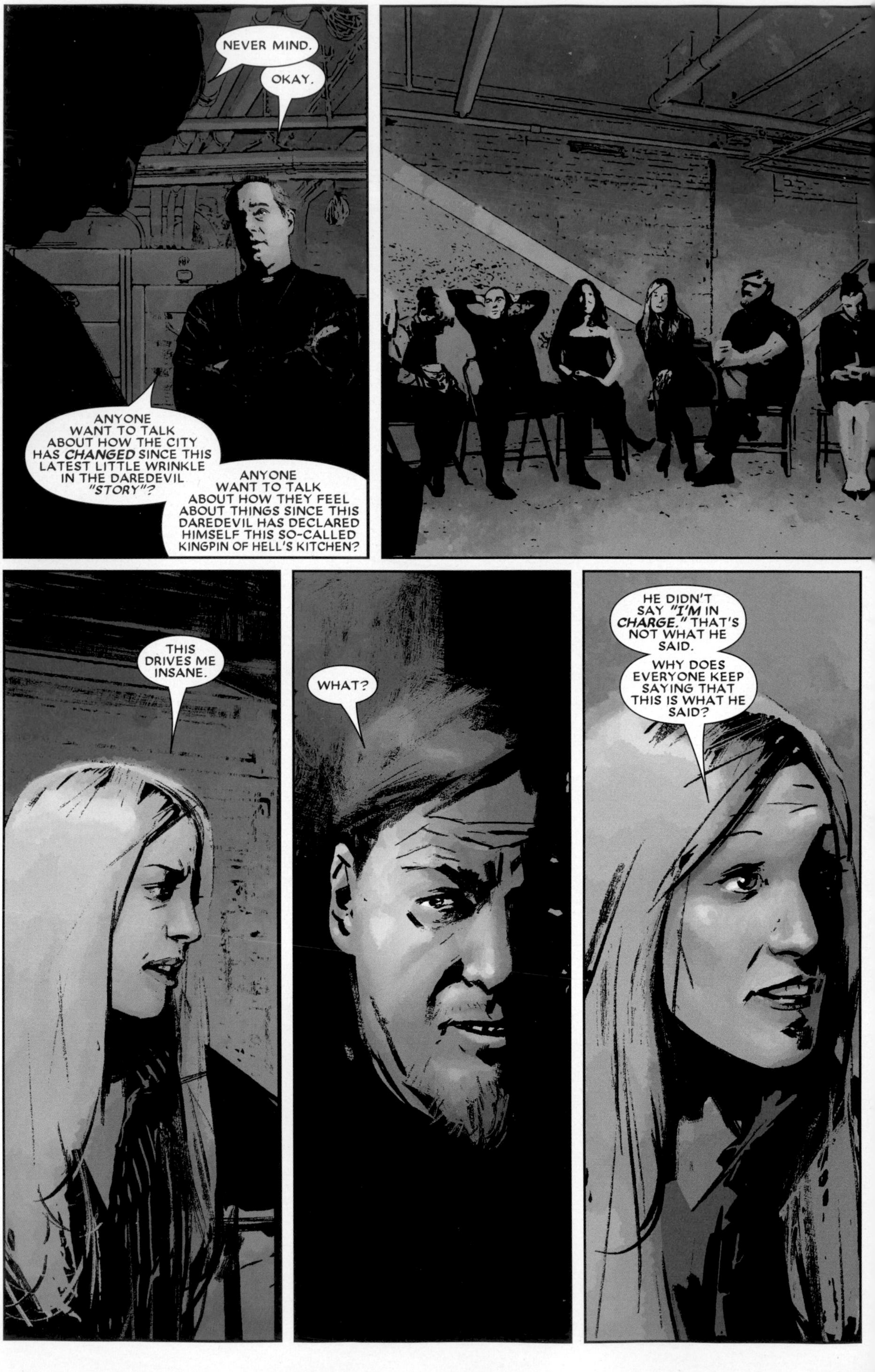
NEVER MIND.
OKAY.
ANYONE WANT TO TALK ABOUT HOW THE CITY HAS *CHANGED* SINCE THIS LATEST LITTLE WRINKLE IN THE DAREDEVIL *"STORY"*?
ANYONE WANT TO TALK ABOUT HOW THEY FEEL ABOUT THINGS SINCE THIS DAREDEVIL HAS DECLARED HIMSELF THIS SO-CALLED KINGPIN OF HELL'S KITCHEN?
THIS DRIVES ME INSANE.
WHAT?
HE DIDN'T SAY *"I'M IN CHARGE."* THAT'S NOT WHAT HE SAID.
WHY DOES EVERYONE KEEP SAYING THAT THIS IS WHAT HE SAID?

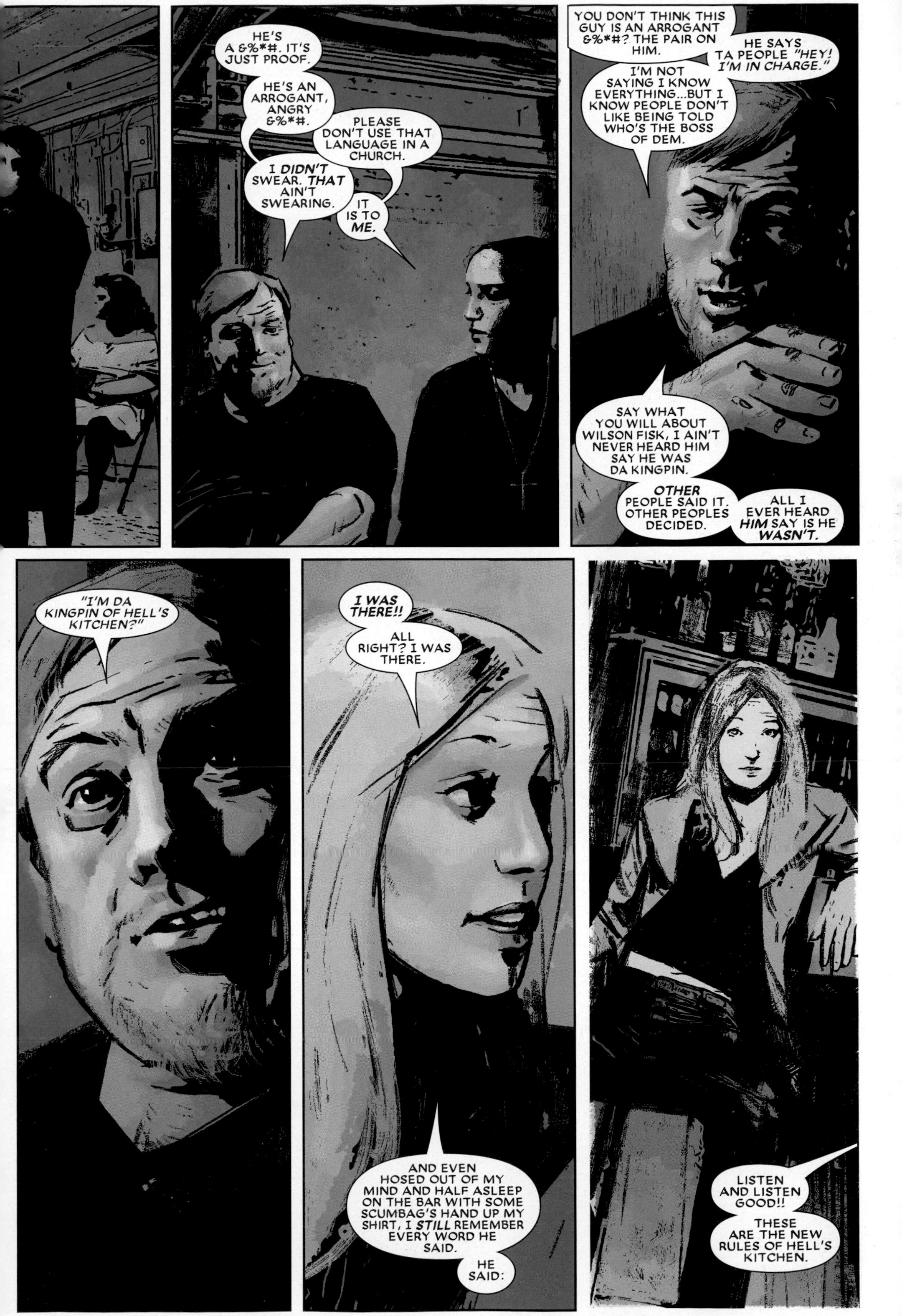
HE'S A &%*#. IT'S JUST PROOF.
HE'S AN ARROGANT, ANGRY &%*#.
PLEASE DON'T USE THAT LANGUAGE IN A CHURCH.
I DIDN'T SWEAR. THAT AIN'T SWEARING.
IT IS TO ME.
YOU DON'T THINK THIS GUY IS AN ARROGANT &%*#? THE PAIR ON HIM.
HE SAYS TA PEOPLE "HEY! I'M IN CHARGE."
I'M NOT SAYING I KNOW EVERYTHING...BUT I KNOW PEOPLE DON'T LIKE BEING TOLD WHO'S THE BOSS OF DEM.
SAY WHAT YOU WILL ABOUT WILSON FISK, I AIN'T NEVER HEARD HIM SAY HE WAS DA KINGPIN.
OTHER PEOPLE SAID IT. OTHER PEOPLES DECIDED.
ALL I EVER HEARD HIM SAY IS HE WASN'T.
"I'M DA KINGPIN OF HELL'S KITCHEN?"
I WAS THERE!!
ALL RIGHT? I WAS THERE.
AND EVEN HOSED OUT OF MY MIND AND HALF ASLEEP ON THE BAR WITH SOME SCUMBAG'S HAND UP MY SHIRT, I STILL REMEMBER EVERY WORD HE SAID.
HE SAID:
LISTEN AND LISTEN GOOD!!
THESE ARE THE NEW RULES OF HELL'S KITCHEN.

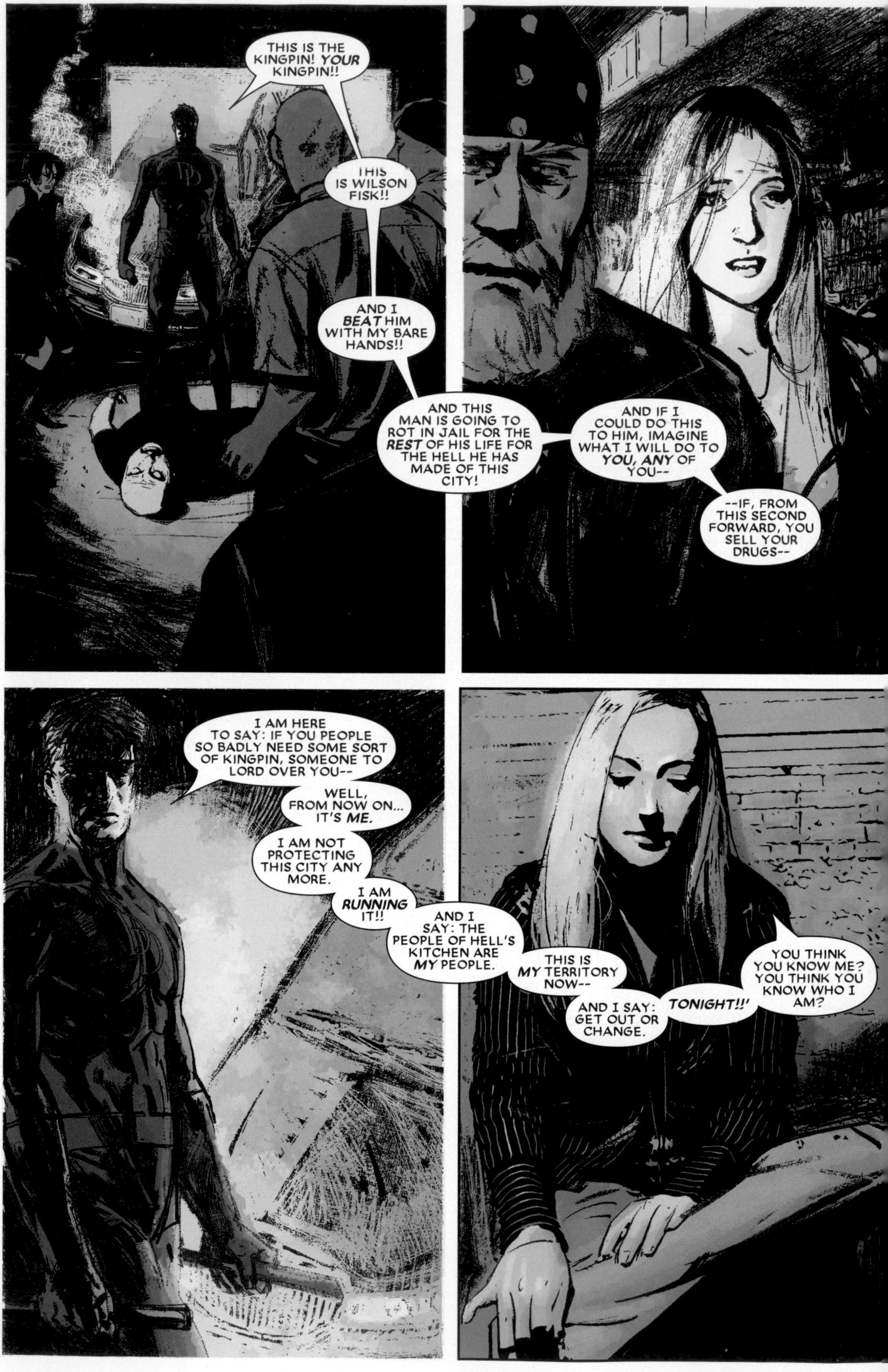
THIS IS THE KINGPIN! YOUR KINGPIN!!
THIS IS WILSON FISK!!
AND I BEAT HIM WITH MY BARE HANDS!!
AND THIS MAN IS GOING TO ROT IN JAIL FOR THE REST OF HIS LIFE FOR THE HELL HE HAS MADE OF THIS CITY!
AND IF I COULD DO THIS TO HIM, IMAGINE WHAT I WILL DO TO YOU, ANY OF YOU--
--IF, FROM THIS SECOND FORWARD, YOU SELL YOUR DRUGS--
I AM HERE TO SAY: IF YOU PEOPLE SO BADLY NEED SOME SORT OF KINGPIN, SOMEONE TO LORD OVER YOU--
WELL, FROM NOW ON... IT'S ME.
I AM NOT PROTECTING THIS CITY ANY MORE.
I AM RUNNING IT!!
AND I SAY: THE PEOPLE OF HELL'S KITCHEN ARE MY PEOPLE.
THIS IS MY TERRITORY NOW--
AND I SAY: GET OUT OR CHANGE.
TONIGHT!!'
YOU THINK YOU KNOW ME? YOU THINK YOU KNOW WHO I AM?

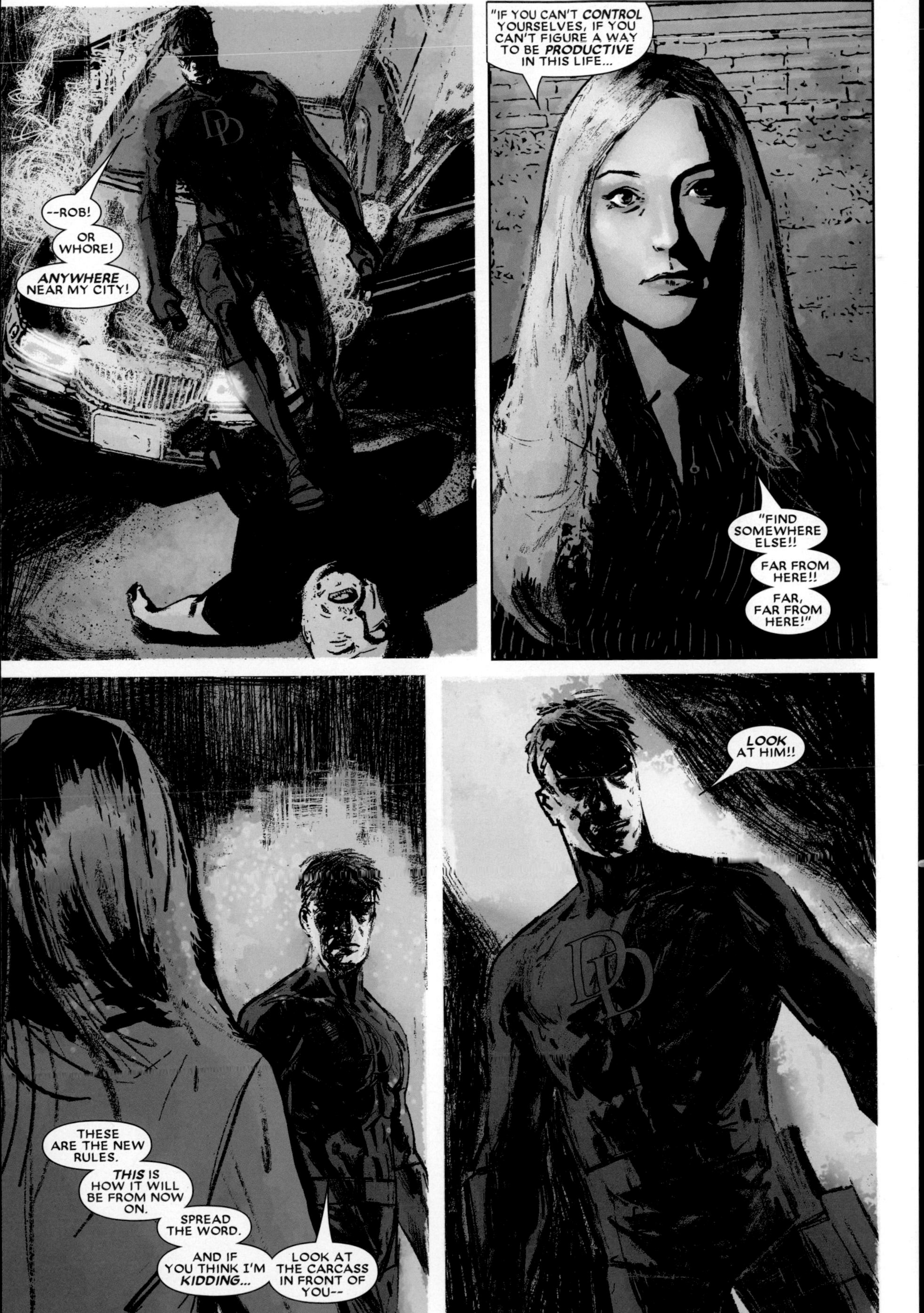
--ROB!
OR WHORE!
ANYWHERE NEAR MY CITY!
"IF YOU CAN'T CONTROL YOURSELVES, IF YOU CAN'T FIGURE A WAY TO BE PRODUCTIVE IN THIS LIFE...
"FIND SOMEWHERE ELSE!!
FAR FROM HERE!!
FAR, FAR FROM HERE!"
THESE ARE THE NEW RULES.
THIS IS HOW IT WILL BE FROM NOW ON.
SPREAD THE WORD.
AND IF YOU THINK I'M KIDDING...
LOOK AT THE CARCASS IN FRONT OF YOU--
LOOK AT HIM!!

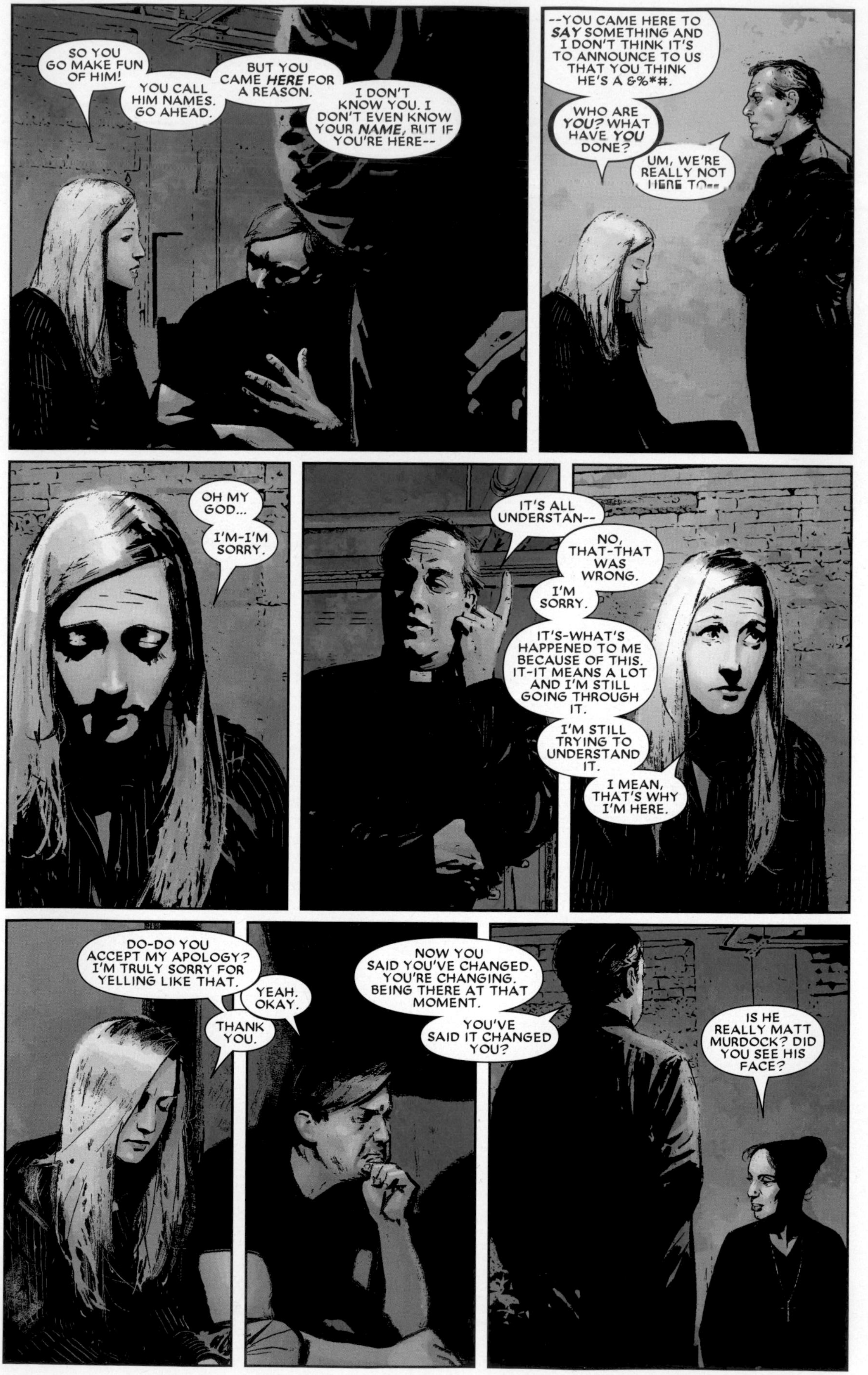
SO YOU GO MAKE FUN OF HIM!
YOU CALL HIM NAMES. GO AHEAD.
BUT YOU CAME HERE FOR A REASON.
I DON'T KNOW YOU. I DON'T EVEN KNOW YOUR NAME, BUT IF YOU'RE HERE--
--YOU CAME HERE TO SAY SOMETHING AND I DON'T THINK IT'S TO ANNOUNCE TO US THAT YOU THINK HE'S A &%*#.
WHO ARE YOU? WHAT HAVE YOU DONE?
UM, WE'RE REALLY NOT HERE TO--
OH MY GOD...
I'M-I'M SORRY.
IT'S ALL UNDERSTAN--
NO, THAT-THAT WAS WRONG.
I'M SORRY.
IT'S-WHAT'S HAPPENED TO ME BECAUSE OF THIS. IT-IT MEANS A LOT AND I'M STILL GOING THROUGH IT.
I'M STILL TRYING TO UNDERSTAND IT.
I MEAN, THAT'S WHY I'M HERE.
DO-DO YOU ACCEPT MY APOLOGY? I'M TRULY SORRY FOR YELLING LIKE THAT.
YEAH. OKAY.
THANK YOU.
NOW YOU SAID YOU'VE CHANGED. YOU'RE CHANGING. BEING THERE AT THAT MOMENT.
YOU'VE SAID IT CHANGED YOU?
IS HE REALLY MATT MURDOCK? DID YOU SEE HIS FACE?

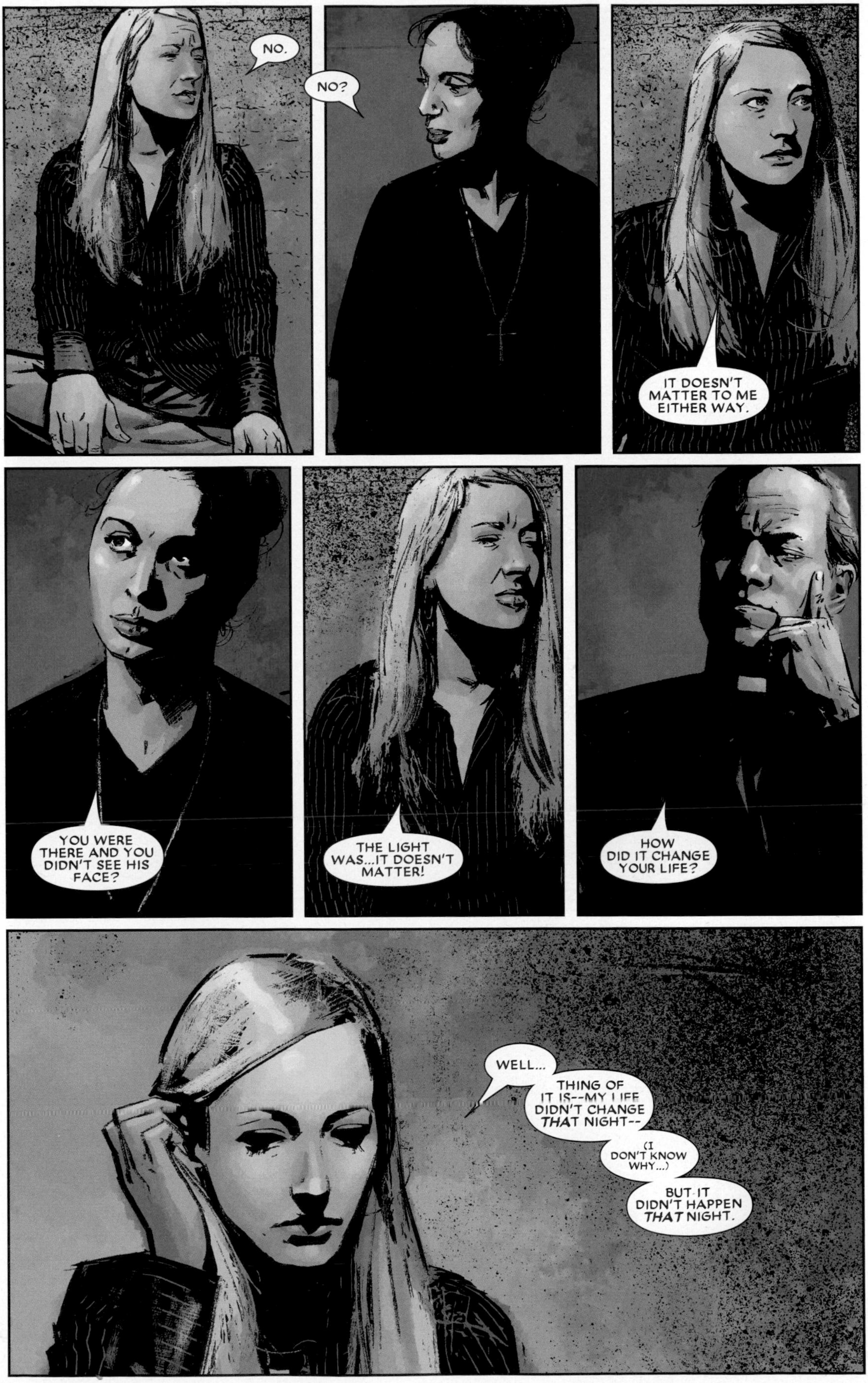
NO.
NO?
IT DOESN'T MATTER TO ME EITHER WAY.
YOU WERE THERE AND YOU DIDN'T SEE HIS FACE?
THE LIGHT WAS...IT DOESN'T MATTER!
HOW DID IT CHANGE YOUR LIFE?
WELL...
THING OF IT IS--MY LIFE DIDN'T CHANGE *THAT* NIGHT--
(I DON'T KNOW WHY...)
BUT IT DIDN'T HAPPEN *THAT* NIGHT.

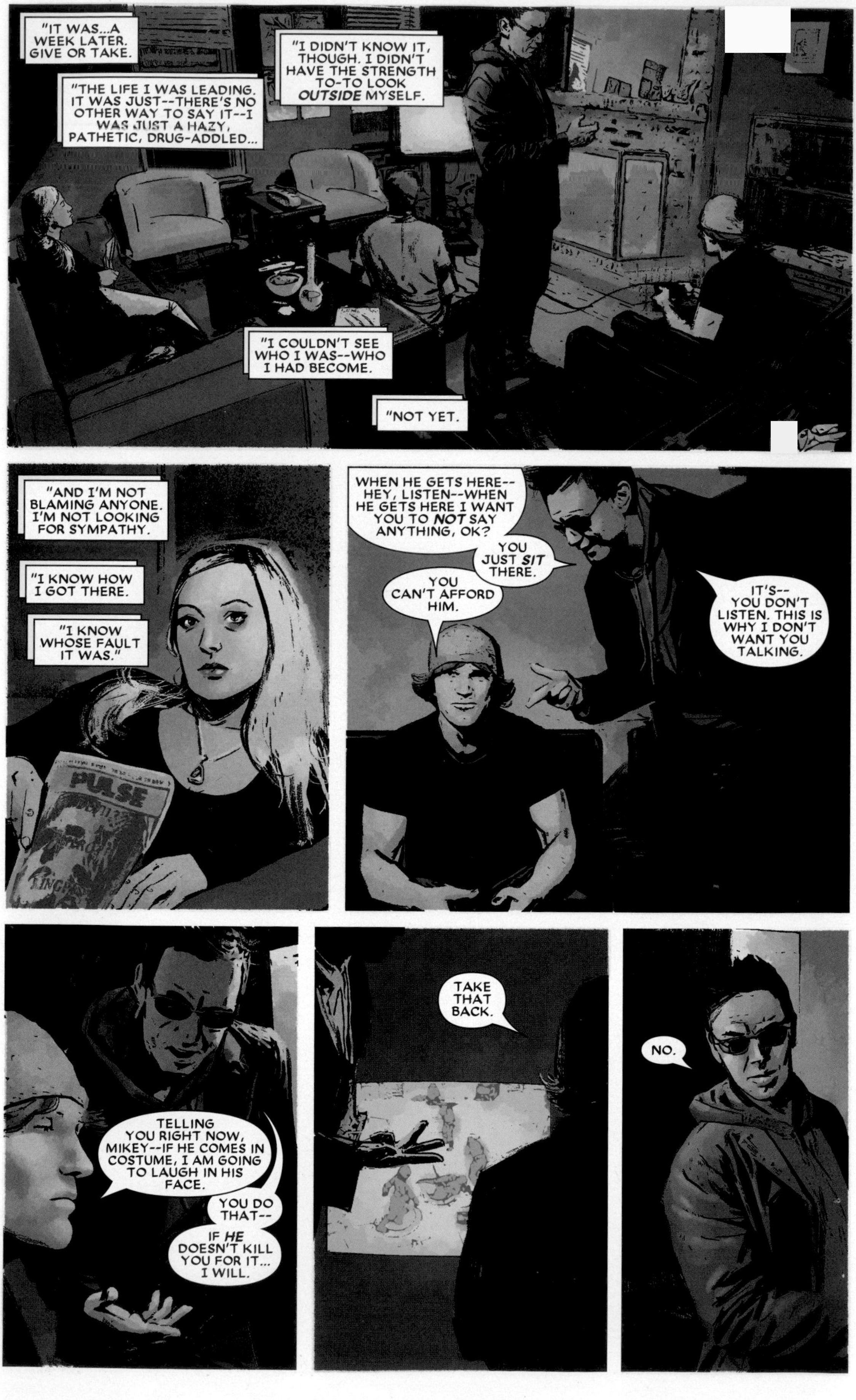
"IT WAS...A WEEK LATER. GIVE OR TAKE.
"THE LIFE I WAS LEADING. IT WAS JUST--THERE'S NO OTHER WAY TO SAY IT--I WAS JUST A HAZY, PATHETIC, DRUG-ADDLED...
"I DIDN'T KNOW IT, THOUGH. I DIDN'T HAVE THE STRENGTH TO-TO LOOK OUTSIDE MYSELF.
"I COULDN'T SEE WHO I WAS--WHO I HAD BECOME.
"NOT YET.
"AND I'M NOT BLAMING ANYONE. I'M NOT LOOKING FOR SYMPATHY.
"I KNOW HOW I GOT THERE.
"I KNOW WHOSE FAULT IT WAS."
PULSE
WHEN HE GETS HERE--HEY, LISTEN--WHEN HE GETS HERE I WANT YOU TO NOT SAY ANYTHING, OK?
YOU JUST SIT THERE.
YOU CAN'T AFFORD HIM.
IT'S--YOU DON'T LISTEN. THIS IS WHY I DON'T WANT YOU TALKING.
TELLING YOU RIGHT NOW, MIKEY--IF HE COMES IN COSTUME, I AM GOING TO LAUGH IN HIS FACE.
YOU DO THAT--
IF HE DOESN'T KILL YOU FOR IT... I WILL.
TAKE THAT BACK.
NO.

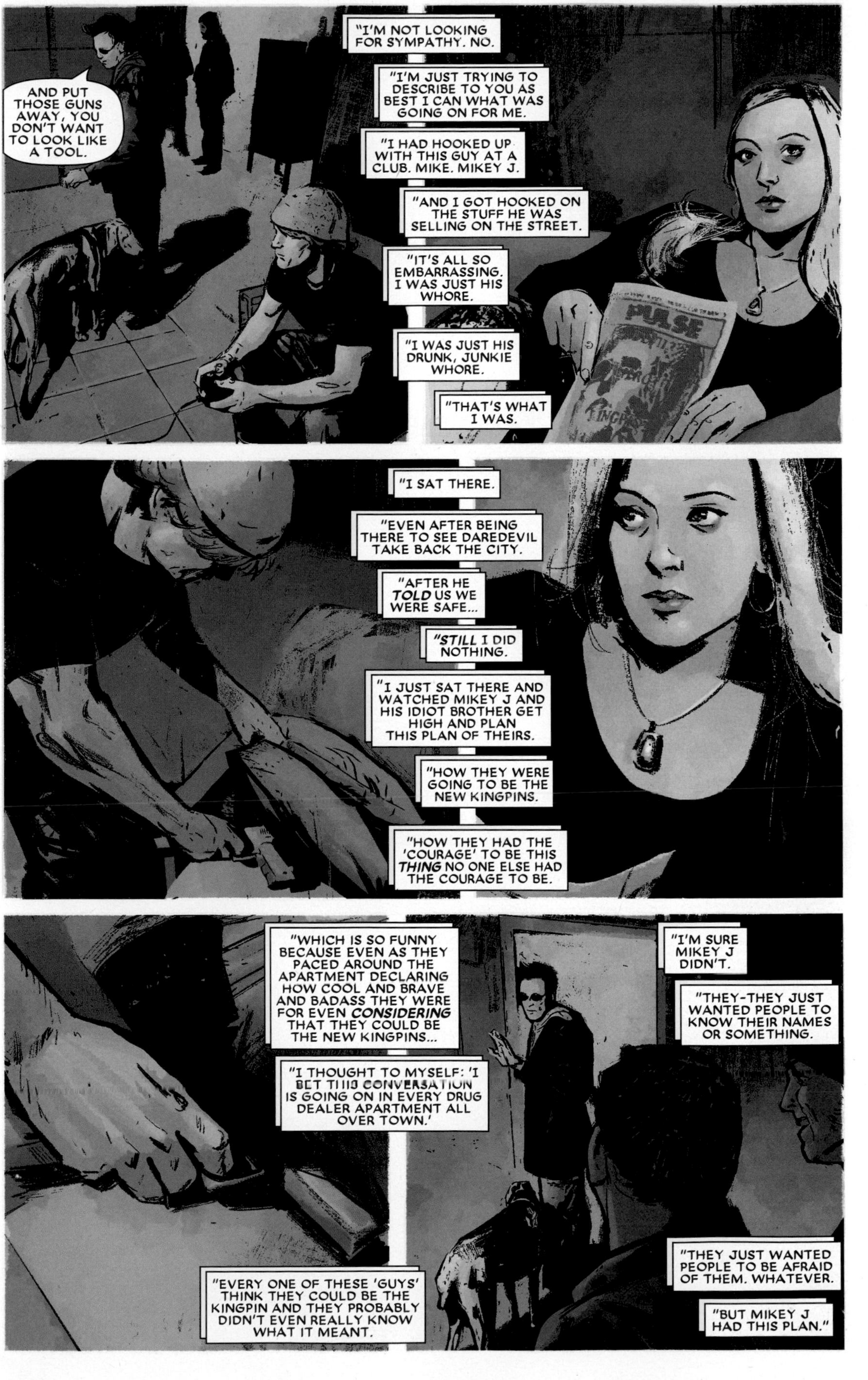

AND PUT THOSE GUNS AWAY, YOU DON'T WANT TO LOOK LIKE A TOOL.
"I'M NOT LOOKING FOR SYMPATHY. NO.
"I'M JUST TRYING TO DESCRIBE TO YOU AS BEST I CAN WHAT WAS GOING ON FOR ME.
"I HAD HOOKED UP WITH THIS GUY AT A CLUB. MIKE. MIKEY J.
"AND I GOT HOOKED ON THE STUFF HE WAS SELLING ON THE STREET.
"IT'S ALL SO EMBARRASSING. I WAS JUST HIS WHORE.
"I WAS JUST HIS DRUNK, JUNKIE WHORE.
"THAT'S WHAT I WAS.
PULSE
"I SAT THERE.
"EVEN AFTER BEING THERE TO SEE DAREDEVIL TAKE BACK THE CITY.
"AFTER HE *TOLD* US WE WERE SAFE...
"*STILL* I DID NOTHING.
"I JUST SAT THERE AND WATCHED MIKEY J AND HIS IDIOT BROTHER GET HIGH AND PLAN THIS PLAN OF THEIRS.
"HOW THEY WERE GOING TO BE THE NEW KINGPINS.
"HOW THEY HAD THE 'COURAGE' TO BE THIS *THING* NO ONE ELSE HAD THE COURAGE TO BE.
"WHICH IS SO FUNNY BECAUSE EVEN AS THEY PACED AROUND THE APARTMENT DECLARING HOW COOL AND BRAVE AND BADASS THEY WERE FOR EVEN *CONSIDERING* THAT THEY COULD BE THE NEW KINGPINS...
"I THOUGHT TO MYSELF: 'I BET THIS CONVERSATION IS GOING ON IN EVERY DRUG DEALER APARTMENT ALL OVER TOWN.'
"EVERY ONE OF THESE 'GUYS' THINK THEY COULD BE THE KINGPIN AND THEY PROBABLY DIDN'T EVEN REALLY KNOW WHAT IT MEANT.
"I'M SURE MIKEY J DIDN'T.
"THEY-THEY JUST WANTED PEOPLE TO KNOW THEIR NAMES OR SOMETHING.
"THEY JUST WANTED PEOPLE TO BE AFRAID OF THEM. WHATEVER.
"BUT MIKEY J HAD THIS PLAN."

"MIKEY J KNEW SOMEONE WHO KNEW SOMEONE WHO KNEW A GUY NAMED...
"...BULLET.
"SO THEY CALLED A MEETING."

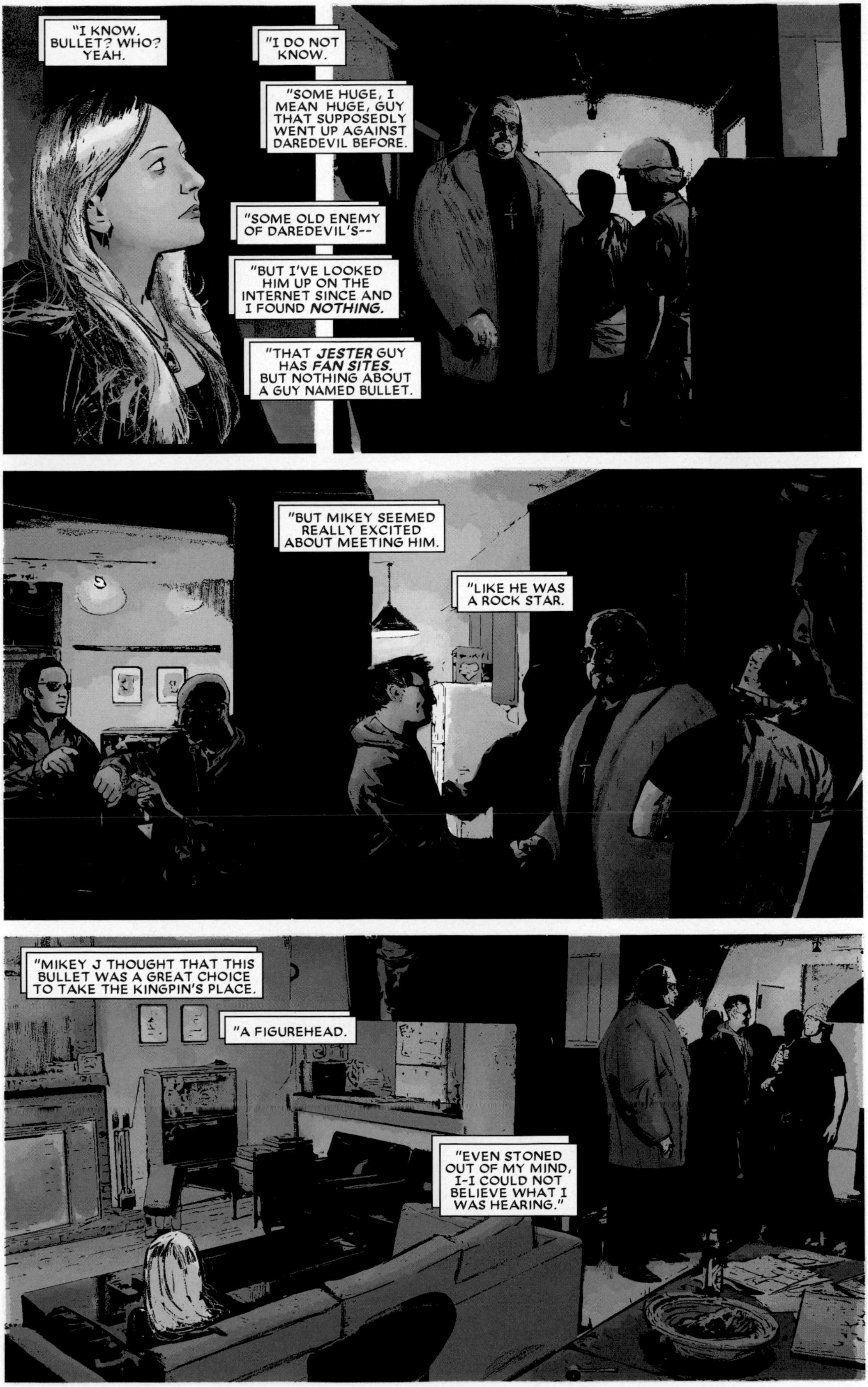
"I KNOW. BULLET? WHO? YEAH.
"I DO NOT KNOW.
"SOME HUGE, I MEAN HUGE, GUY THAT SUPPOSEDLY WENT UP AGAINST DAREDEVIL BEFORE.
"SOME OLD ENEMY OF DAREDEVIL'S--
"BUT I'VE LOOKED HIM UP ON THE INTERNET SINCE AND I FOUND NOTHING.
"THAT JESTER GUY HAS FAN SITES. BUT NOTHING ABOUT A GUY NAMED BULLET.
"BUT MIKEY SEEMED REALLY EXCITED ABOUT MEETING HIM.
"LIKE HE WAS A ROCK STAR.
"MIKEY J THOUGHT THAT THIS BULLET WAS A GREAT CHOICE TO TAKE THE KINGPIN'S PLACE.
"A FIGUREHEAD.
"EVEN STONED OUT OF MY MIND, I-I COULD NOT BELIEVE WHAT I WAS HEARING."

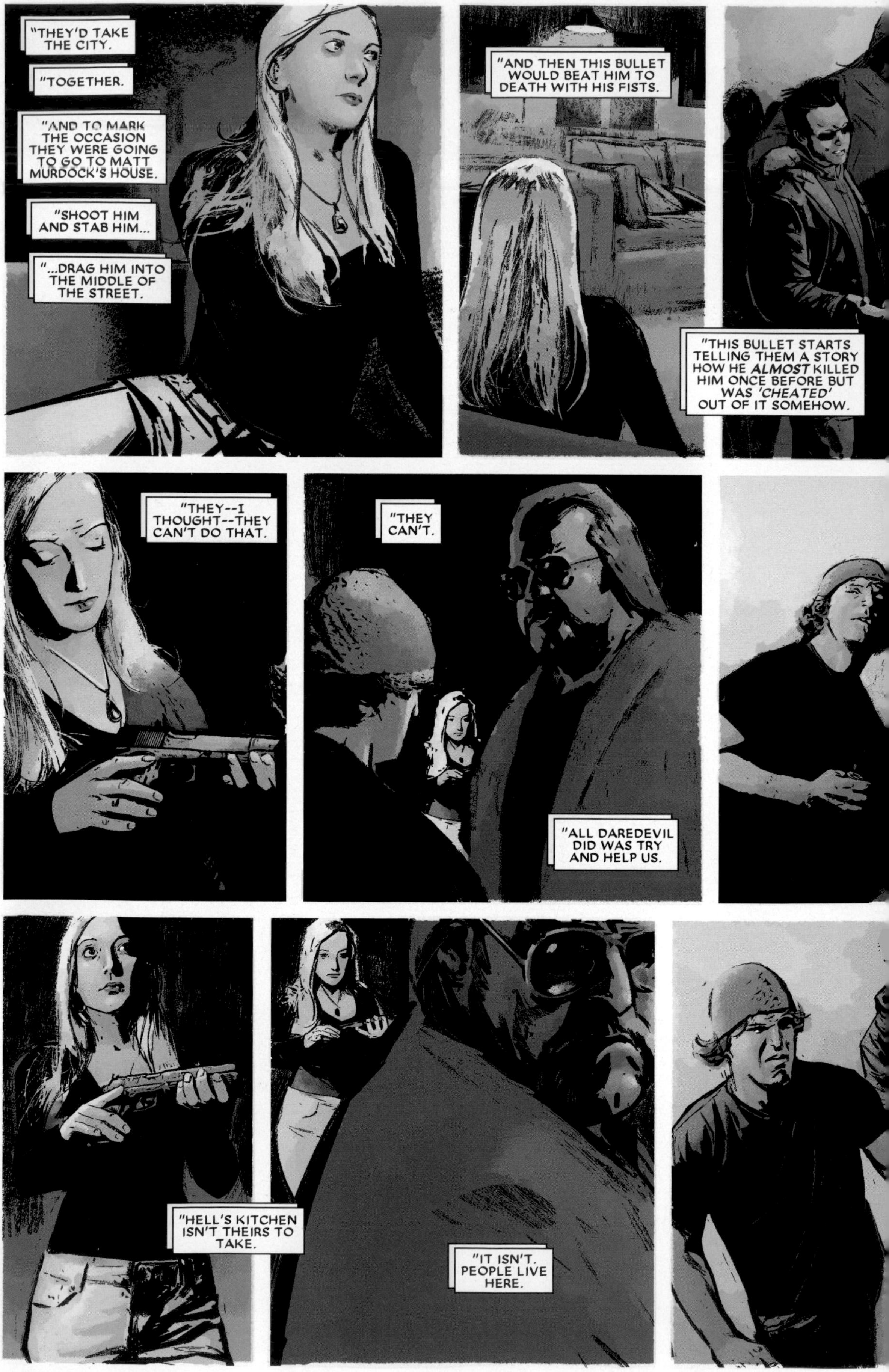
"THEY'D TAKE THE CITY.
"TOGETHER.
"AND TO MARK THE OCCASION THEY WERE GOING TO GO TO MATT MURDOCK'S HOUSE.
"SHOOT HIM AND STAB HIM...
"...DRAG HIM INTO THE MIDDLE OF THE STREET.
"AND THEN THIS BULLET WOULD BEAT HIM TO DEATH WITH HIS FISTS.
"THIS BULLET STARTS TELLING THEM A STORY HOW HE ALMOST KILLED HIM ONCE BEFORE BUT WAS 'CHEATED' OUT OF IT SOMEHOW.
"THEY--I THOUGHT--THEY CAN'T DO THAT.
"THEY CAN'T.
"ALL DAREDEVIL DID WAS TRY AND HELP US.
"HELL'S KITCHEN ISN'T THEIRS TO TAKE.
"IT ISN'T. PEOPLE LIVE HERE.

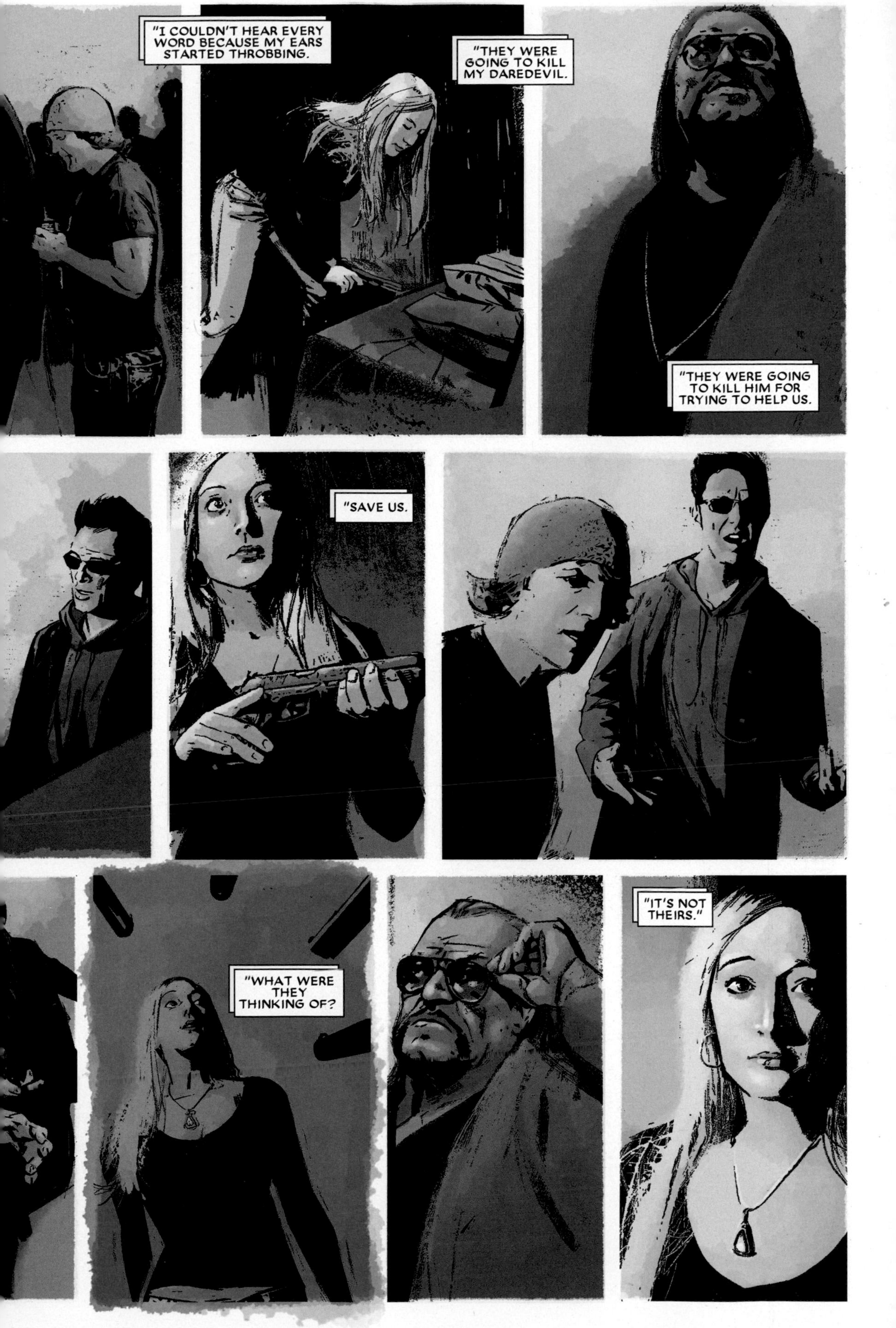
"I COULDN'T HEAR EVERY WORD BECAUSE MY EARS STARTED THROBBING.
"THEY WERE GOING TO KILL MY DAREDEVIL.
"THEY WERE GOING TO KILL HIM FOR TRYING TO HELP US.
"SAVE US.
"WHAT WERE THEY THINKING OF?
"IT'S NOT THEIRS."

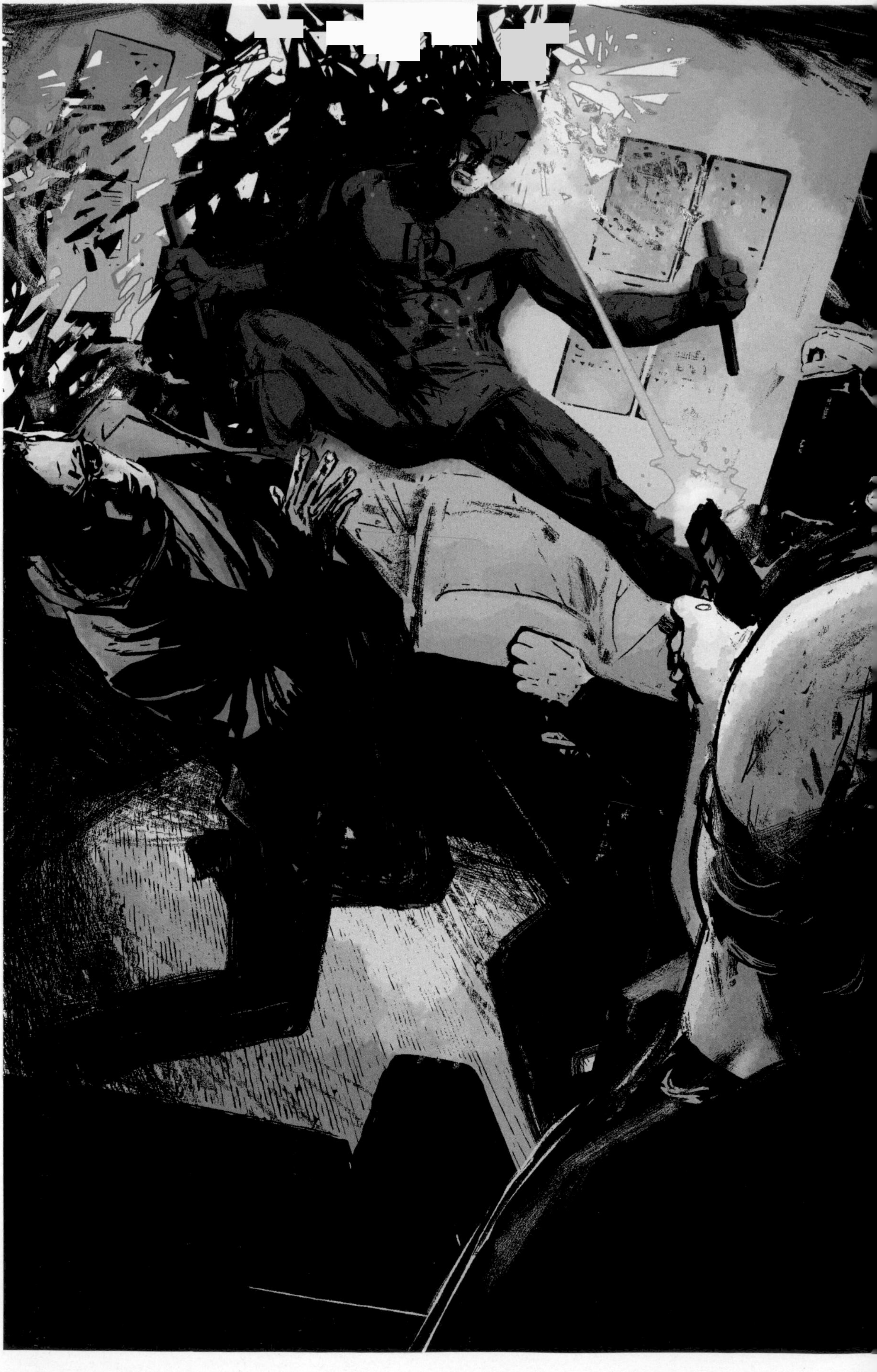

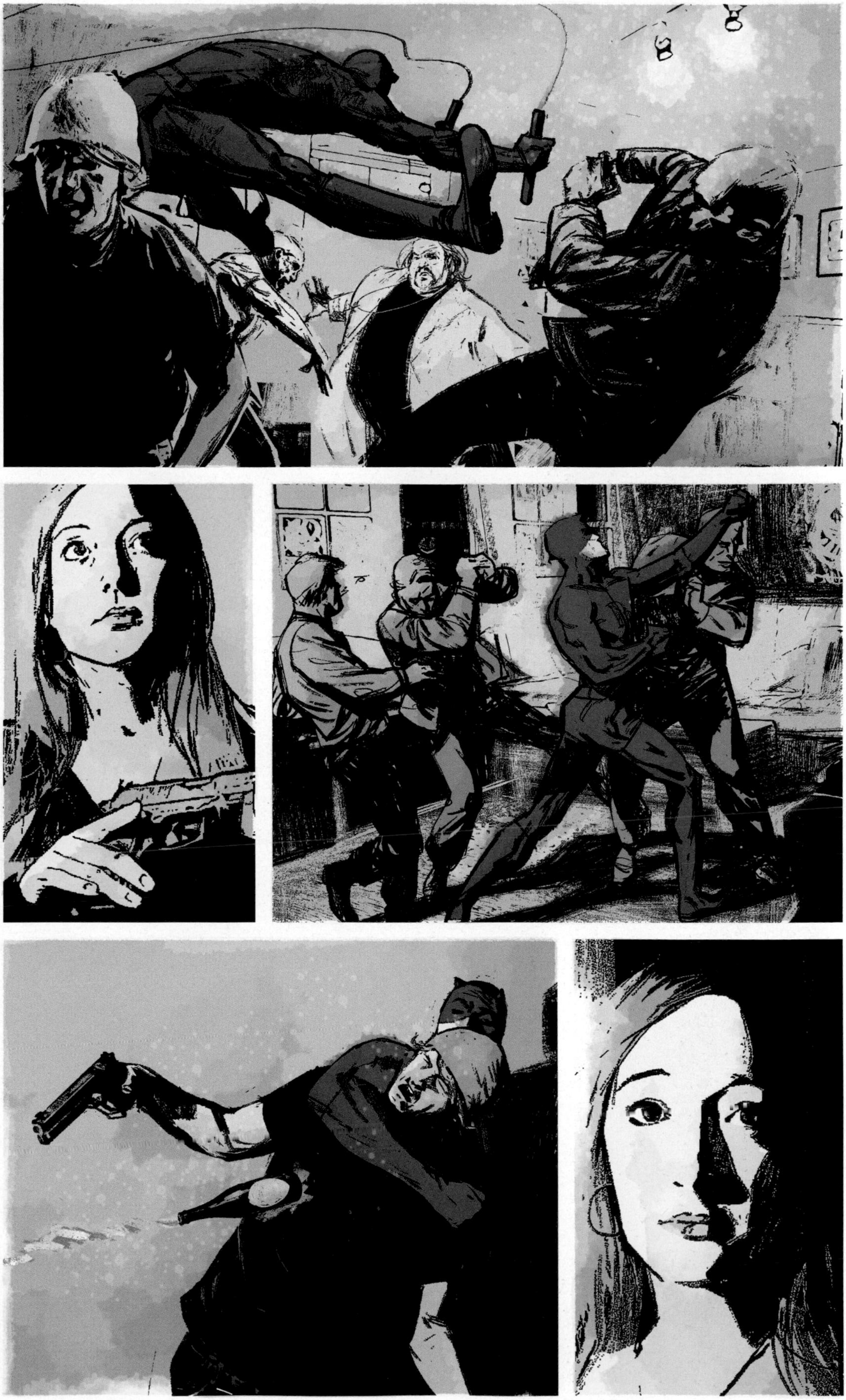

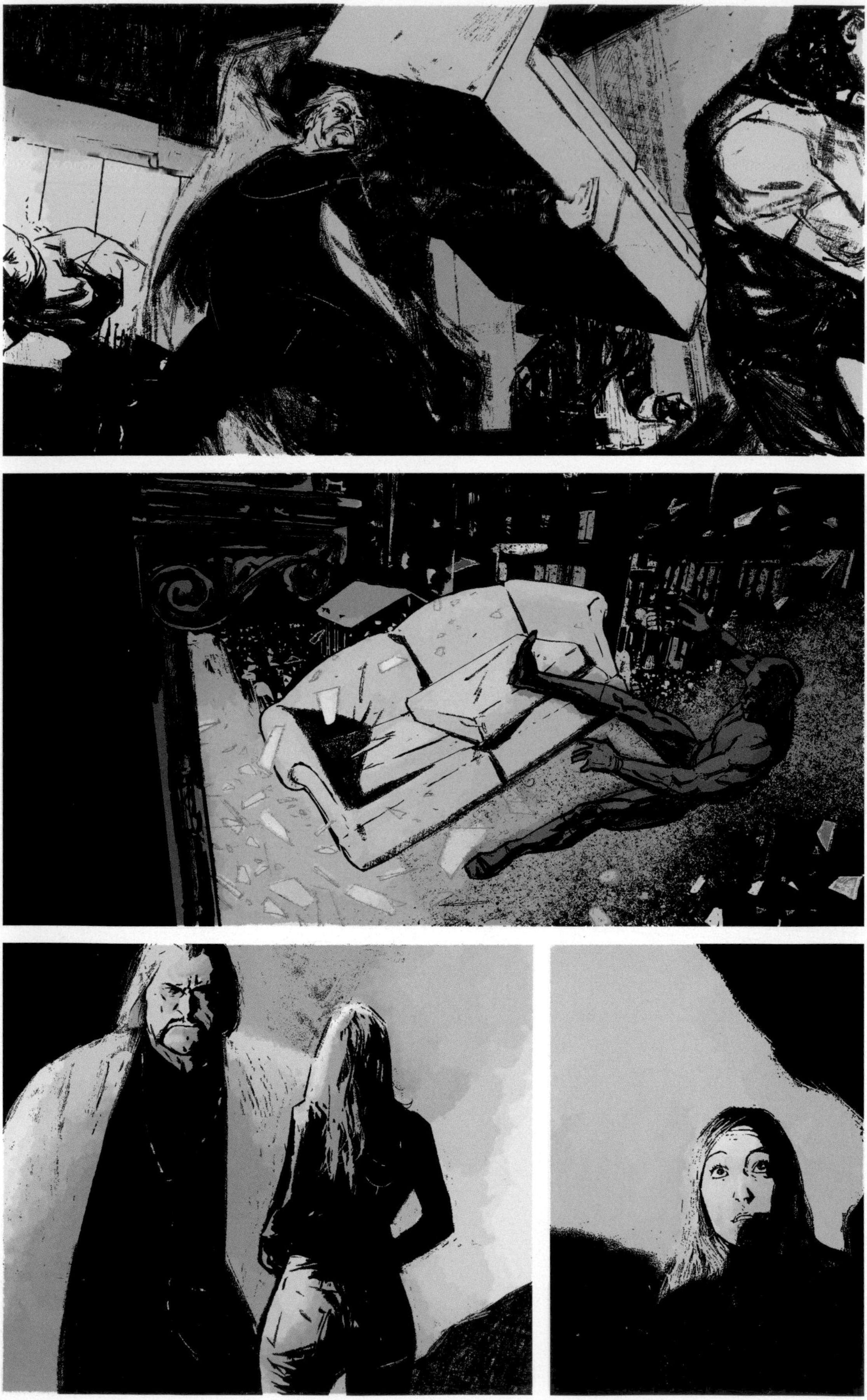

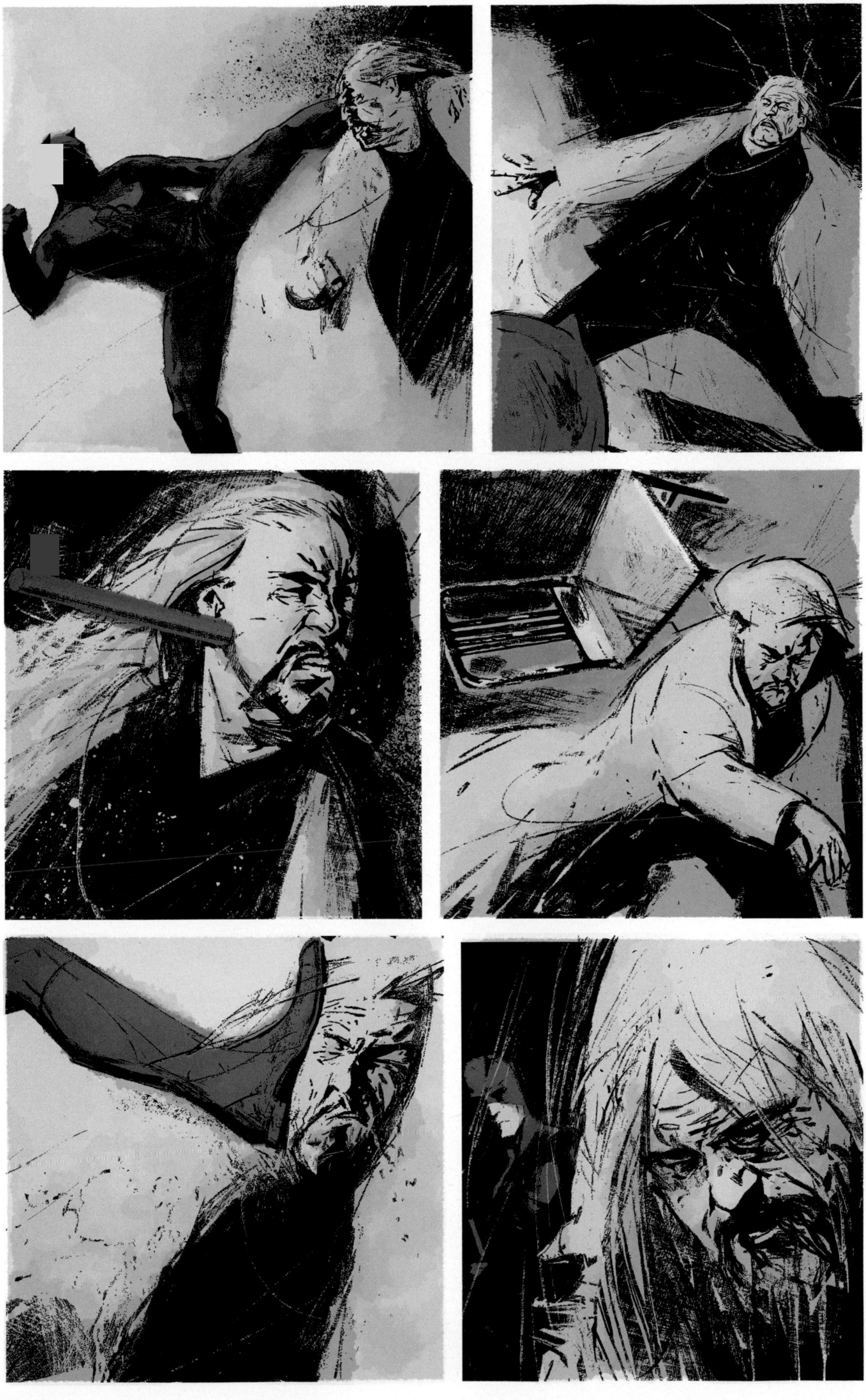

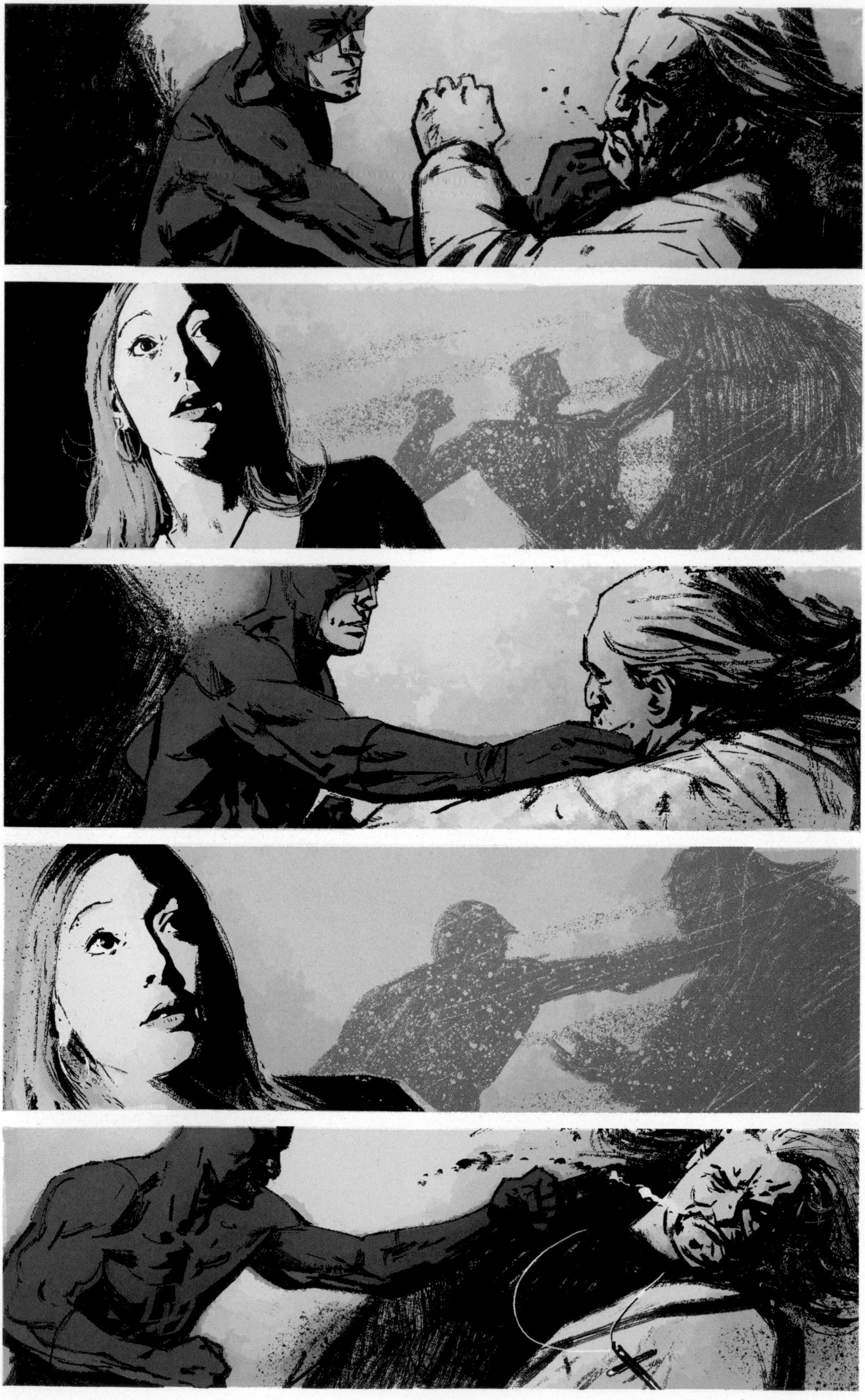

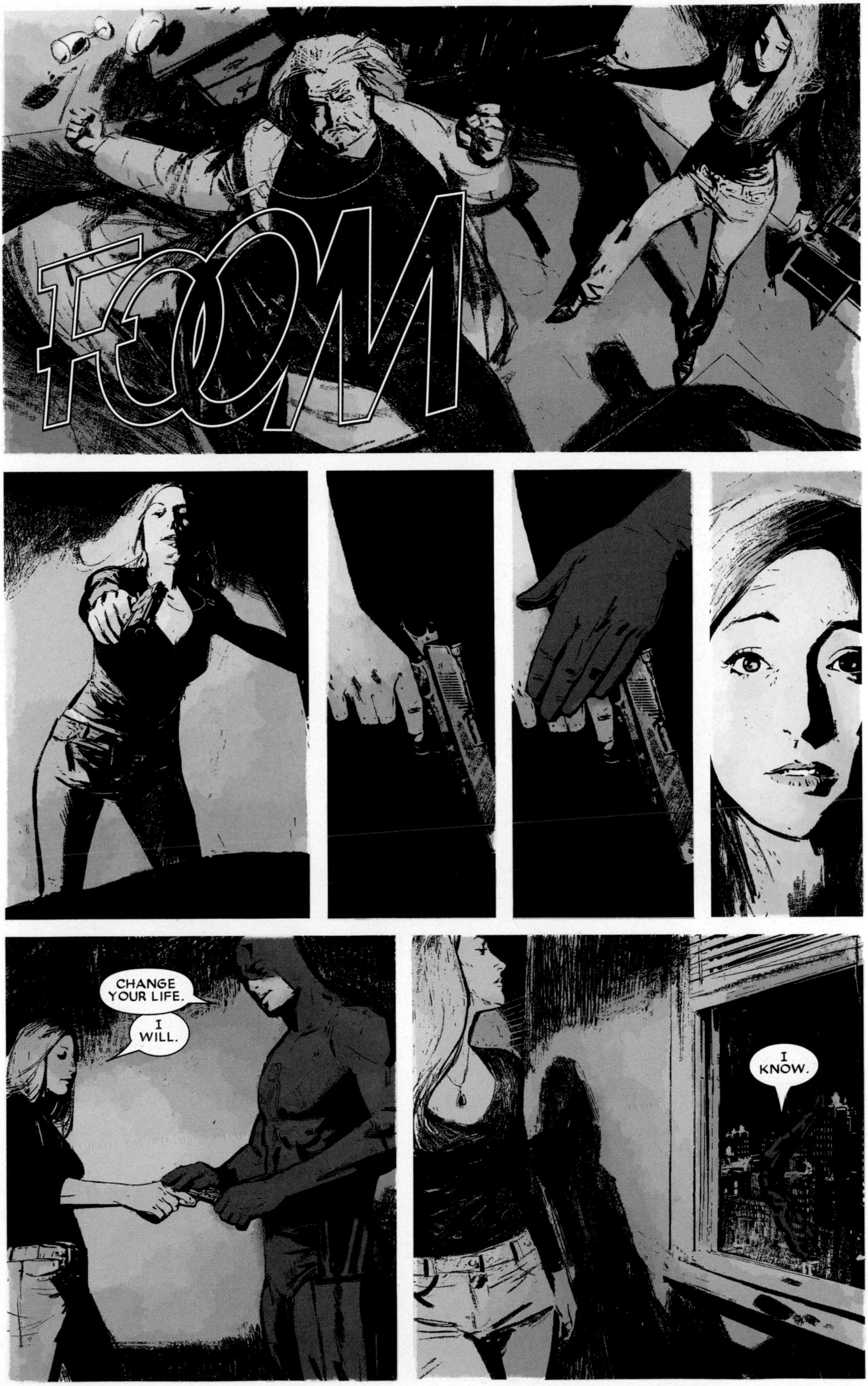
FOOM
CHANGE YOUR LIFE.
I WILL.
I KNOW.

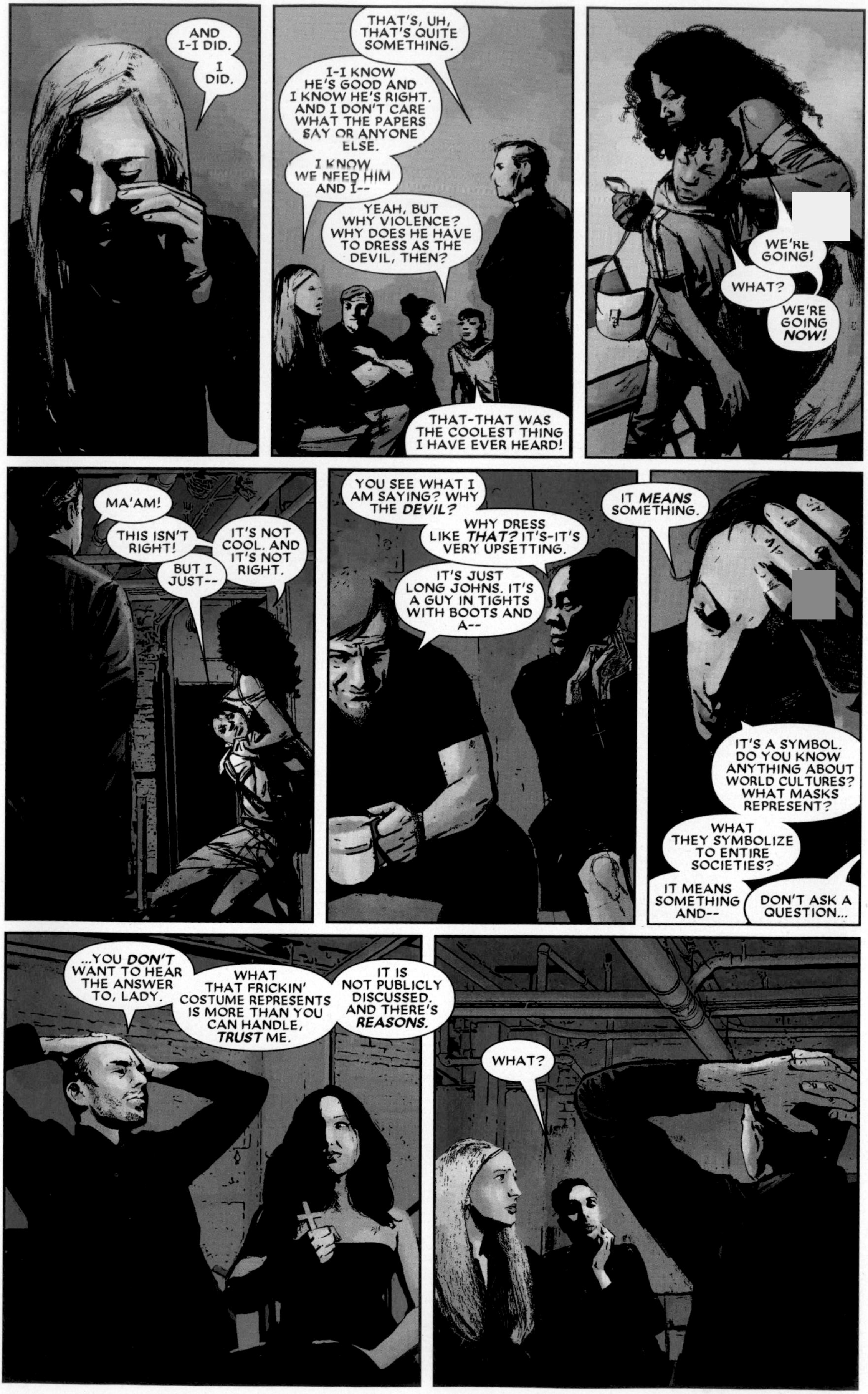

AND I-I DID.
I DID.
THAT'S, UH, THAT'S QUITE SOMETHING.
I-I KNOW HE'S GOOD AND I KNOW HE'S RIGHT. AND I DON'T CARE WHAT THE PAPERS SAY OR ANYONE ELSE.
I KNOW WE NEED HIM AND I--
YEAH, BUT WHY VIOLENCE? WHY DOES HE HAVE TO DRESS AS THE DEVIL, THEN?
THAT-THAT WAS THE COOLEST THING I HAVE EVER HEARD!
WE'RE GOING!
WHAT?
WE'RE GOING *NOW!*
MA'AM!
THIS ISN'T RIGHT!
IT'S NOT COOL. AND IT'S NOT RIGHT.
BUT I JUST--
YOU SEE WHAT I AM SAYING? WHY THE *DEVIL?*
WHY DRESS LIKE *THAT?* IT'S-IT'S VERY UPSETTING.
IT'S JUST LONG JOHNS. IT'S A GUY IN TIGHTS WITH BOOTS AND A--
IT *MEANS* SOMETHING.
IT'S A SYMBOL. DO YOU KNOW ANYTHING ABOUT WORLD CULTURES? WHAT MASKS REPRESENT?
WHAT THEY SYMBOLIZE TO ENTIRE SOCIETIES?
IT MEANS SOMETHING AND--
DON'T ASK A QUESTION...
...YOU *DON'T* WANT TO HEAR THE ANSWER TO, LADY.
WHAT THAT FRICKIN' COSTUME REPRESENTS IS MORE THAN YOU CAN HANDLE, *TRUST* ME.
IT IS NOT PUBLICLY DISCUSSED. AND THERE'S *REASONS.*
WHAT?

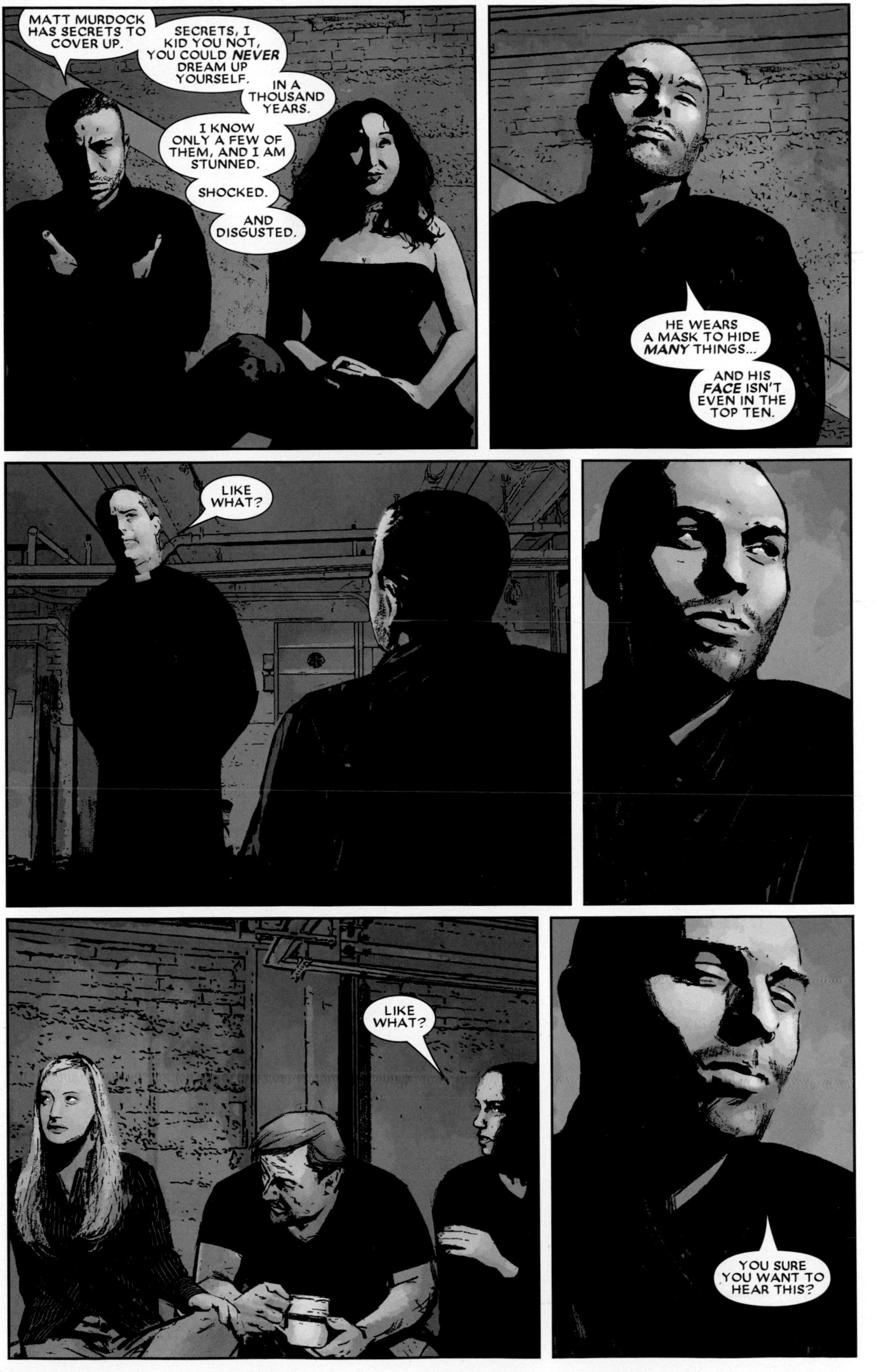
MATT MURDOCK HAS SECRETS TO COVER UP.
SECRETS, I KID YOU NOT, YOU COULD NEVER DREAM UP YOURSELF.
IN A THOUSAND YEARS.
I KNOW ONLY A FEW OF THEM, AND I AM STUNNED.
SHOCKED.
AND DISGUSTED.
HE WEARS A MASK TO HIDE MANY THINGS...
AND HIS FACE ISN'T EVEN IN THE TOP TEN.
LIKE WHAT?
LIKE WHAT?
YOU SURE YOU WANT TO HEAR THIS?

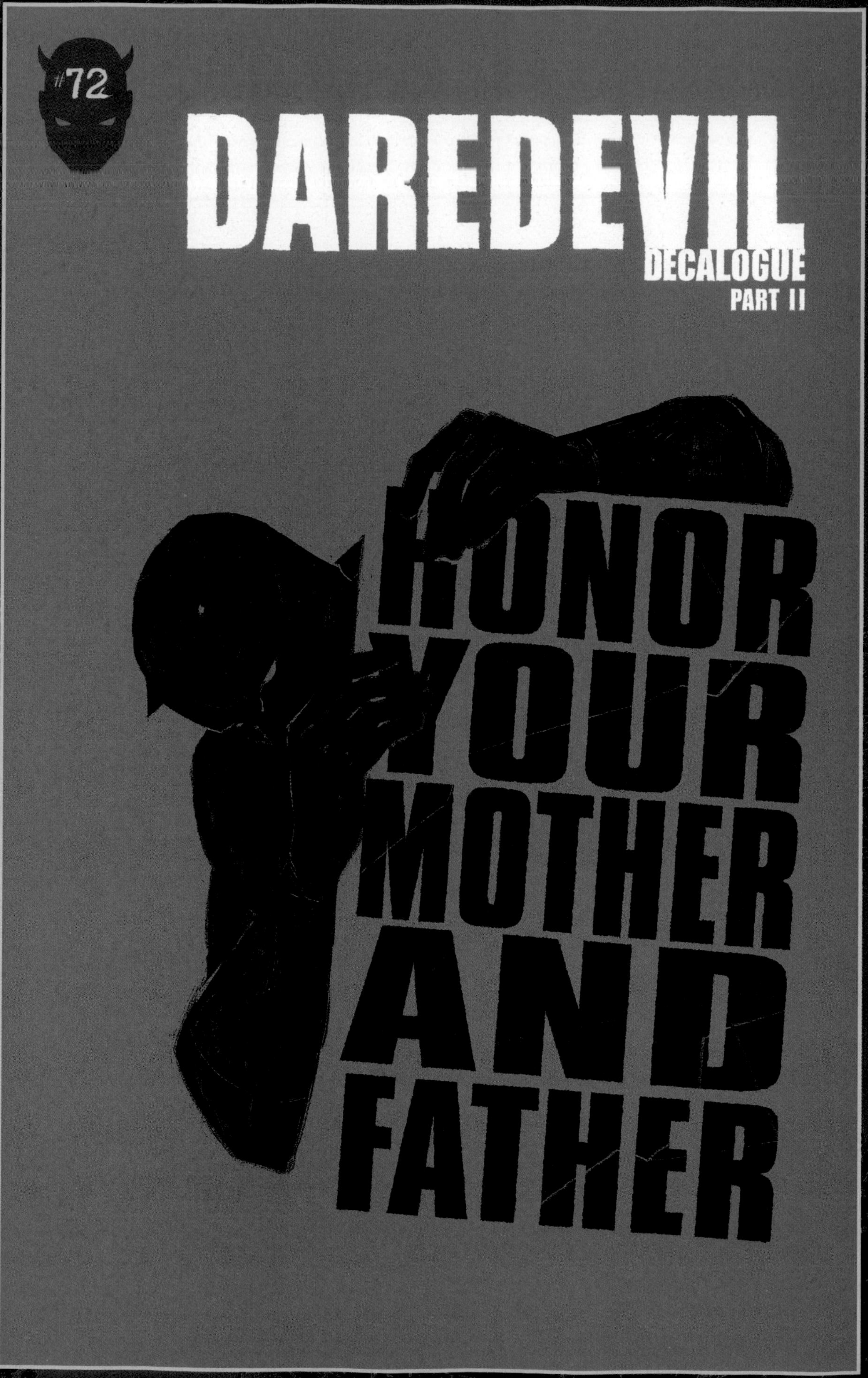
#72
DAREDEVIL
DECALOGUE
PART II
HONOR YOUR MOTHER AND FATHER

DAREDEVIL

DECALOGUE
PART III

#73

THOU SHALL NOT LIE

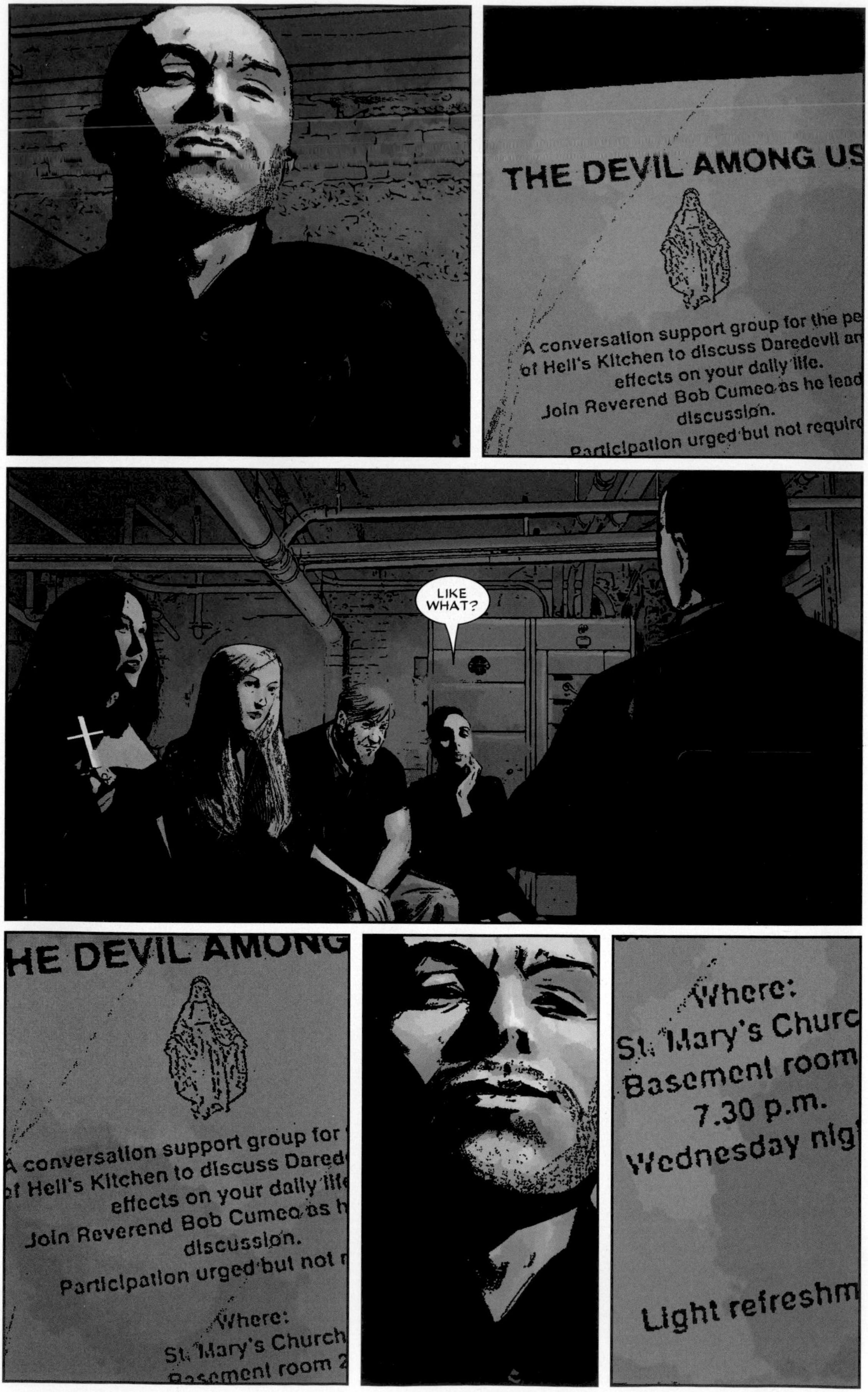
THE DEVIL AMONG US
A conversation support group for the pe
of Hell's Kitchen to discuss Daredevil an
effects on your daily life.
Join Reverend Bob Cumeo as he lead
discussion.
Participation urged but not requir
LIKE WHAT?
HE DEVIL AMONG
A conversation support group for
of Hell's Kitchen to discuss Dared
effects on your daily life
Join Reverend Bob Cumeo as h
discussion.
Participation urged but not
Where:
St. Mary's Church
Basement room 2
Where:
St. Mary's Churc
Basement room
7.30 p.m.
Wednesday nig
Light refreshm

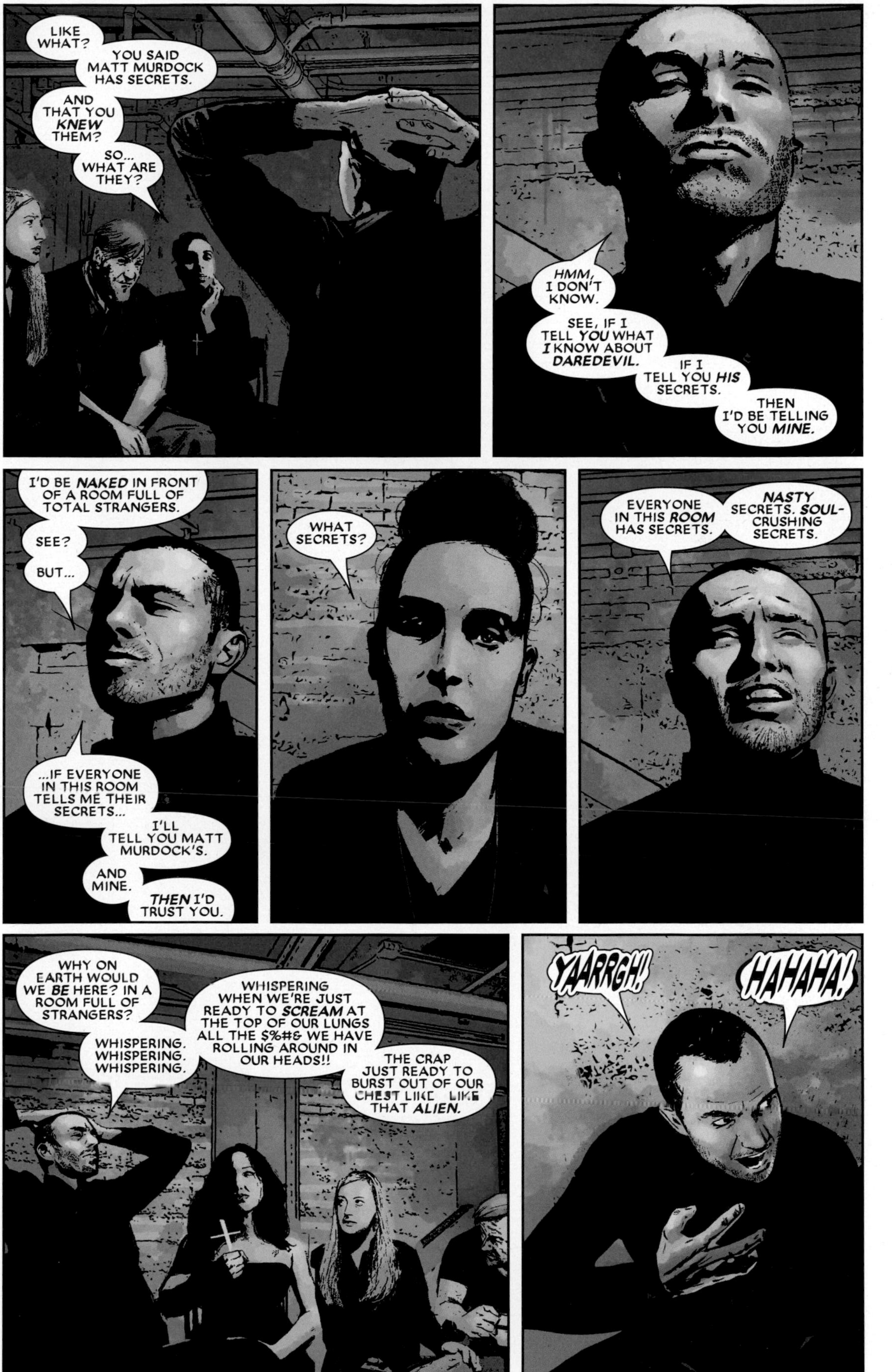

LIKE WHAT?
YOU SAID MATT MURDOCK HAS SECRETS.
AND THAT YOU KNEW THEM?
SO... WHAT ARE THEY?
HMM, I DON'T KNOW.
SEE, IF I TELL YOU WHAT I KNOW ABOUT DAREDEVIL.
IF I TELL YOU HIS SECRETS.
THEN I'D BE TELLING YOU MINE.
I'D BE NAKED IN FRONT OF A ROOM FULL OF TOTAL STRANGERS.
SEE?
BUT...
...IF EVERYONE IN THIS ROOM TELLS ME THEIR SECRETS...
I'LL TELL YOU MATT MURDOCK'S.
AND MINE.
THEN I'D TRUST YOU.
WHAT SECRETS?
EVERYONE IN THIS ROOM HAS SECRETS.
NASTY SECRETS. SOUL-CRUSHING SECRETS.
WHY ON EARTH WOULD WE BE HERE? IN A ROOM FULL OF STRANGERS?
WHISPERING. WHISPERING. WHISPERING.
WHISPERING WHEN WE'RE JUST READY TO SCREAM AT THE TOP OF OUR LUNGS ALL THE $%#& WE HAVE ROLLING AROUND IN OUR HEADS!!
THE CRAP JUST READY TO BURST OUT OF OUR CHEST LIKE LIKE THAT ALIEN.
YAARRGH!
HAHAHA!

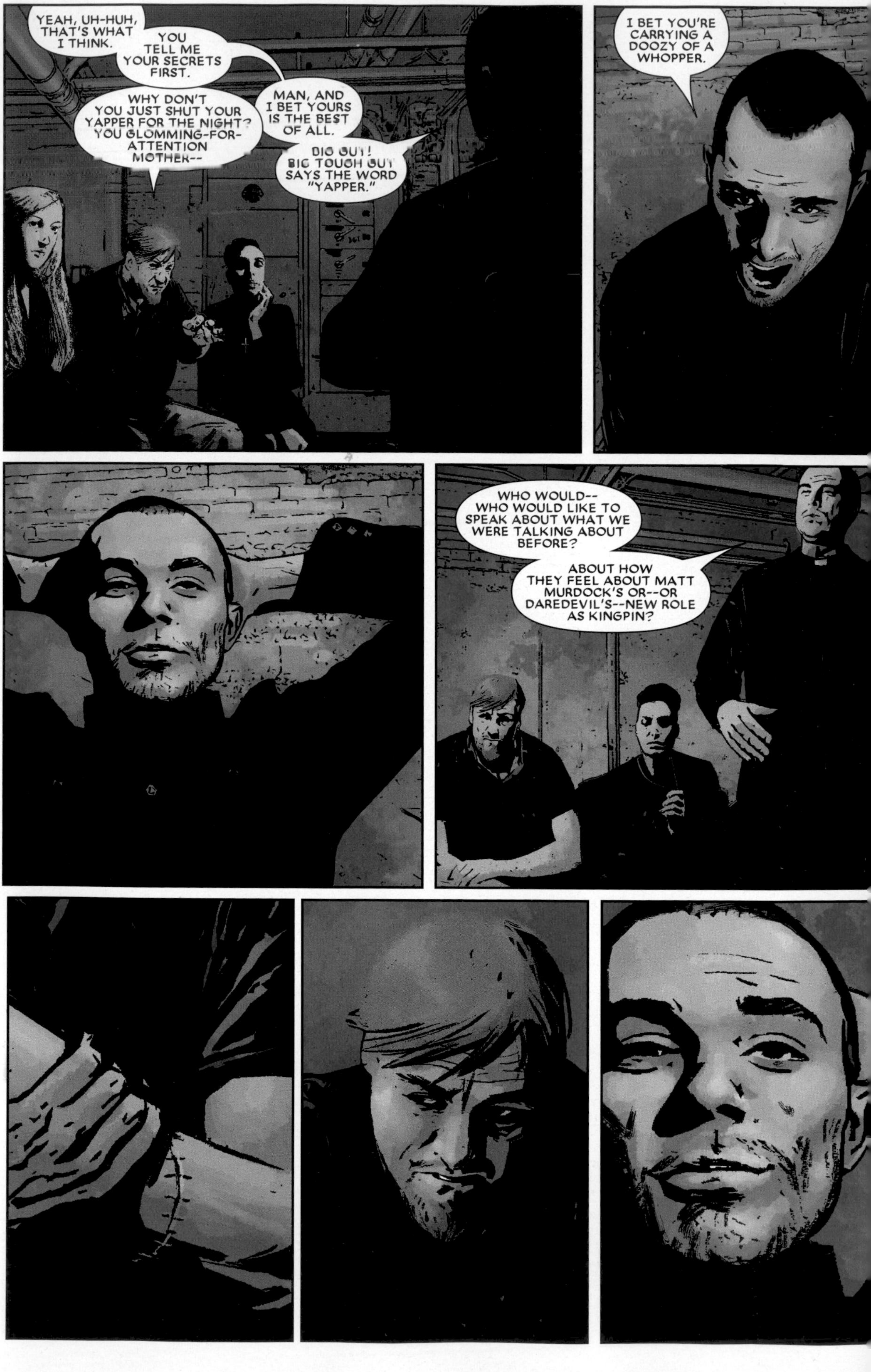
YEAH, UH-HUH, THAT'S WHAT I THINK.
YOU TELL ME YOUR SECRETS FIRST.
WHY DON'T YOU JUST SHUT YOUR YAPPER FOR THE NIGHT? YOU GLOMMING-FOR-ATTENTION MOTHER--
MAN, AND I BET YOURS IS THE BEST OF ALL.
BIG GUY! BIG TOUGH GUY SAYS THE WORD "YAPPER."
I BET YOU'RE CARRYING A DOOZY OF A WHOPPER.
WHO WOULD-- WHO WOULD LIKE TO SPEAK ABOUT WHAT WE WERE TALKING ABOUT BEFORE?
ABOUT HOW THEY FEEL ABOUT MATT MURDOCK'S OR--OR DAREDEVIL'S--NEW ROLE AS KINGPIN?

SHUT UP!

SHUT UP, MAN.

I MEAN IT, DON'T--

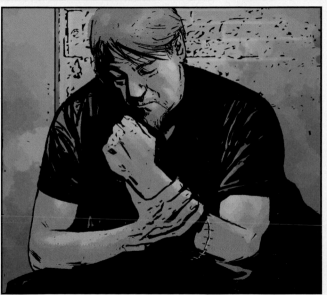

ANYONE?

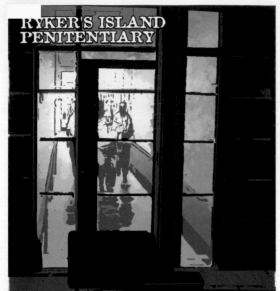

RYKER'S ISLAND
PENITENTIARY

DO NOT REMOVE
...S FROM
...ITHOUT
...ATION

HI, DAD.

WHAT THE HELL ARE *YOU* DOING HERE?

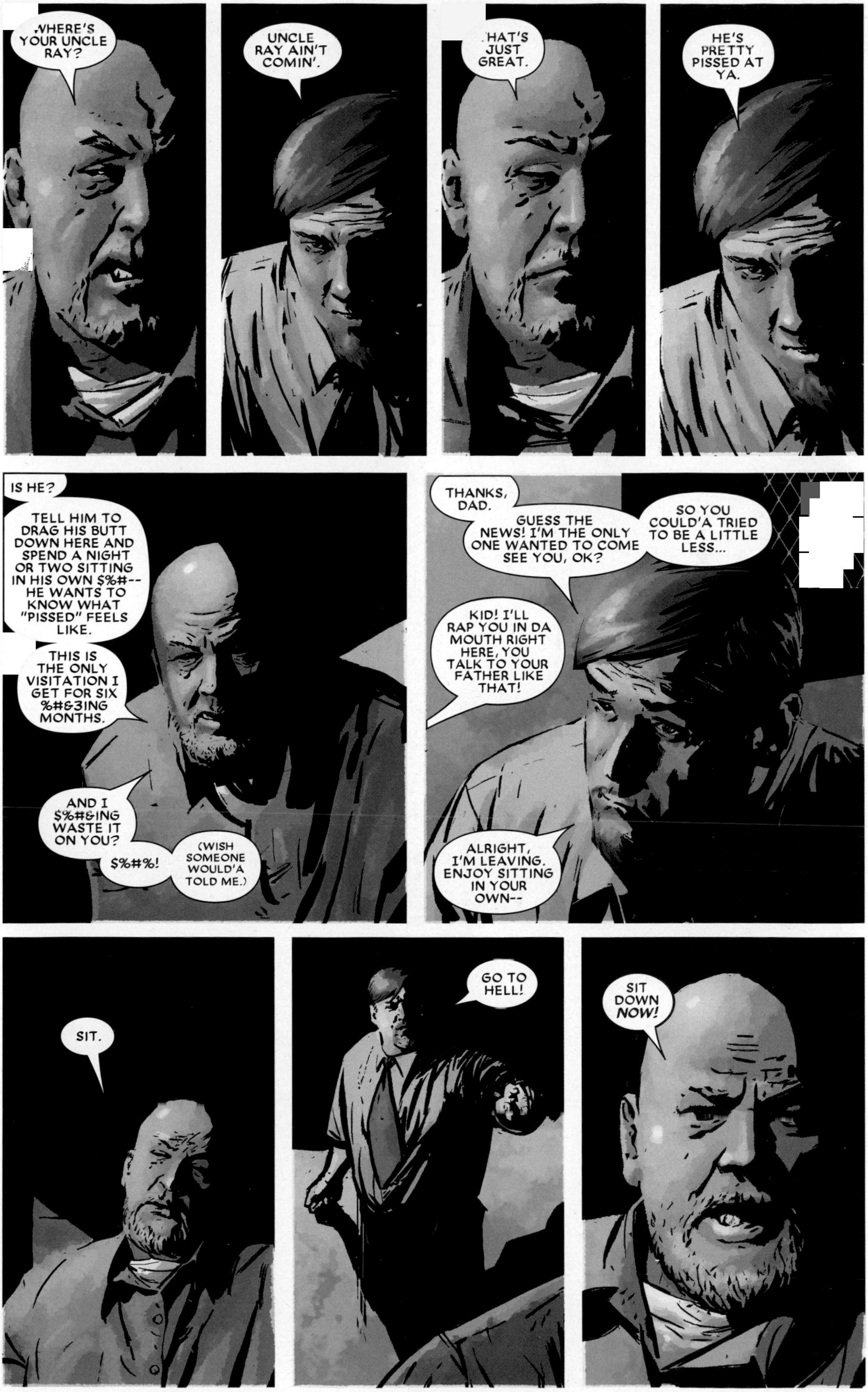
WHERE'S YOUR UNCLE RAY?
UNCLE RAY AIN'T COMIN'.
THAT'S JUST GREAT.
HE'S PRETTY PISSED AT YA.
IS HE?
TELL HIM TO DRAG HIS BUTT DOWN HERE AND SPEND A NIGHT OR TWO SITTING IN HIS OWN $%#--HE WANTS TO KNOW WHAT "PISSED" FEELS LIKE.
THIS IS THE ONLY VISITATION I GET FOR SIX %#&3ING MONTHS.
AND I $%#&ING WASTE IT ON YOU?
$%#%!
(WISH SOMEONE WOULD'A TOLD ME.)
THANKS, DAD.
GUESS THE NEWS! I'M THE ONLY ONE WANTED TO COME SEE YOU, OK?
SO YOU COULD'A TRIED TO BE A LITTLE LESS...
KID! I'LL RAP YOU IN DA MOUTH RIGHT HERE, YOU TALK TO YOUR FATHER LIKE THAT!
ALRIGHT, I'M LEAVING. ENJOY SITTING IN YOUR OWN--
SIT.
GO TO HELL!
SIT DOWN NOW!

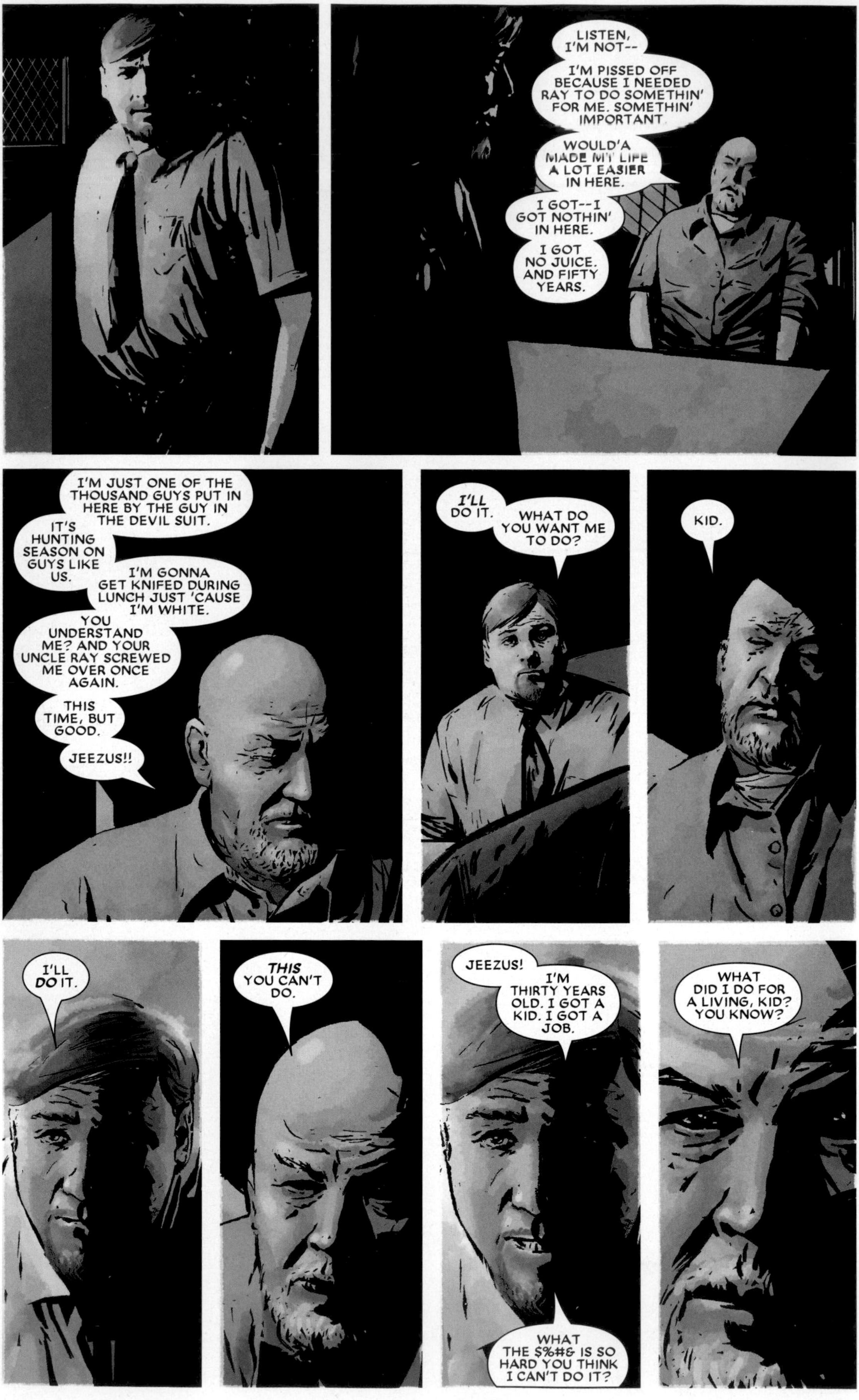
LISTEN, I'M NOT--
I'M PISSED OFF BECAUSE I NEEDED RAY TO DO SOMETHIN' FOR ME. SOMETHIN' IMPORTANT.
WOULD'A MADE MY LIFE A LOT EASIER IN HERE.
I GOT--I GOT NOTHIN' IN HERE.
I GOT NO JUICE. AND FIFTY YEARS.
I'M JUST ONE OF THE THOUSAND GUYS PUT IN HERE BY THE GUY IN THE DEVIL SUIT.
IT'S HUNTING SEASON ON GUYS LIKE US.
I'M GONNA GET KNIFED DURING LUNCH JUST 'CAUSE I'M WHITE.
YOU UNDERSTAND ME? AND YOUR UNCLE RAY SCREWED ME OVER ONCE AGAIN.
THIS TIME, BUT GOOD.
JEEZUS!!
I'LL DO IT.
WHAT DO YOU WANT ME TO DO?
KID.
I'LL *DO* IT.
THIS YOU CAN'T DO.
JEEZUS!
I'M THIRTY YEARS OLD. I GOT A KID. I GOT A JOB.
WHAT THE $%#& IS SO HARD YOU THINK I CAN'T DO IT?
WHAT DID I DO FOR A LIVING, KID? YOU KNOW?

KINDA.

"KINDA."

"KINDA" AND YOU STILL WANT TO DO WHAT I NEED TO HAVE DONE.

I WANNA HELP YOU.

YOU KNOW WHERE JOSIE'S BAR IS?

YEAH, IT'S CLOSED UP.

THE FRONT OF IT IS, NOT THE BACK.

THERE'S A BACK?

SHUT UP. YOU GO THERE.

YOU TELL HIM YOU'RE MY SON.

YOU DON'T TAKE NO $%#& OFF OF NO ONE THERE. YOU GOT A PIECE?

A PIECE? YOU GOT A PIECE?

NO.

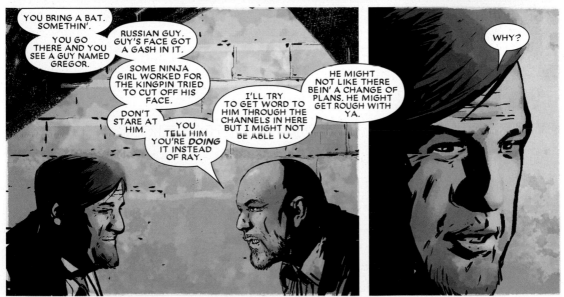

YOU BRING A BAT. SOMETHIN'.

YOU GO THERE AND YOU SEE A GUY NAMED GREGOR.

RUSSIAN GUY. GUY'S FACE GOT A GASH IN IT.

SOME NINJA GIRL WORKED FOR THE KINGPIN TRIED TO CUT OFF HIS FACE.

DON'T STARE AT HIM.

YOU TELL HIM YOU'RE DOING IT INSTEAD OF RAY.

I'LL TRY TO GET WORD TO HIM THROUGH THE CHANNELS IN HERE BUT I MIGHT NOT BE ABLE TO.

HE MIGHT NOT LIKE THERE BEIN' A CHANGE OF PLANS. HE MIGHT GET ROUGH WITH YA.

WHY?

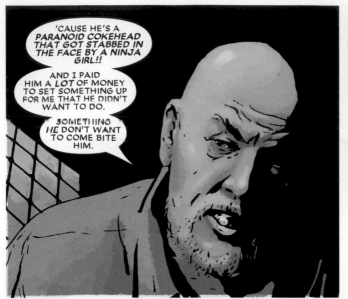

'CAUSE HE'S A *PARANOID COKEHEAD* THAT GOT STABBED IN THE FACE BY A *NINJA GIRL!!*

AND I PAID HIM A *LOT* OF MONEY TO SET SOMETHING UP FOR ME THAT HE *DIDN'T WANT* TO DO.

SOMETHING *HE* DON'T WANT TO COME BITE *HIM.*

WHAT IS IT?

JUST *GO* THERE.

I CAN'T TELL YOU *HERE.*

KID, IF YOU SCREW THIS UP...

IF YOU DROP THE BALL ON THIS LIKE YOU ALWAYS DO...

JUST-- DON'T COME *NEAR* THIS PLACE.

YOU UNDERSTAND ME?

YES, SIR.

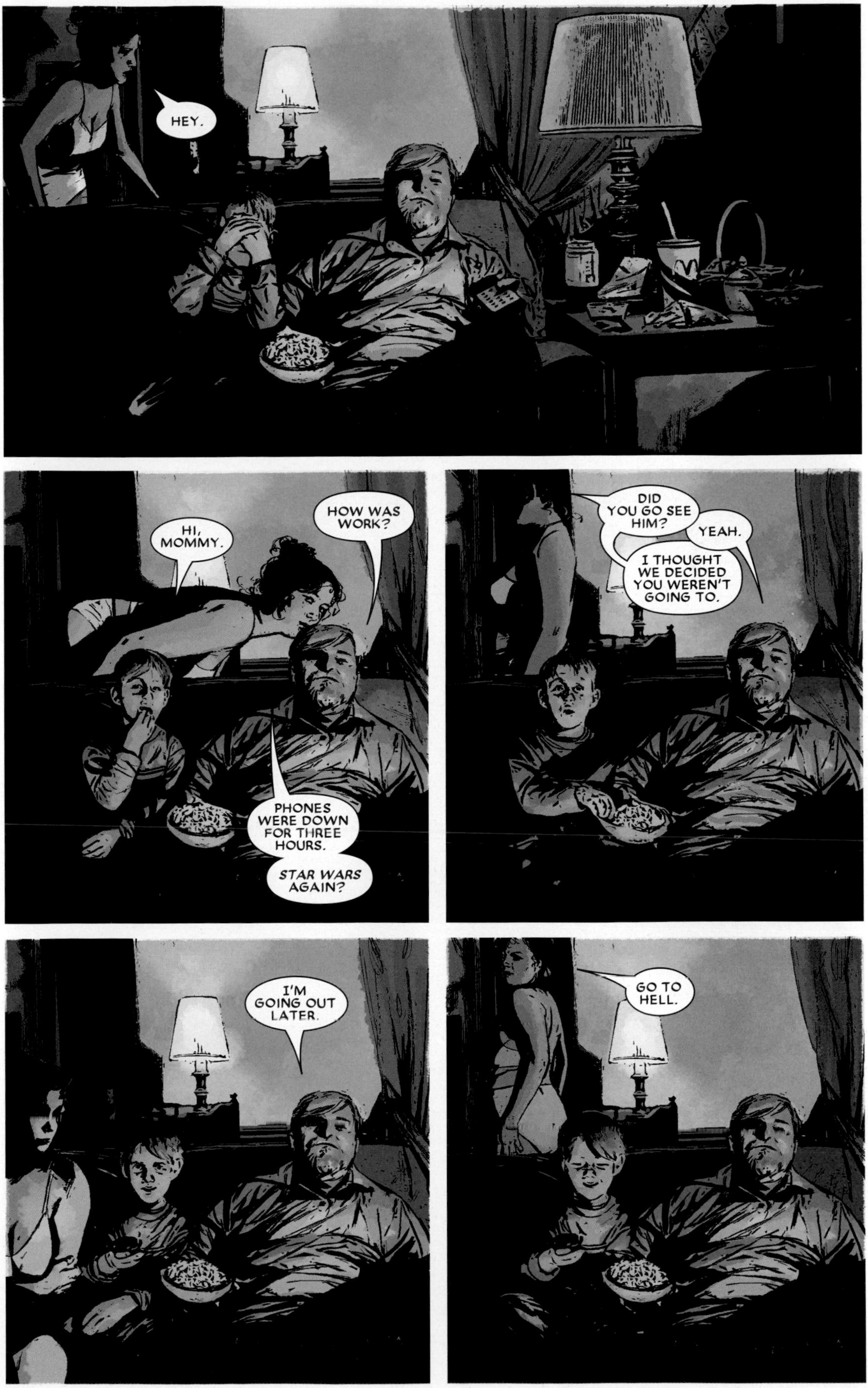

HEY.
HI, MOMMY.
HOW WAS WORK?
PHONES WERE DOWN FOR THREE HOURS.
STAR WARS AGAIN?
DID YOU GO SEE HIM?
YEAH.
I THOUGHT WE DECIDED YOU WEREN'T GOING TO.
I'M GOING OUT LATER.
GO TO HELL.

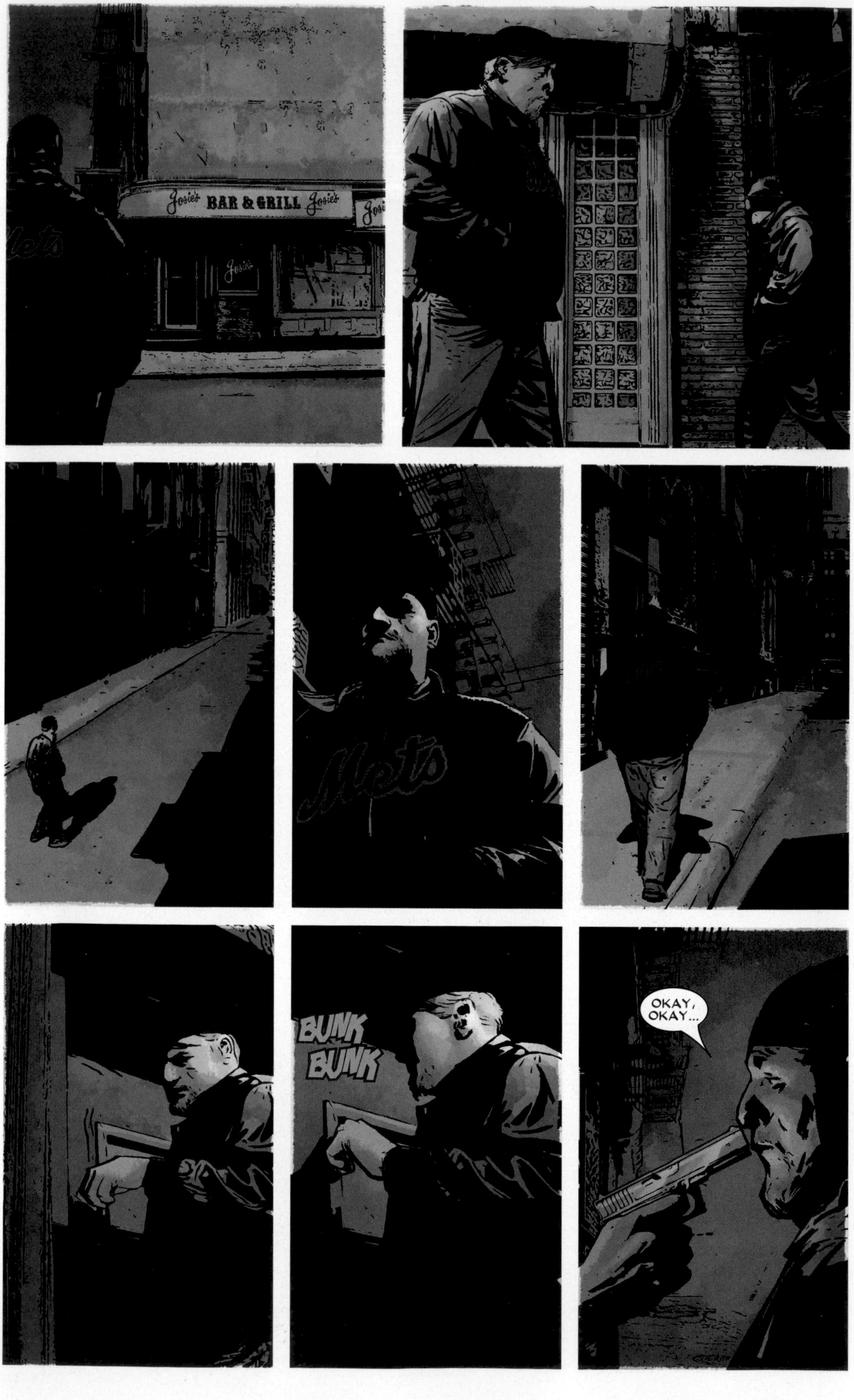
Josie's BAR & GRILL Josie's
Josie's
Mets
Mets
BUNK
BUNK
OKAY, OKAY...

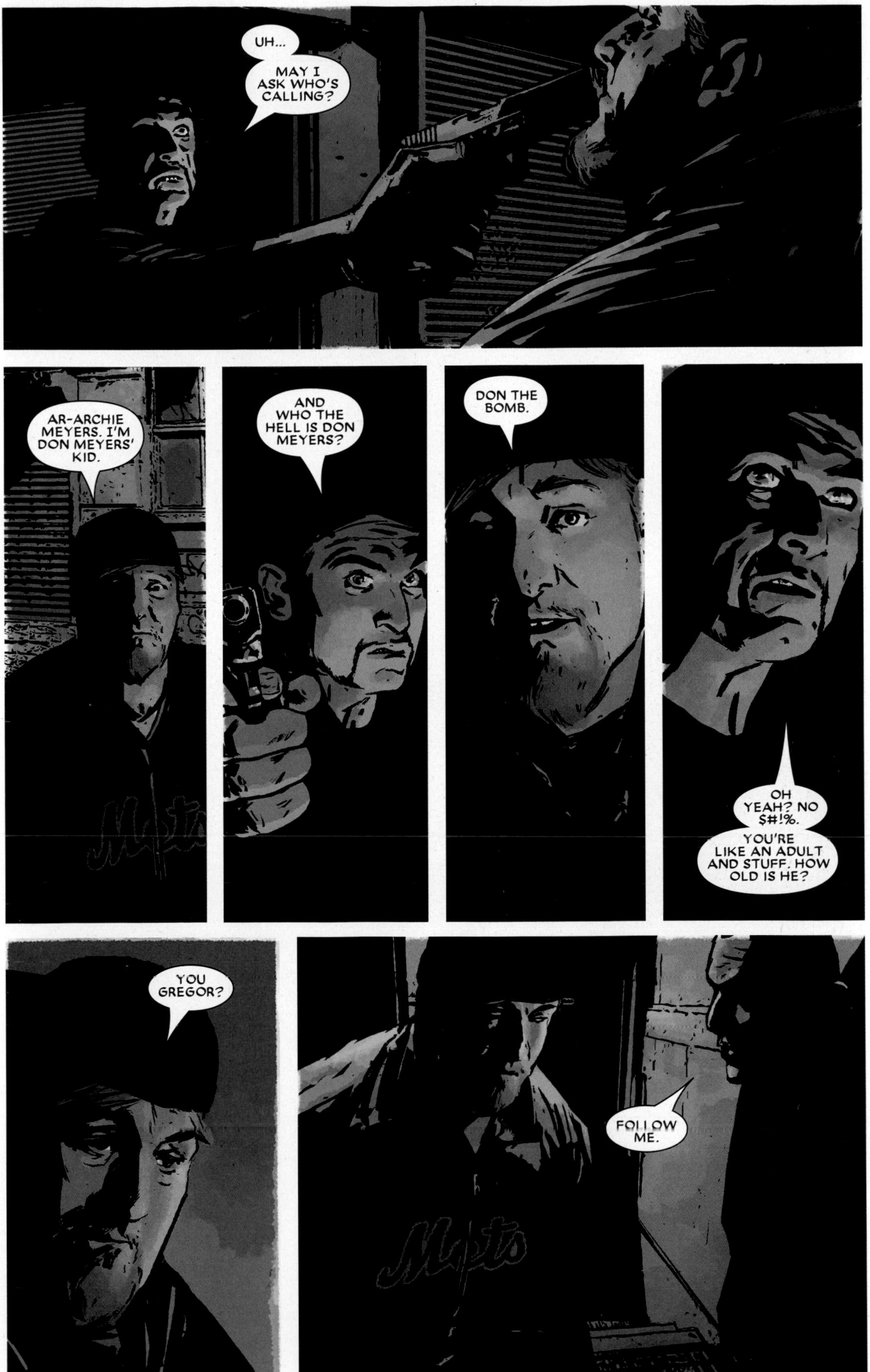
UH...
MAY I ASK WHO'S CALLING?
AR-ARCHIE MEYERS. I'M DON MEYERS' KID.
AND WHO THE HELL IS DON MEYERS?
DON THE BOMB.
OH YEAH? NO $#!%.
YOU'RE LIKE AN ADULT AND STUFF. HOW OLD IS HE?
YOU GREGOR?
FOLLOW ME.

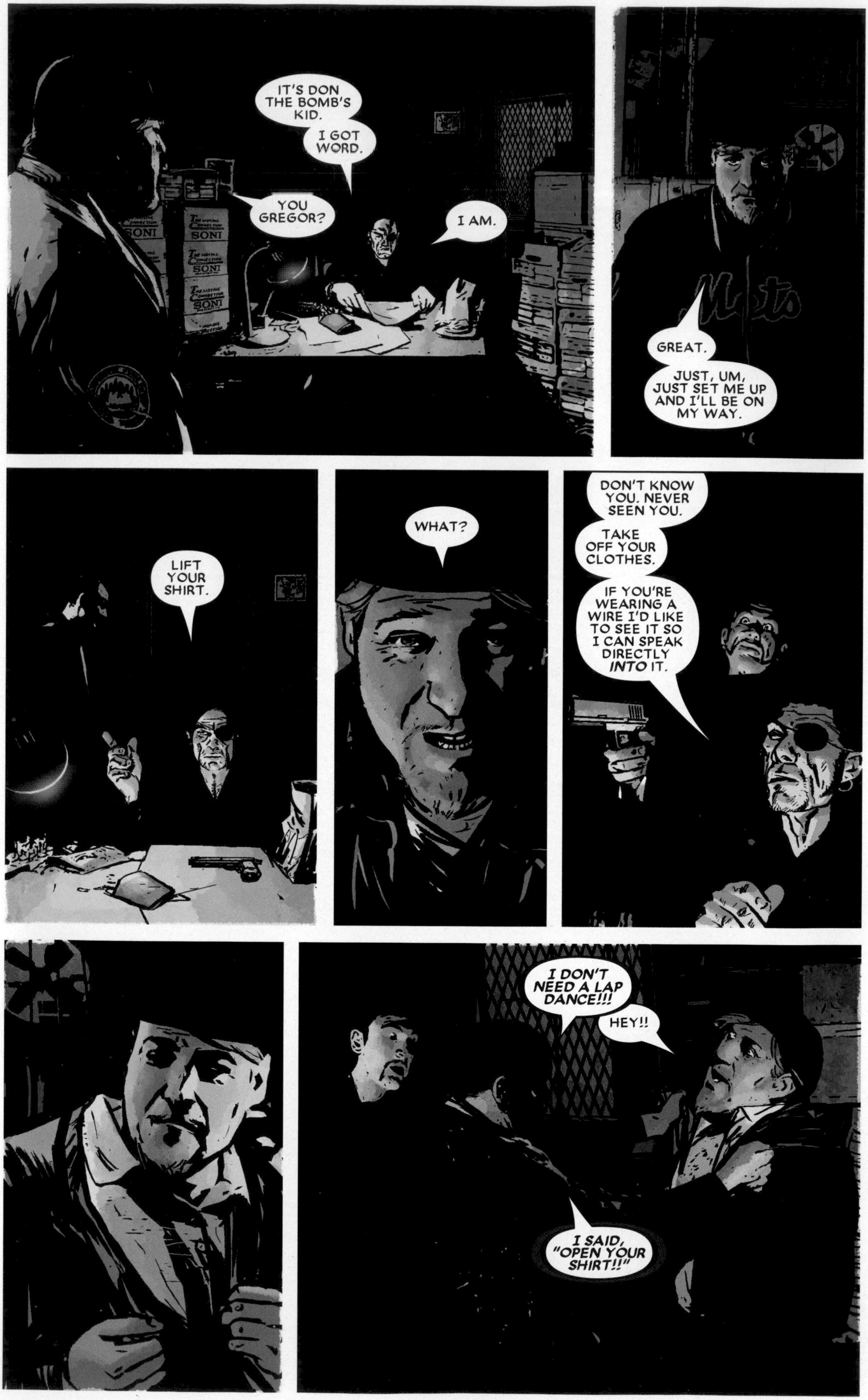
IT'S DON THE BOMB'S KID.
I GOT WORD.
YOU GREGOR?
I AM.
GREAT.
JUST, UM, JUST SET ME UP AND I'LL BE ON MY WAY.
LIFT YOUR SHIRT.
WHAT?
DON'T KNOW YOU. NEVER SEEN YOU.
TAKE OFF YOUR CLOTHES.
IF YOU'RE WEARING A WIRE I'D LIKE TO SEE IT SO I CAN SPEAK DIRECTLY *INTO* IT.
I DON'T NEED A LAP DANCE!!!
HEY!!
I SAID, "OPEN YOUR SHIRT!!"

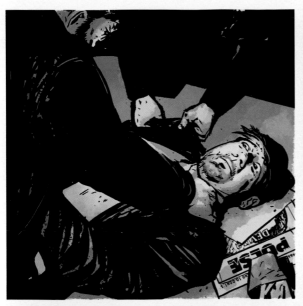

SORRY ABOUT THAT. HOW'S YOUR FATHER?

ROTTING IN PRISON.

THE FOOD AIN'T AS BAD AS THEY SAY.

DON'T WORRY ABOUT HIM.

ONCE DAREDEVIL GOES TO JAIL ALL THE CASES ARE GOING TO GET OVERTURNED.

EVERY SINGLE ONE.

LAWYER FRIEND TOLD ME THAT.

HE TOLD ME ONCE THE FEDS COME DOWN ON MURDOCK... EVERY SINGLE CASE MURDOCK EVER TRIED GETS THROWN OUT.

EVERY SINGLE GUY THAT WENT TO JAIL 'CAUSE DAREDEVIL BEAT ON HIM... GETS LET OUT OF PRISON.

EVERY ONE.

SEE, MY LAWYER FRIEND THINKS THAT'S WHY THE FEDS AIN'T *EVER* GONNA PUT THE HAMMER DOWN ON MURDOCK.

BECAUSE OF THE TIDAL WAVE THAT'LL COME AFTER IT.

BUT I THINK THEY WILL.

I THINK ALL THOSE FEDS ARE GREEDY-- HOW YOU SAY?

GREEDY?

THE GLORY HOUNDS. THIS, YES.

LOOKING FOR A TV SHOW TO BE ON.

I SAY TO YOU, YOUR FATHER WILL GET OUT OF THERE SOON ENOUGH.

BUT THAT'S FOR THEN, THIS IS FOR NOW.

YOU KNOW WHAT THIS IS?

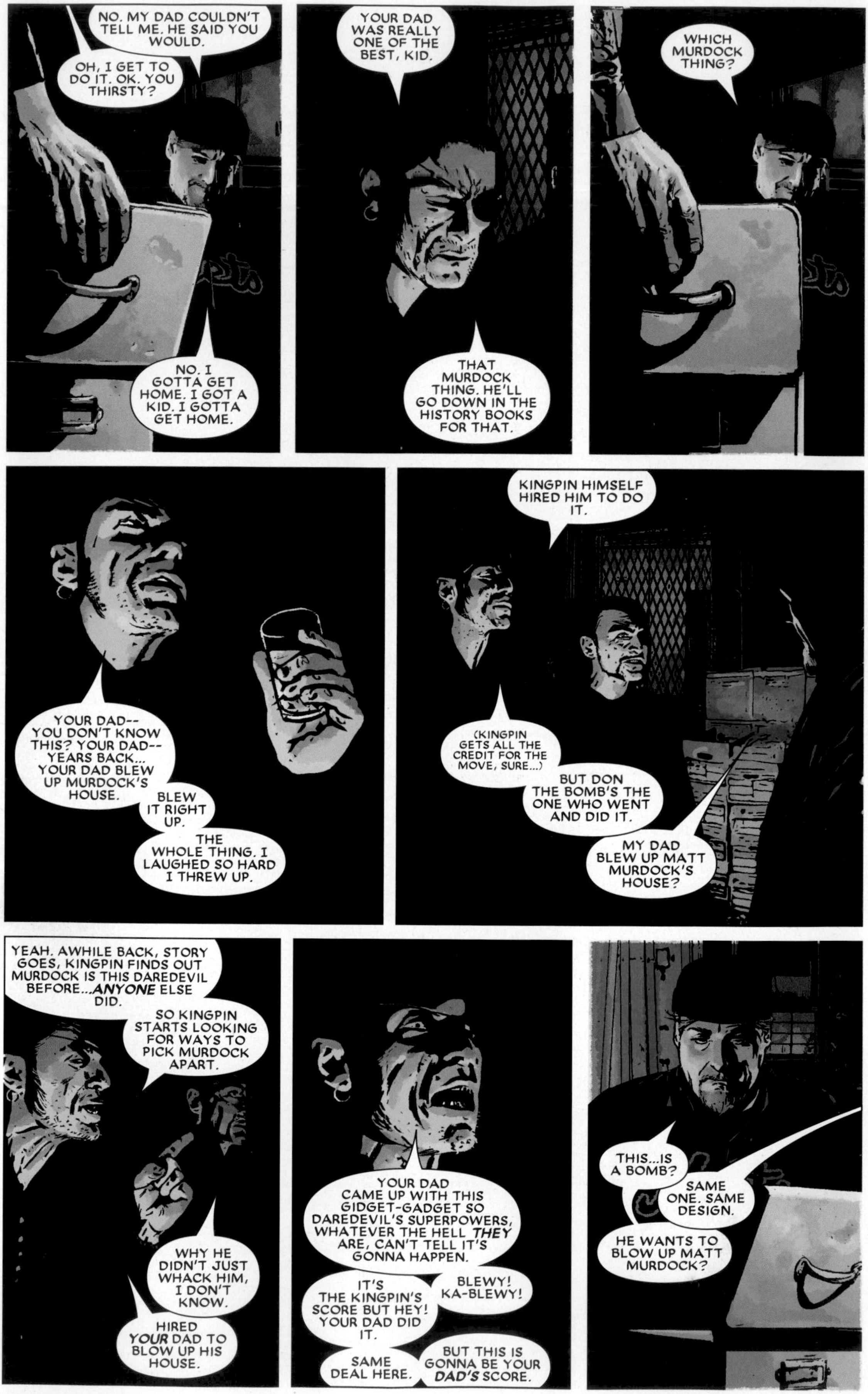
NO. MY DAD COULDN'T TELL ME. HE SAID YOU WOULD.
OH, I GET TO DO IT. OK. YOU THIRSTY?
NO. I GOTTA GET HOME. I GOT A KID. I GOTTA GET HOME.
YOUR DAD WAS REALLY ONE OF THE BEST, KID.
THAT MURDOCK THING. HE'LL GO DOWN IN THE HISTORY BOOKS FOR THAT.
WHICH MURDOCK THING?
YOUR DAD-- YOU DON'T KNOW THIS? YOUR DAD-- YEARS BACK... YOUR DAD BLEW UP MURDOCK'S HOUSE.
BLEW IT RIGHT UP.
THE WHOLE THING. I LAUGHED SO HARD I THREW UP.
KINGPIN HIMSELF HIRED HIM TO DO IT.
(KINGPIN GETS ALL THE CREDIT FOR THE MOVE, SURE...)
BUT DON THE BOMB'S THE ONE WHO WENT AND DID IT.
MY DAD BLEW UP MATT MURDOCK'S HOUSE?
YEAH. AWHILE BACK, STORY GOES, KINGPIN FINDS OUT MURDOCK IS THIS DAREDEVIL BEFORE...*ANYONE* ELSE DID.
SO KINGPIN STARTS LOOKING FOR WAYS TO PICK MURDOCK APART.
WHY HE DIDN'T JUST WHACK HIM, I DON'T KNOW.
HIRED *YOUR* DAD TO BLOW UP HIS HOUSE.
YOUR DAD CAME UP WITH THIS GIDGET-GADGET SO DAREDEVIL'S SUPERPOWERS, WHATEVER THE HELL *THEY* ARE, CAN'T TELL IT'S GONNA HAPPEN.
BLEWY! KA-BLEWY!
IT'S THE KINGPIN'S SCORE BUT HEY! YOUR DAD DID IT.
SAME DEAL HERE.
BUT THIS IS GONNA BE YOUR *DAD'S* SCORE.
THIS...IS A BOMB?
SAME ONE. SAME DESIGN.
HE WANTS TO BLOW UP MATT MURDOCK?

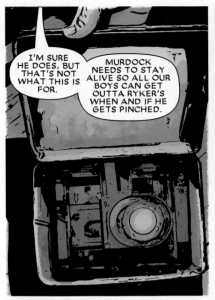

I'M SURE HE DOES, BUT THAT'S NOT WHAT THIS IS FOR.

MURDOCK NEEDS TO STAY ALIVE SO ALL OUR BOYS CAN GET OUTTA RYKER'S WHEN AND IF HE GETS PINCHED.

NO, THIS IS FOR MURDOCK'S BOY--

GUY'S NAME IS FOGGY.

WHICH TO ME, WITH A NAME LIKE THAT, SAYS HE HAD ONE BAD TIME IN THE HIGH SCHOOL.

GUY'S MATT MURDOCK'S BESTEST FRIEND IN THE WHOLE WORLD. SOME WEASEL LAWYER.

YOUR DAD WANTS HIM TO GO BLEWY.

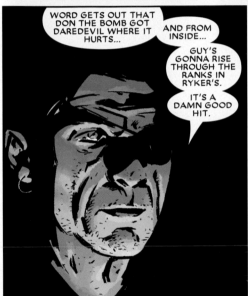

WORD GETS OUT THAT DON THE BOMB GOT DAREDEVIL WHERE IT HURTS...

AND FROM INSIDE...

GUY'S GONNA RISE THROUGH THE RANKS IN RYKER'S.

IT'S A DAMN GOOD HIT.

ALL YOU GOTTA DO IS SLIP IT UNDER HIS CAR AND PUSH THE BLUE BUTTON.

NEXT TIME THE CAR DOOR OPENS AND CLOSES-- BLEWY.

HEY, WHO KNOWS...

...MIGHT BE A NEW CAREER FOR YOU WHEN THE NEXT KINGPIN COMES UP...

AND, HEY, THAT MIGHT BE ME.

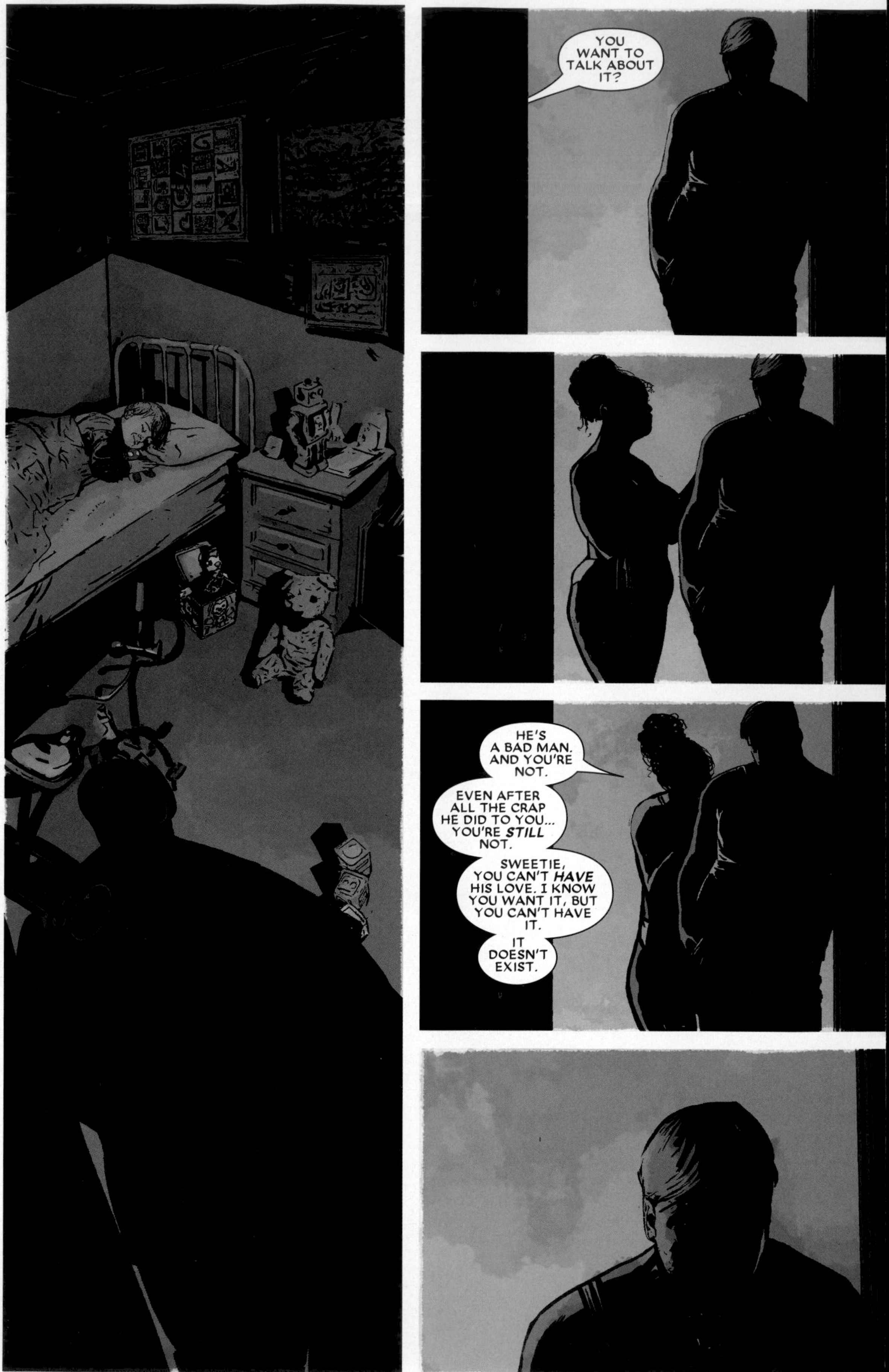
YOU WANT TO TALK ABOUT IT?
HE'S A BAD MAN. AND YOU'RE NOT.
EVEN AFTER ALL THE CRAP HE DID TO YOU... YOU'RE STILL NOT.
SWEETIE, YOU CAN'T HAVE HIS LOVE. I KNOW YOU WANT IT, BUT YOU CAN'T HAVE IT.
IT DOESN'T EXIST.

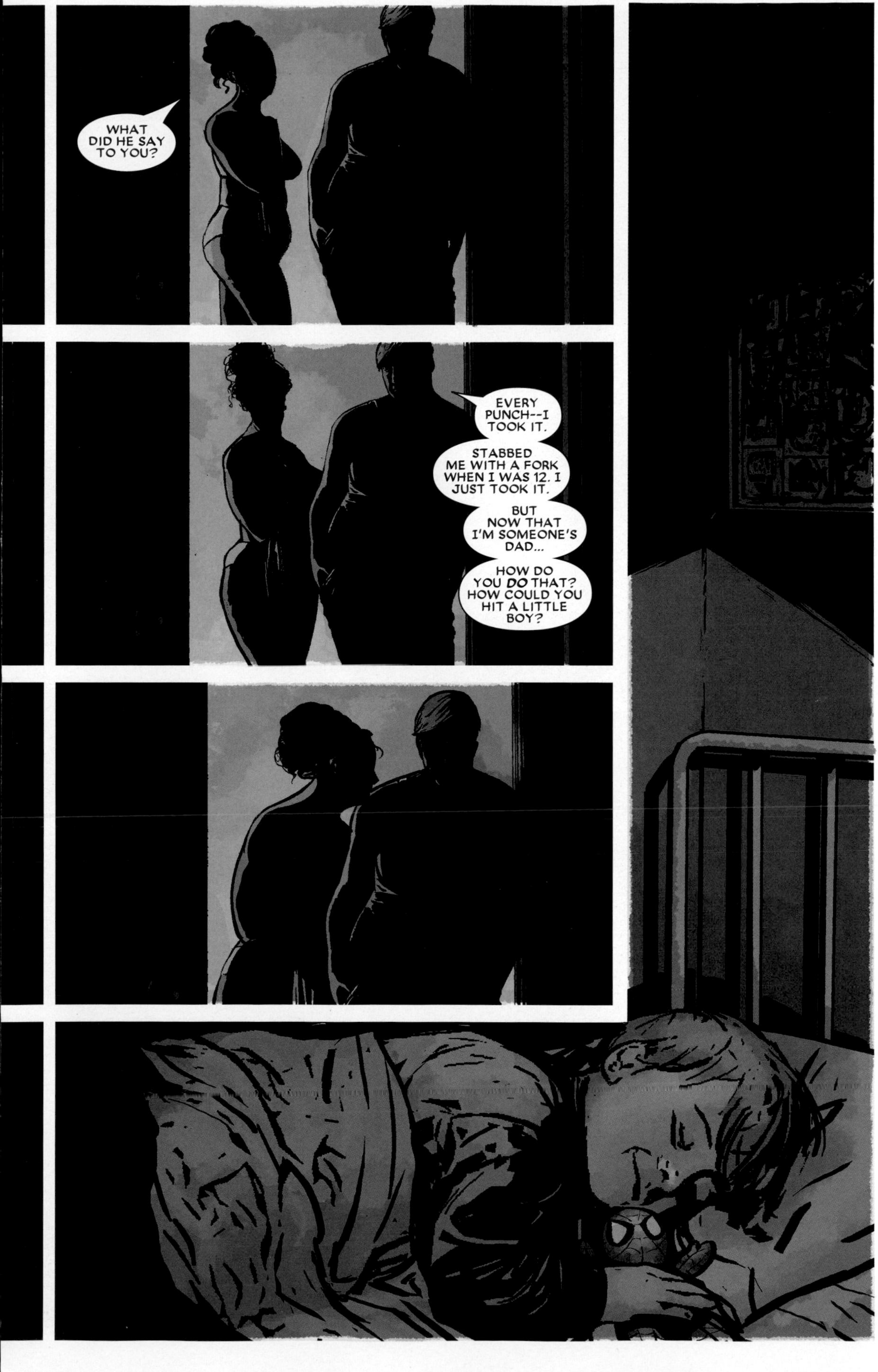
WHAT DID HE SAY TO YOU?
EVERY PUNCH--I TOOK IT.
STABBED ME WITH A FORK WHEN I WAS 12. I JUST TOOK IT.
BUT NOW THAT I'M SOMEONE'S DAD...
HOW DO YOU *DO* THAT? HOW COULD YOU HIT A LITTLE BOY?

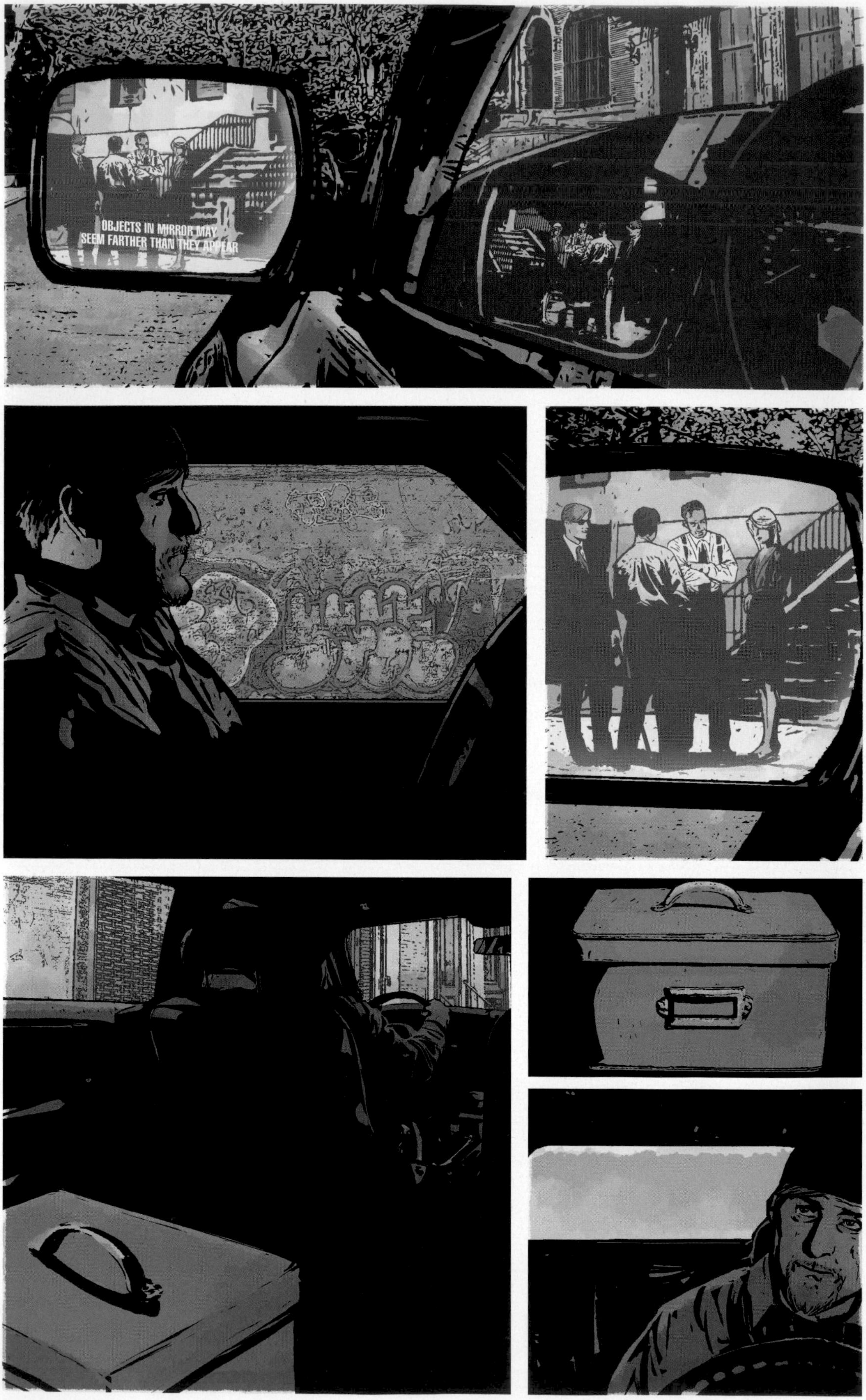
OBJECTS IN MIRROR MAY
SEEM FARTHER THAN THEY APPEAR

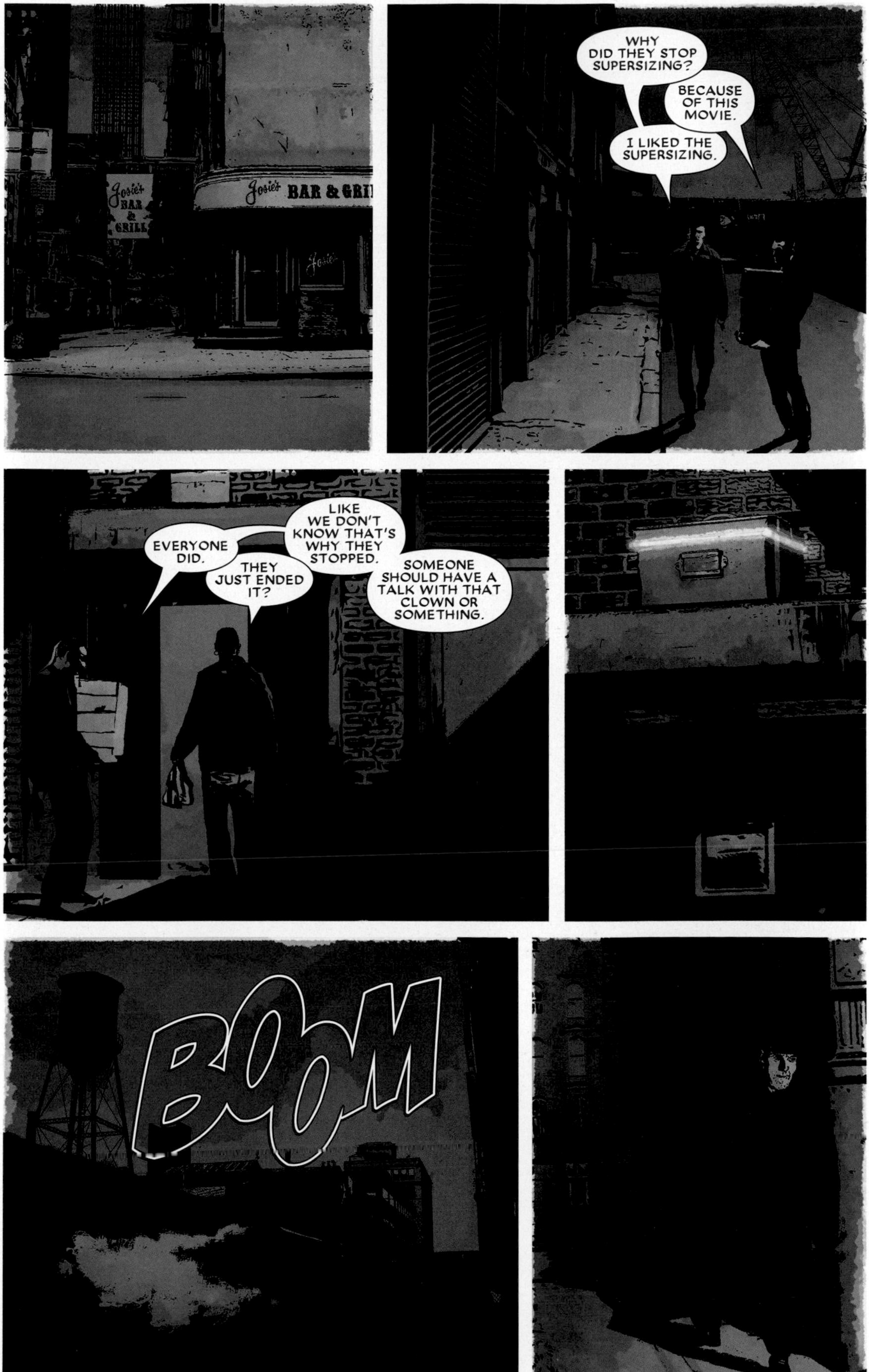
Josie's BAR & GRILL
Josie's BAR & GRILL
Josie's
WHY DID THEY STOP SUPERSIZING?
BECAUSE OF THIS MOVIE.
I LIKED THE SUPERSIZING.
EVERYONE DID.
LIKE WE DON'T KNOW THAT'S WHY THEY STOPPED.
THEY JUST ENDED IT?
SOMEONE SHOULD HAVE A TALK WITH THAT CLOWN OR SOMETHING.
BOOM

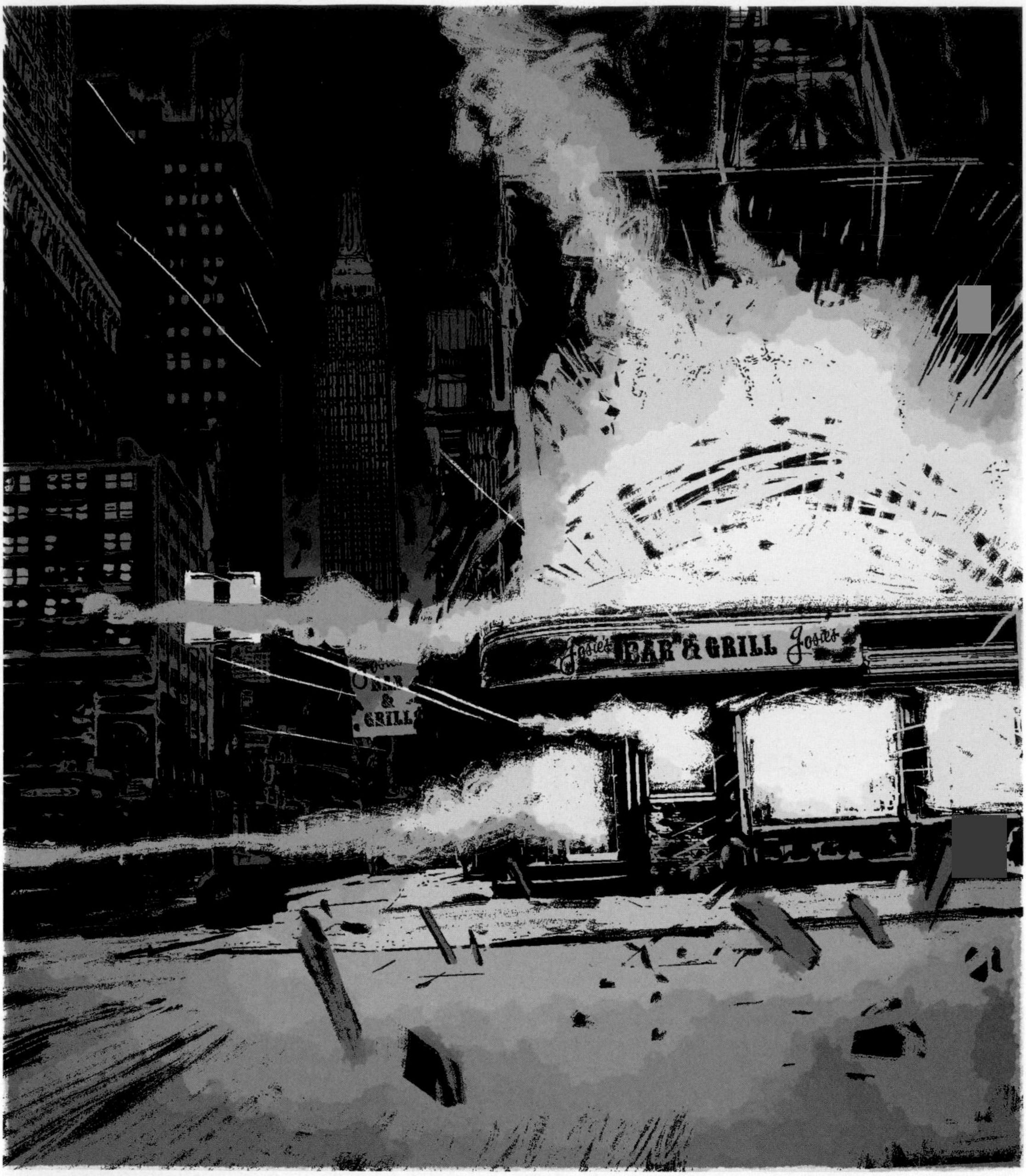
Josie's BAR & GRILL Josie's
& GRILL

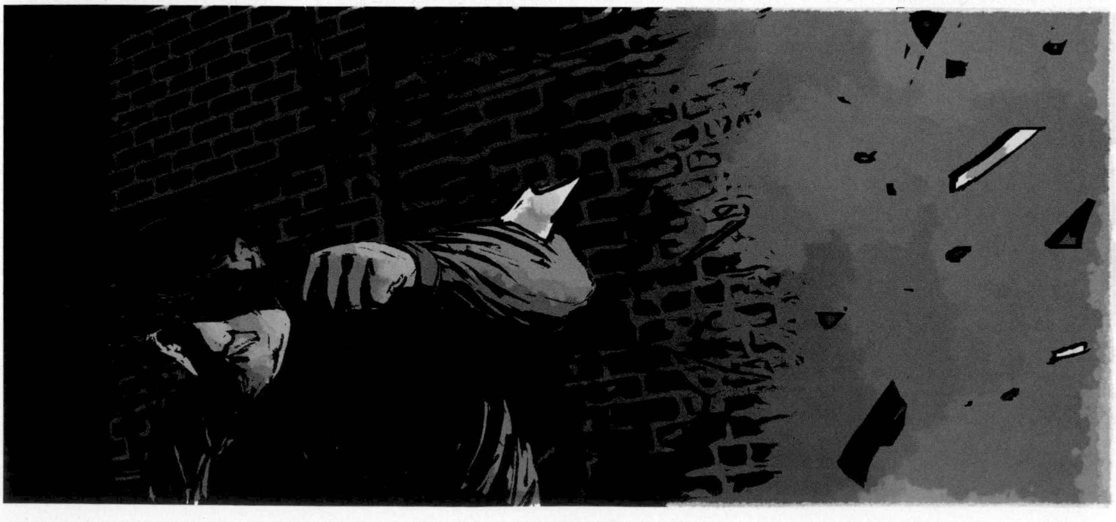

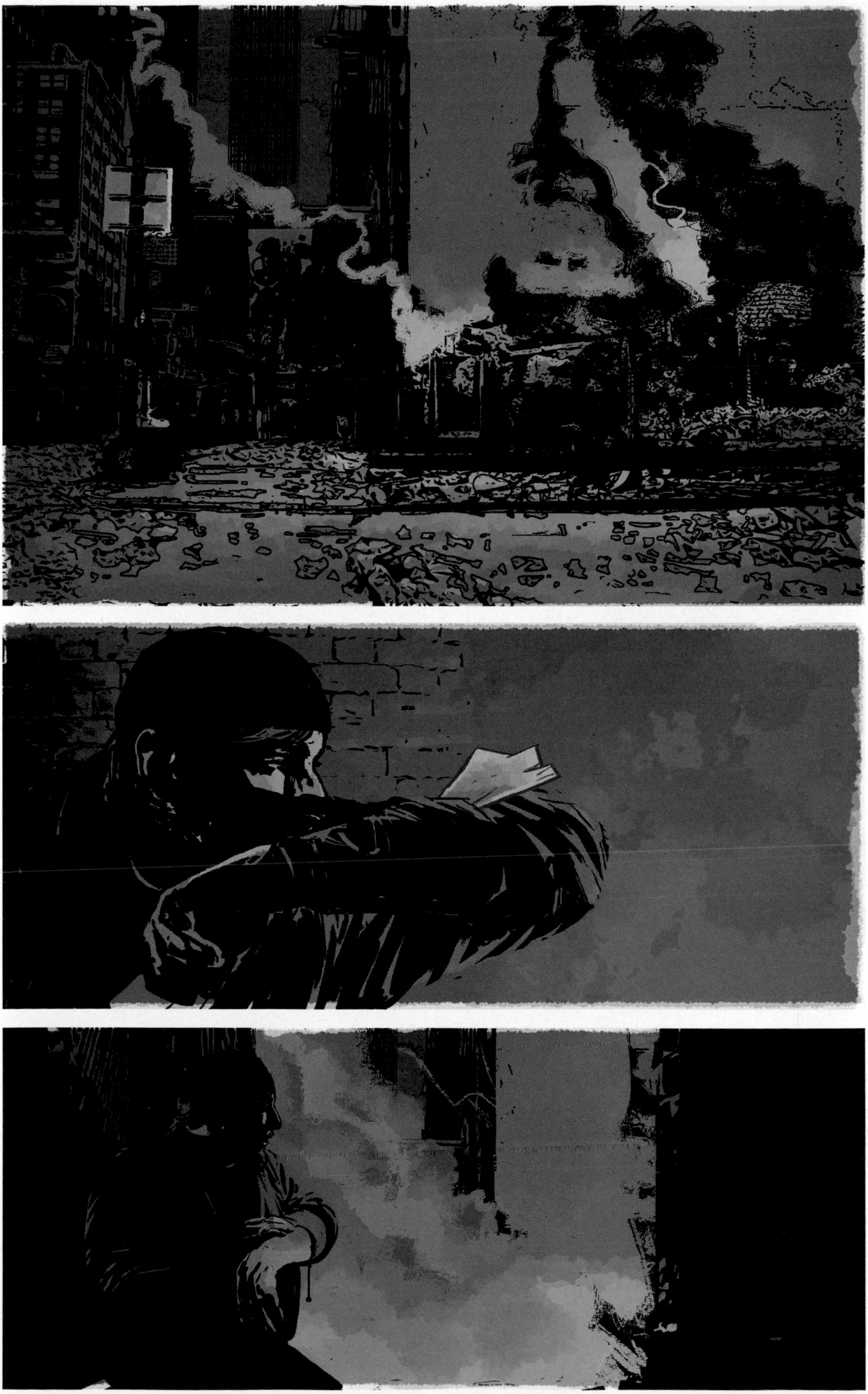

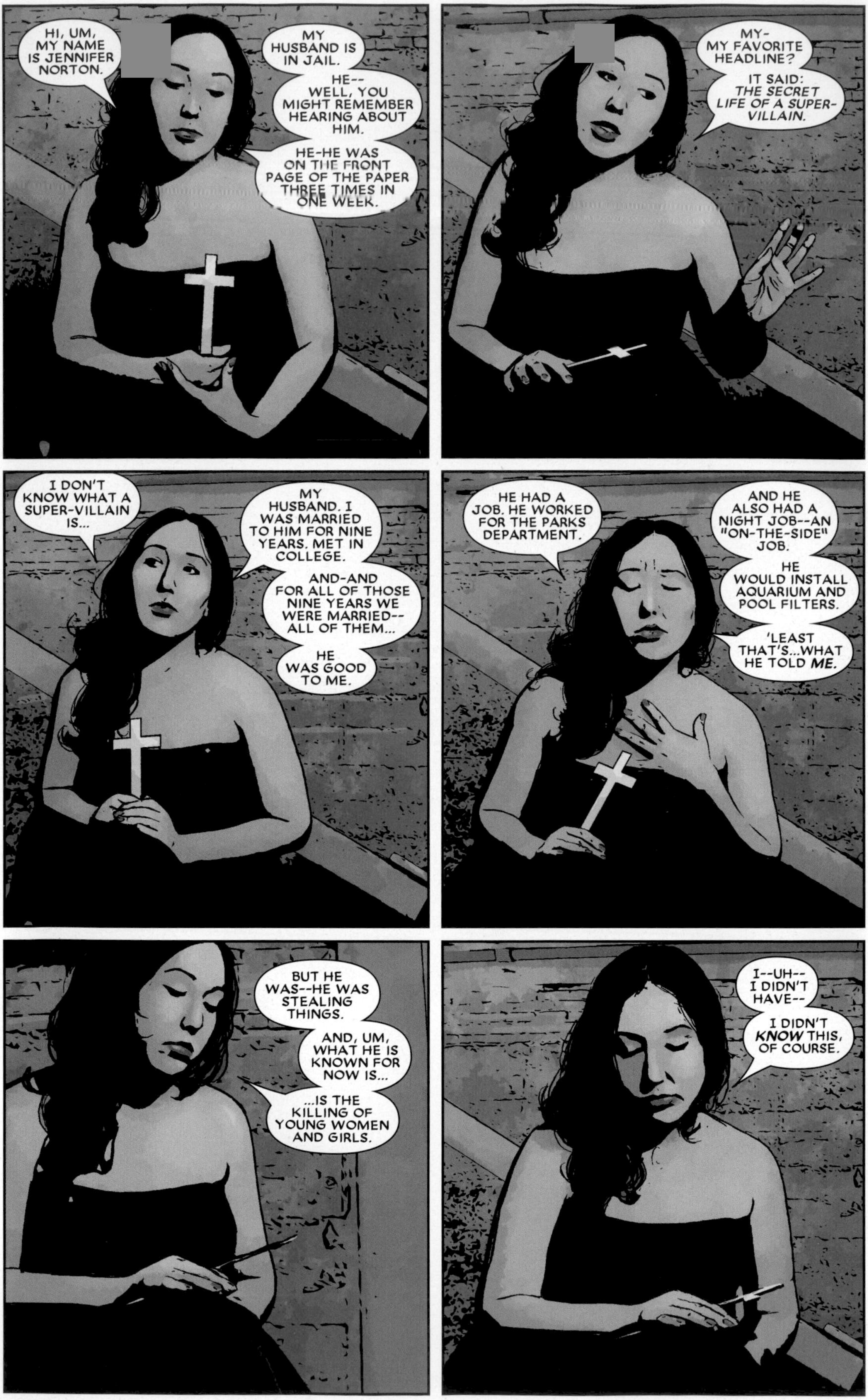
HI, UM, MY NAME IS JENNIFER NORTON.
MY HUSBAND IS IN JAIL.
HE-- WELL, YOU MIGHT REMEMBER HEARING ABOUT HIM.
HE-HE WAS ON THE FRONT PAGE OF THE PAPER THREE TIMES IN ONE WEEK.
MY- MY FAVORITE HEADLINE?
IT SAID: *THE SECRET LIFE OF A SUPER-VILLAIN.*
I DON'T KNOW WHAT A SUPER-VILLAIN IS...
MY HUSBAND. I WAS MARRIED TO HIM FOR NINE YEARS. MET IN COLLEGE.
AND-AND FOR ALL OF THOSE NINE YEARS WE WERE MARRIED-- ALL OF THEM...
HE WAS GOOD TO ME.
HE HAD A JOB. HE WORKED FOR THE PARKS DEPARTMENT.
AND HE ALSO HAD A NIGHT JOB--AN "ON-THE-SIDE" JOB.
HE WOULD INSTALL AQUARIUM AND POOL FILTERS.
'LEAST THAT'S...WHAT HE TOLD *ME.*
BUT HE WAS--HE WAS STEALING THINGS.
AND, UM, WHAT HE IS KNOWN FOR NOW IS...
...IS THE KILLING OF YOUNG WOMEN AND GIRLS.
I--UH-- I DIDN'T HAVE--
I DIDN'T ***KNOW*** THIS, OF COURSE.

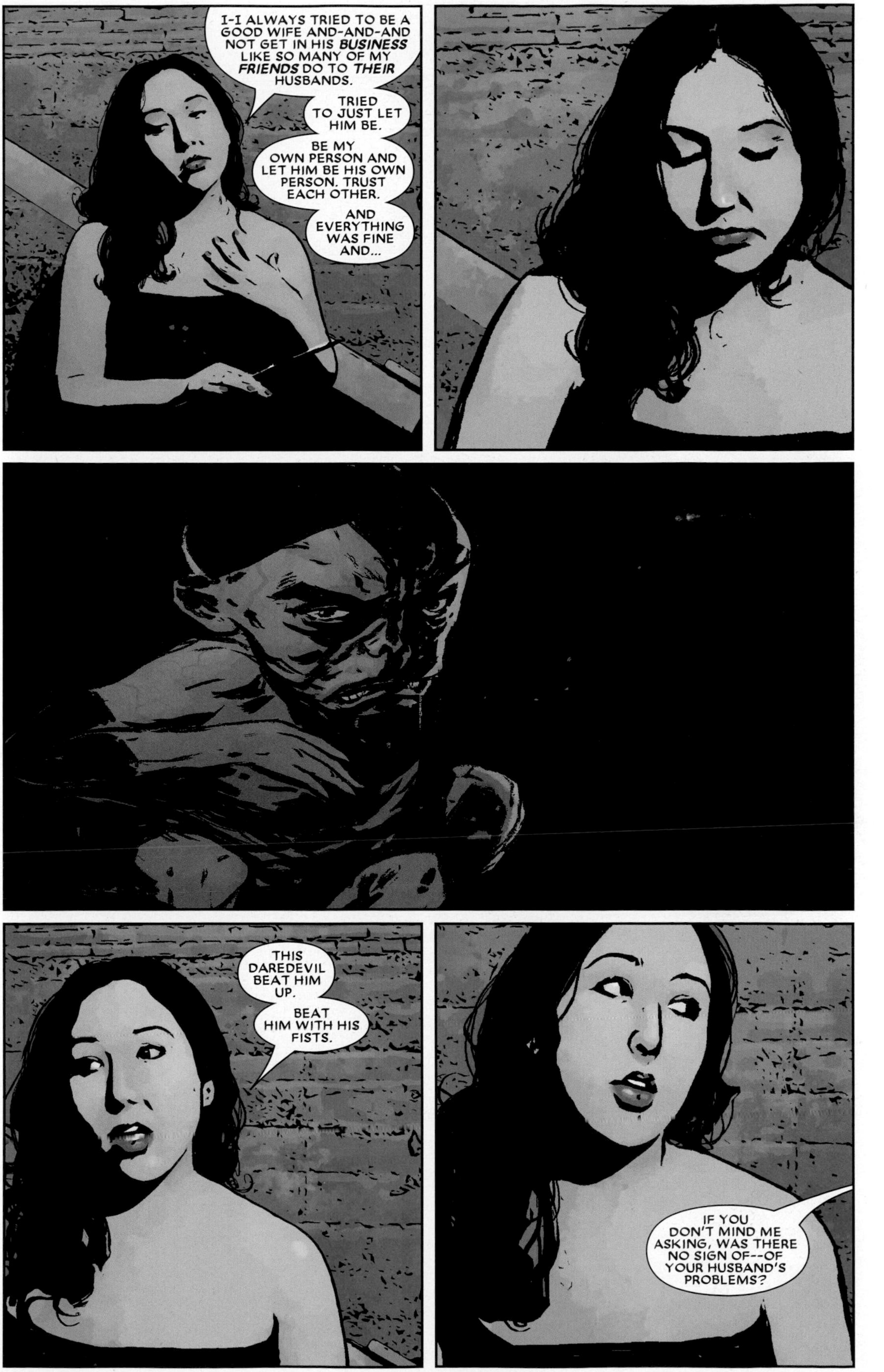
I-I ALWAYS TRIED TO BE A GOOD WIFE AND-AND-AND NOT GET IN HIS *BUSINESS* LIKE SO MANY OF MY *FRIENDS* DO TO *THEIR* HUSBANDS.
TRIED TO JUST LET HIM BE.
BE MY OWN PERSON AND LET HIM BE HIS OWN PERSON. TRUST EACH OTHER.
AND EVERYTHING WAS FINE AND...
THIS DAREDEVIL BEAT HIM UP.
BEAT HIM WITH HIS FISTS.
IF YOU DON'T MIND ME ASKING, WAS THERE NO SIGN OF--OF YOUR HUSBAND'S PROBLEMS?

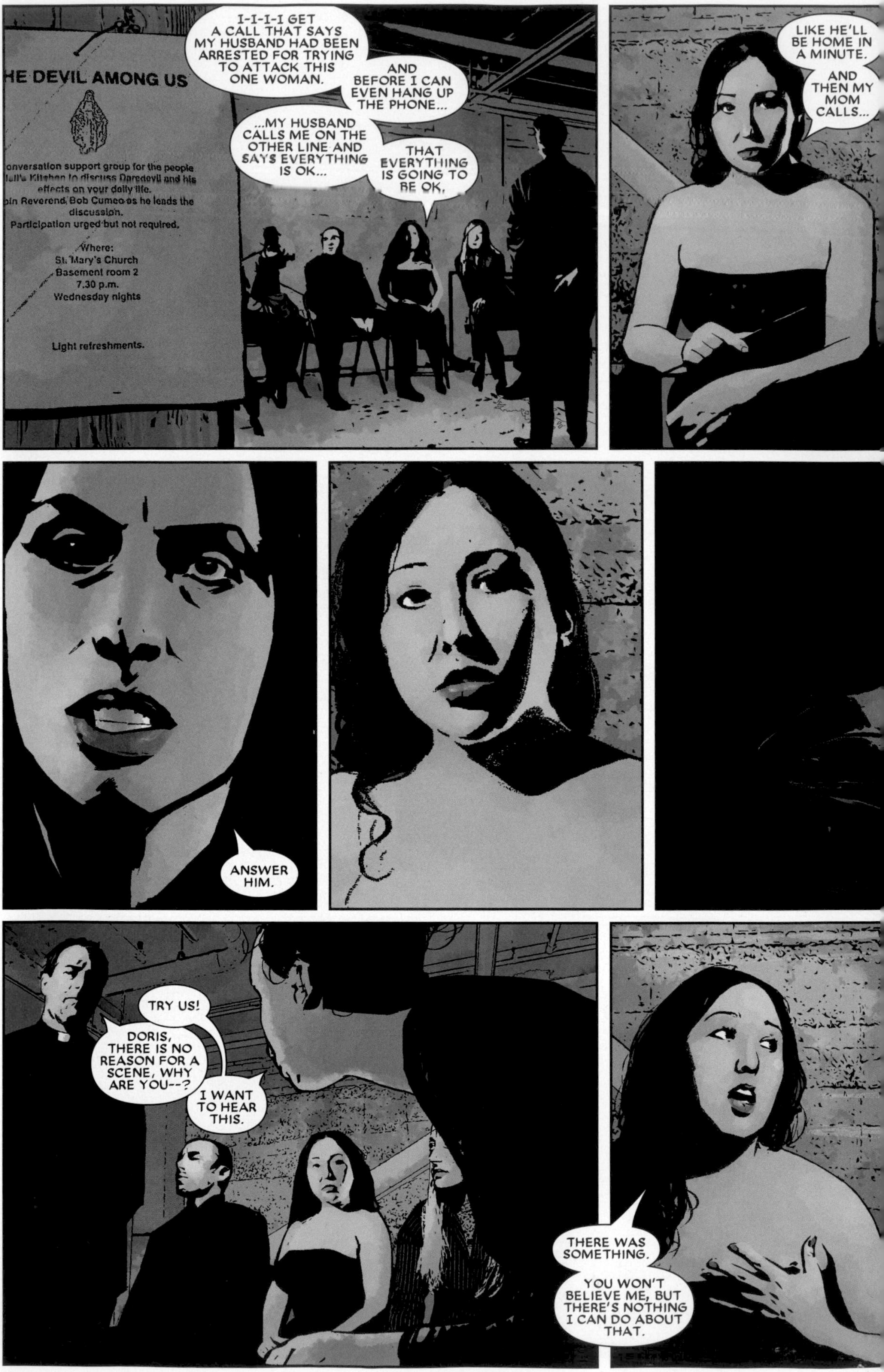
HE DEVIL AMONG US
onversation support group for the people
effects on your daily life.
oin Reverend Bob Cumeo as he leads the discussion.
Participation urged but not required.
Where:
St. Mary's Church
Basement room 2
7.30 p.m.
Wednesday nights
Light refreshments.
I-I-I-I GET A CALL THAT SAYS MY HUSBAND HAD BEEN ARRESTED FOR TRYING TO ATTACK THIS ONE WOMAN.
AND BEFORE I CAN EVEN HANG UP THE PHONE...
...MY HUSBAND CALLS ME ON THE OTHER LINE AND SAYS EVERYTHING IS OK...
THAT EVERYTHING IS GOING TO BE OK,
LIKE HE'LL BE HOME IN A MINUTE.
AND THEN MY MOM CALLS...
ANSWER HIM.
TRY US!
DORIS, THERE IS NO REASON FOR A SCENE, WHY ARE YOU--?
I WANT TO HEAR THIS.
THERE WAS SOMETHING.
YOU WON'T BELIEVE ME, BUT THERE'S NOTHING I CAN DO ABOUT THAT.

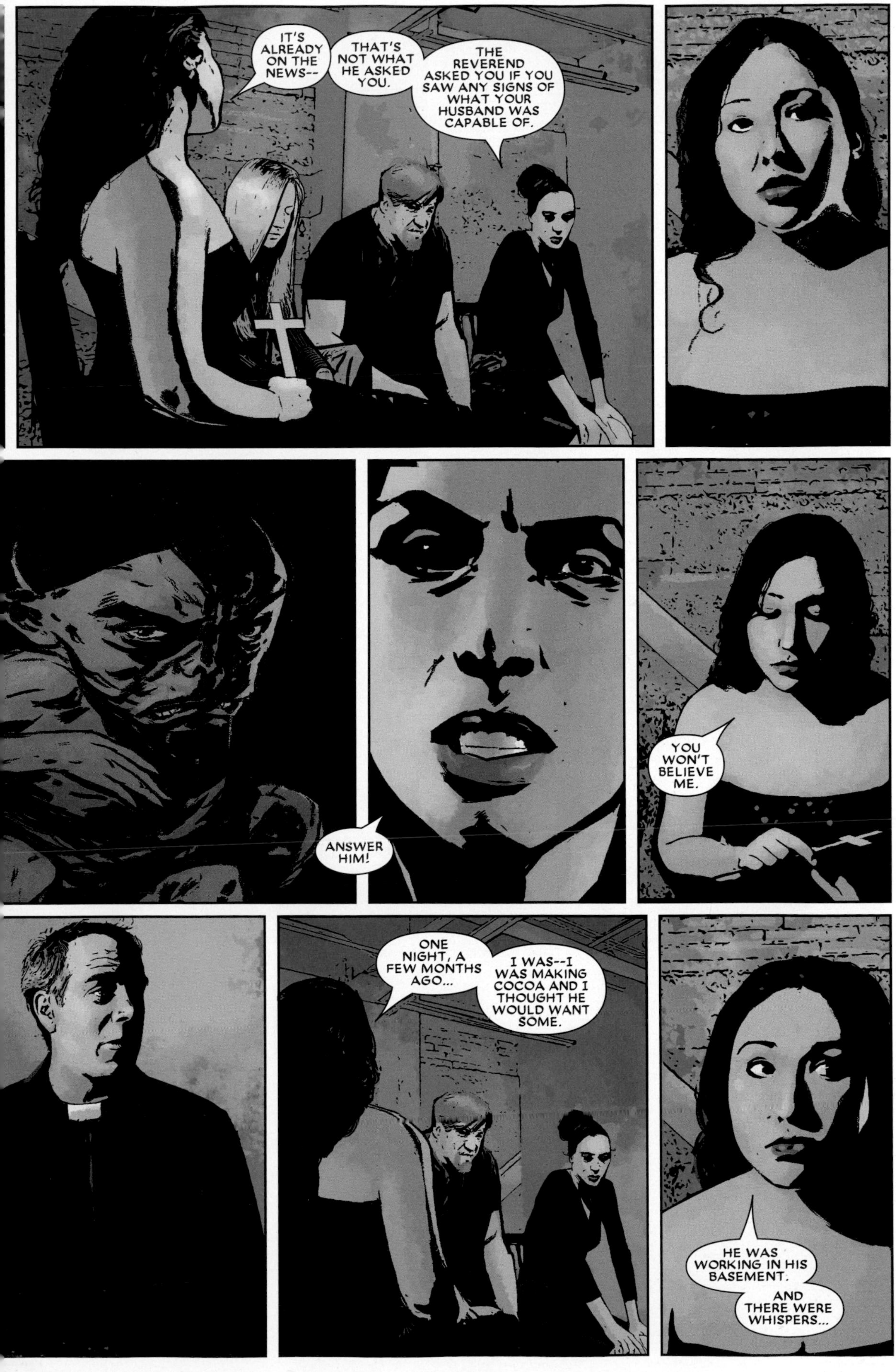
IT'S ALREADY ON THE NEWS--
THAT'S NOT WHAT HE ASKED YOU.
THE REVEREND ASKED YOU IF YOU SAW ANY SIGNS OF WHAT YOUR HUSBAND WAS CAPABLE OF.
ANSWER HIM!
YOU WON'T BELIEVE ME.
ONE NIGHT, A FEW MONTHS AGO...
I WAS--I WAS MAKING COCOA AND I THOUGHT HE WOULD WANT SOME.
HE WAS WORKING IN HIS BASEMENT.
AND THERE WERE WHISPERS...

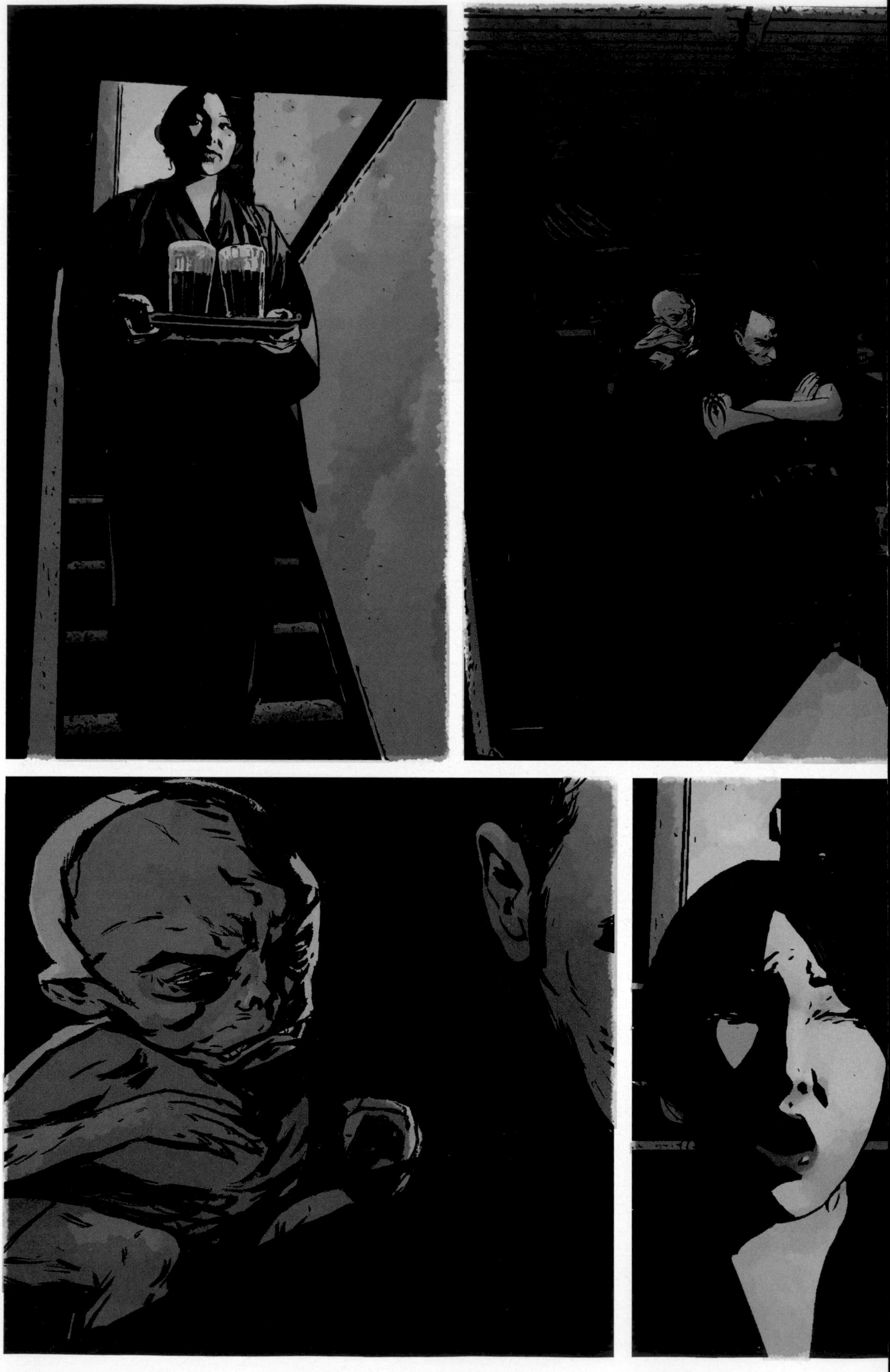

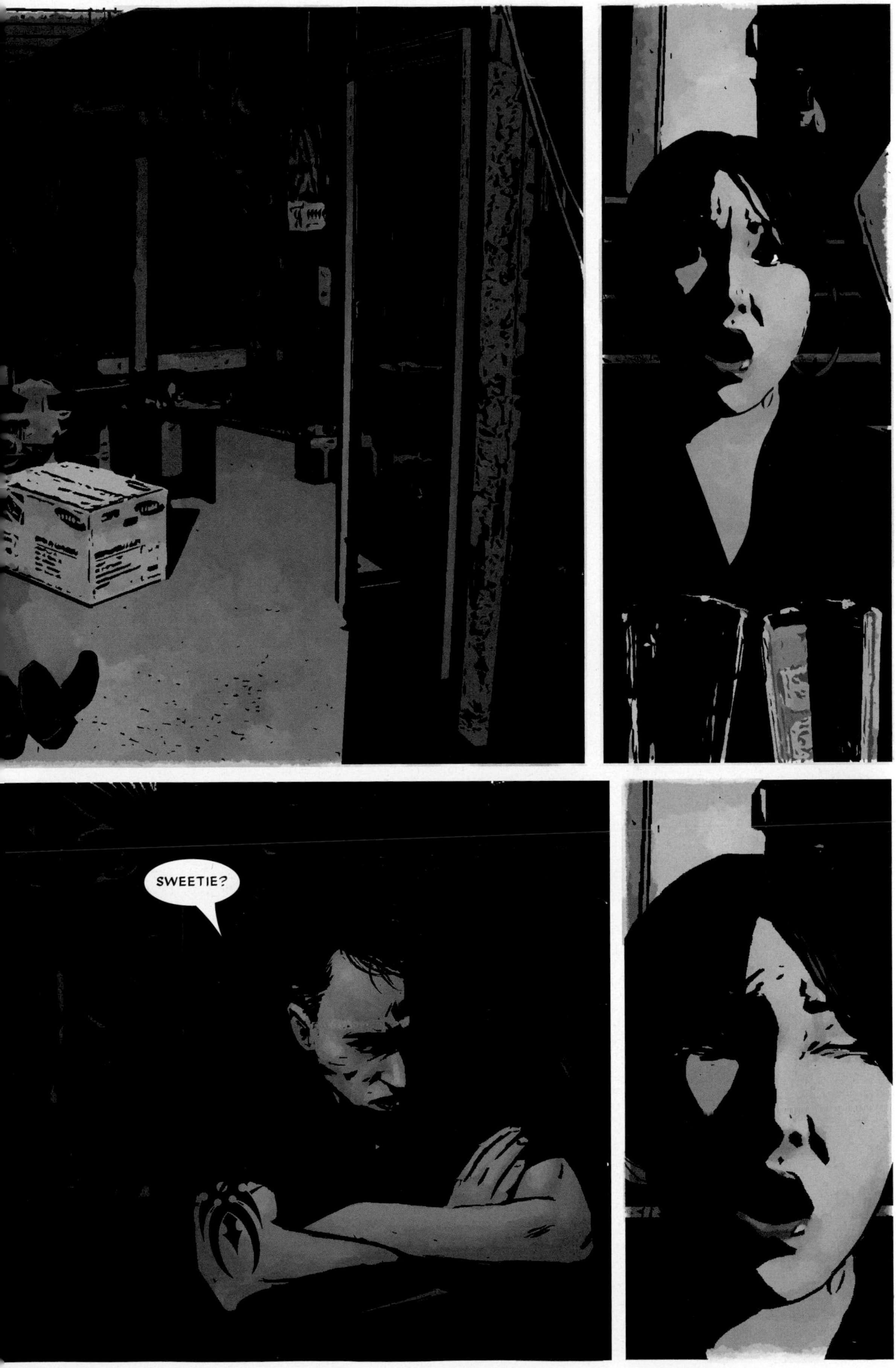
SWEETIE?

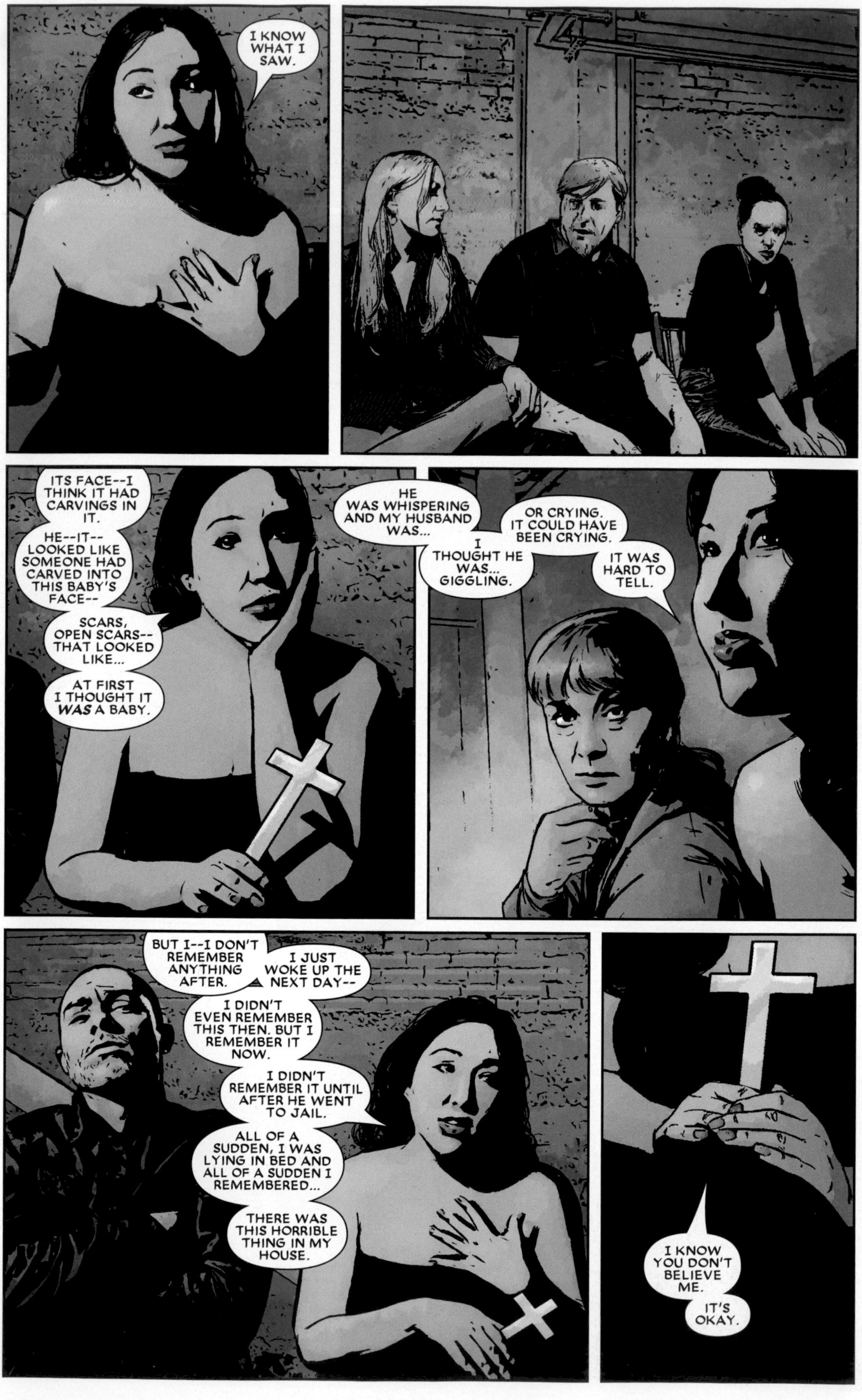
I KNOW WHAT I SAW.
ITS FACE--I THINK IT HAD CARVINGS IN IT.
HE--IT--LOOKED LIKE SOMEONE HAD CARVED INTO THIS BABY'S FACE--
SCARS, OPEN SCARS--THAT LOOKED LIKE...
AT FIRST I THOUGHT IT *WAS* A BABY.
HE WAS WHISPERING AND MY HUSBAND WAS...
I THOUGHT HE WAS... GIGGLING.
OR CRYING. IT COULD HAVE BEEN CRYING.
IT WAS HARD TO TELL.
BUT I--I DON'T REMEMBER ANYTHING AFTER.
I JUST WOKE UP THE NEXT DAY--
I DIDN'T EVEN REMEMBER THIS THEN. BUT I REMEMBER IT NOW.
I DIDN'T REMEMBER IT UNTIL AFTER HE WENT TO JAIL.
ALL OF A SUDDEN, I WAS LYING IN BED AND ALL OF A SUDDEN I REMEMBERED...
THERE WAS THIS HORRIBLE THING IN MY HOUSE.
I KNOW YOU DON'T BELIEVE ME.
IT'S OKAY.

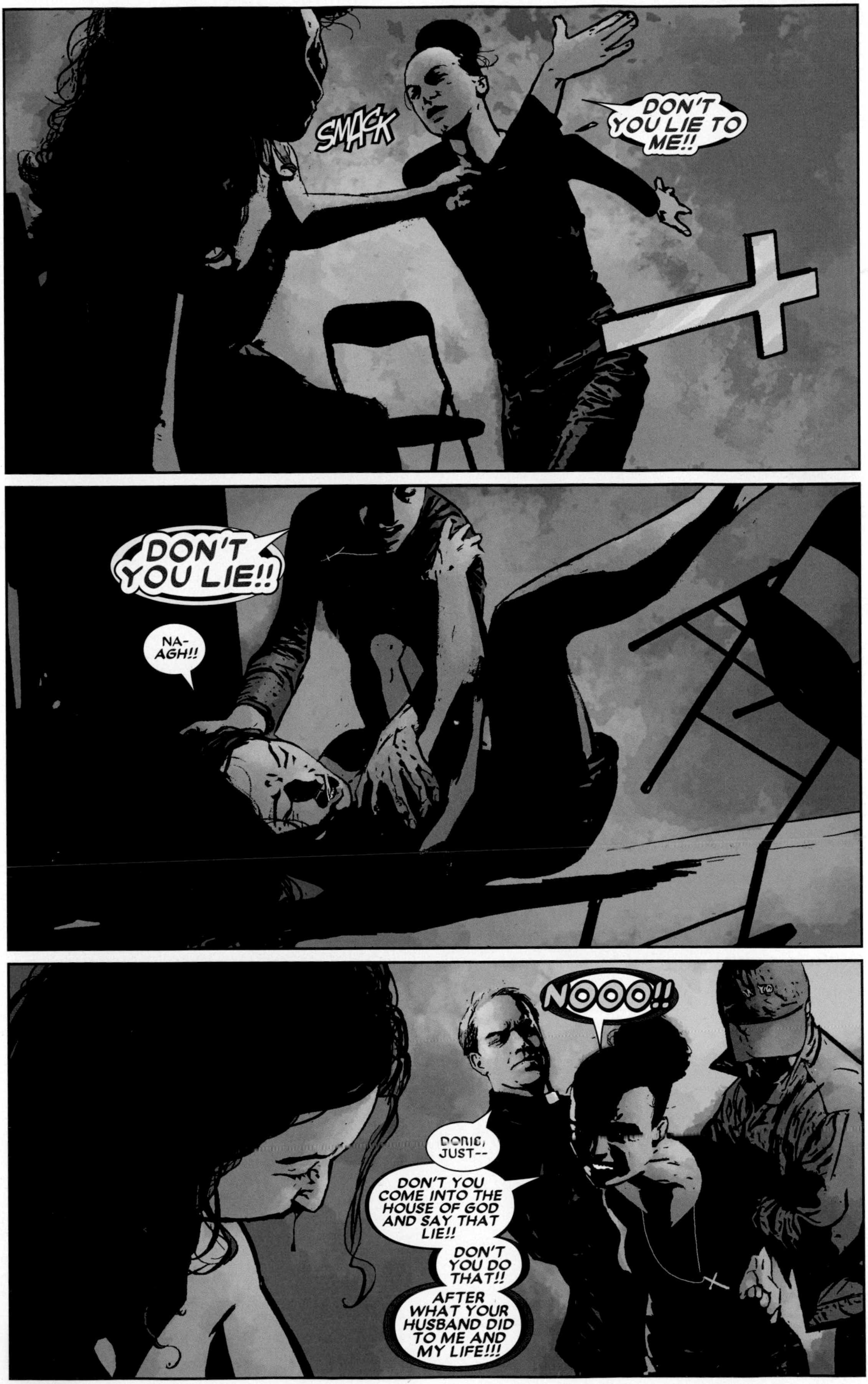
SMACK
DON'T YOU LIE TO ME!!
DON'T YOU LIE!!
NA-AGH!!
NOOO!!
DORIS, JUST--
DON'T YOU COME INTO THE HOUSE OF GOD AND SAY THAT LIE!!
DON'T YOU DO THAT!!
AFTER WHAT YOUR HUSBAND DID TO ME AND MY LIFE!!!

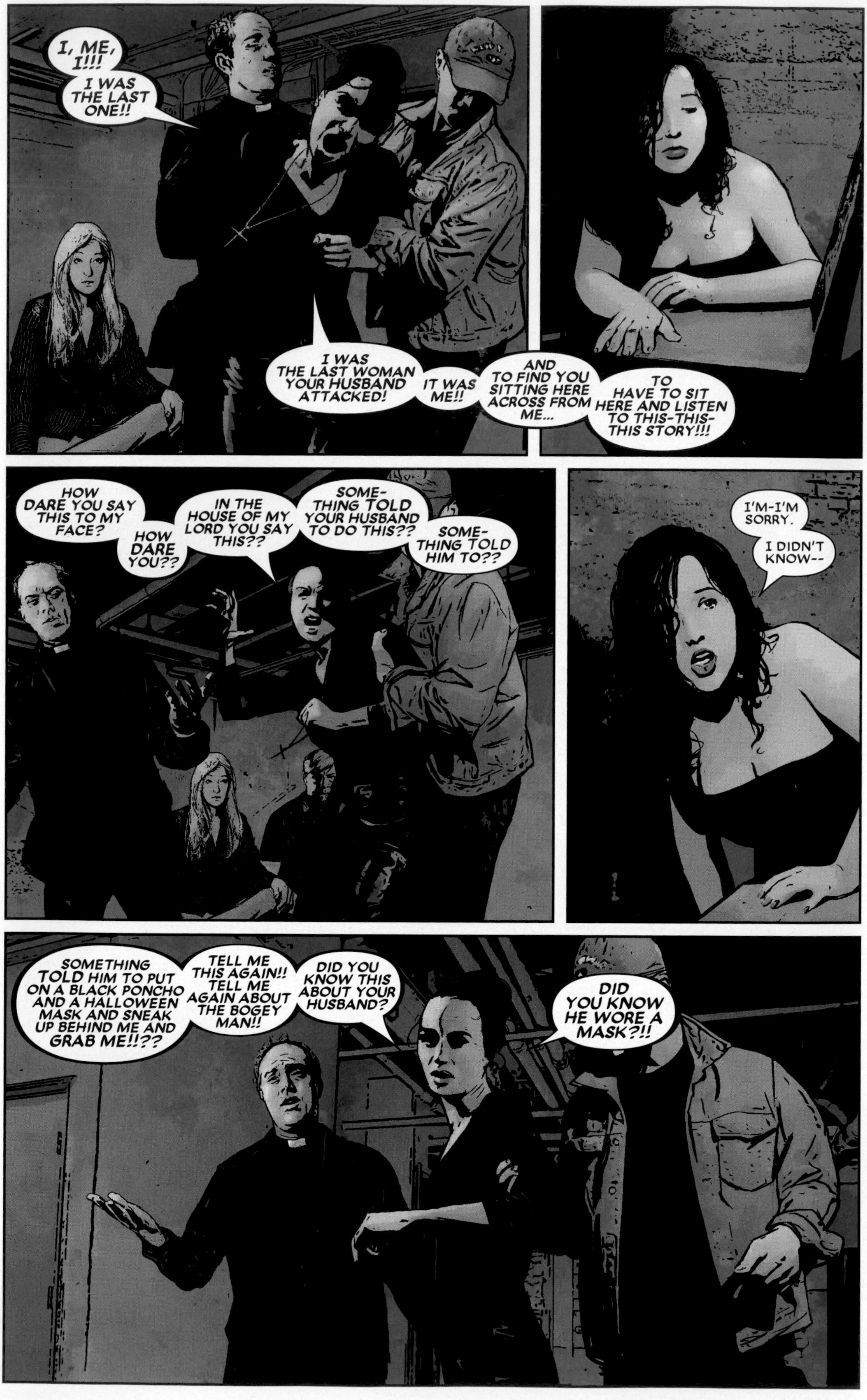
I, ME, I!!! I WAS THE LAST ONE!!
I WAS THE LAST WOMAN YOUR HUSBAND ATTACKED!
IT WAS ME!!
AND TO FIND YOU SITTING HERE ACROSS FROM ME...
TO HAVE TO SIT HERE AND LISTEN TO THIS-THIS-THIS STORY!!!
HOW DARE YOU SAY THIS TO MY FACE?
HOW DARE YOU??
IN THE HOUSE OF MY LORD YOU SAY THIS??
SOME-THING TOLD YOUR HUSBAND TO DO THIS??
SOME-THING TOLD HIM TO??
I'M-I'M SORRY.
I DIDN'T KNOW--
SOMETHING TOLD HIM TO PUT ON A BLACK PONCHO AND A HALLOWEEN MASK AND SNEAK UP BEHIND ME AND GRAB ME!!??
TELL ME THIS AGAIN!! TELL ME AGAIN ABOUT THE BOGEY MAN!!
DID YOU KNOW THIS ABOUT YOUR HUSBAND?
DID YOU KNOW HE WORE A MASK?!!

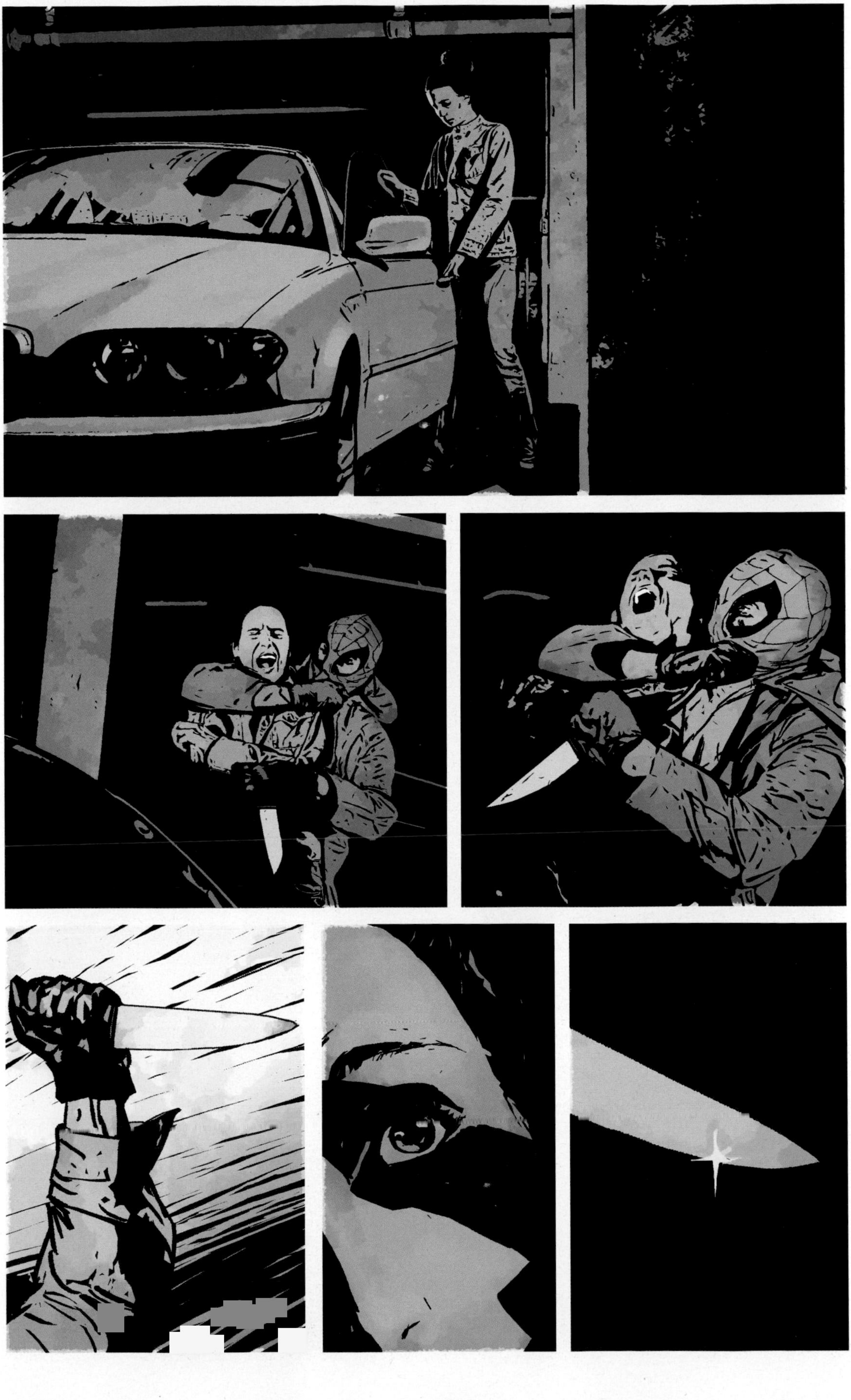

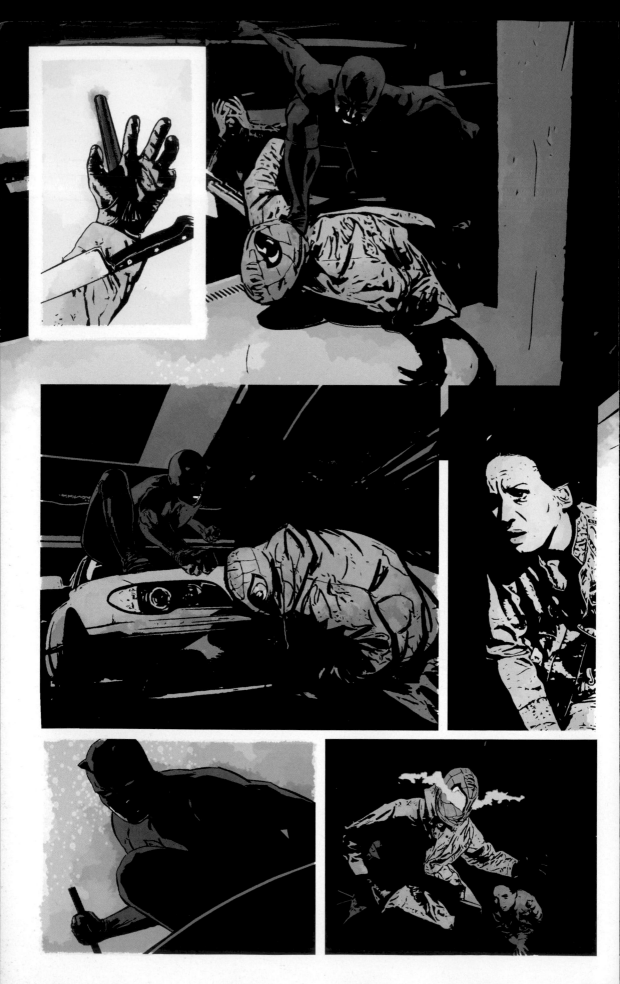

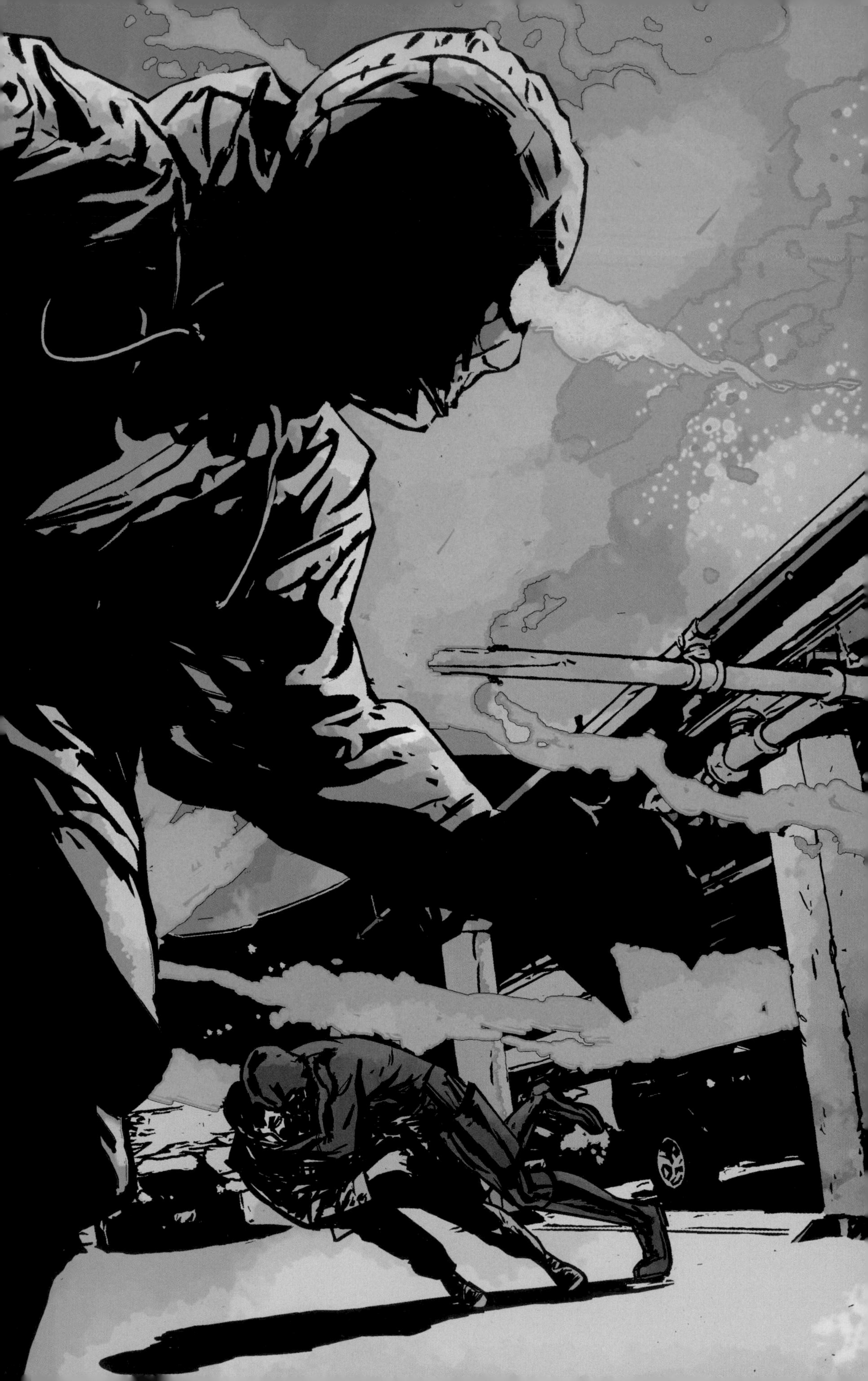

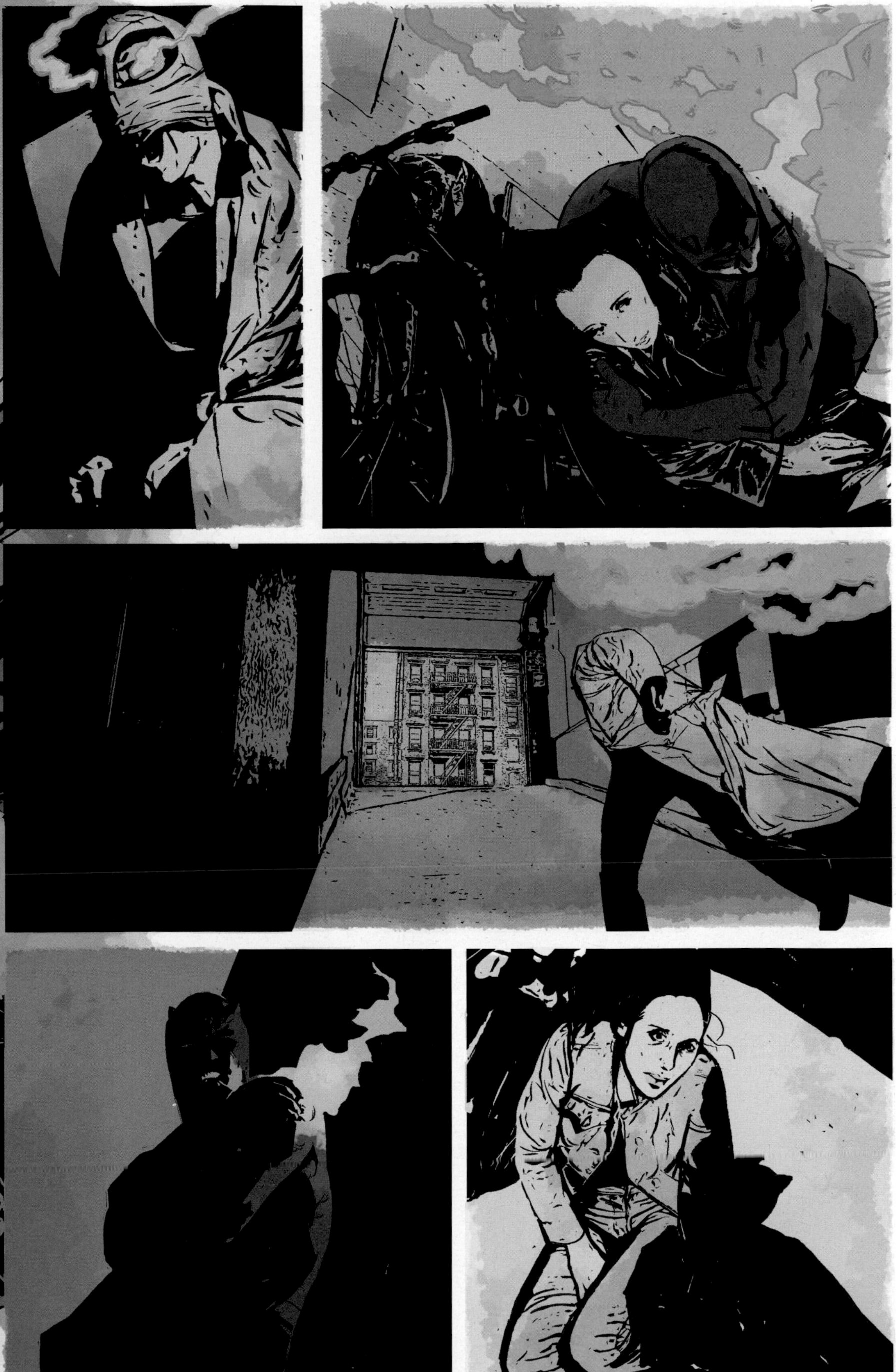

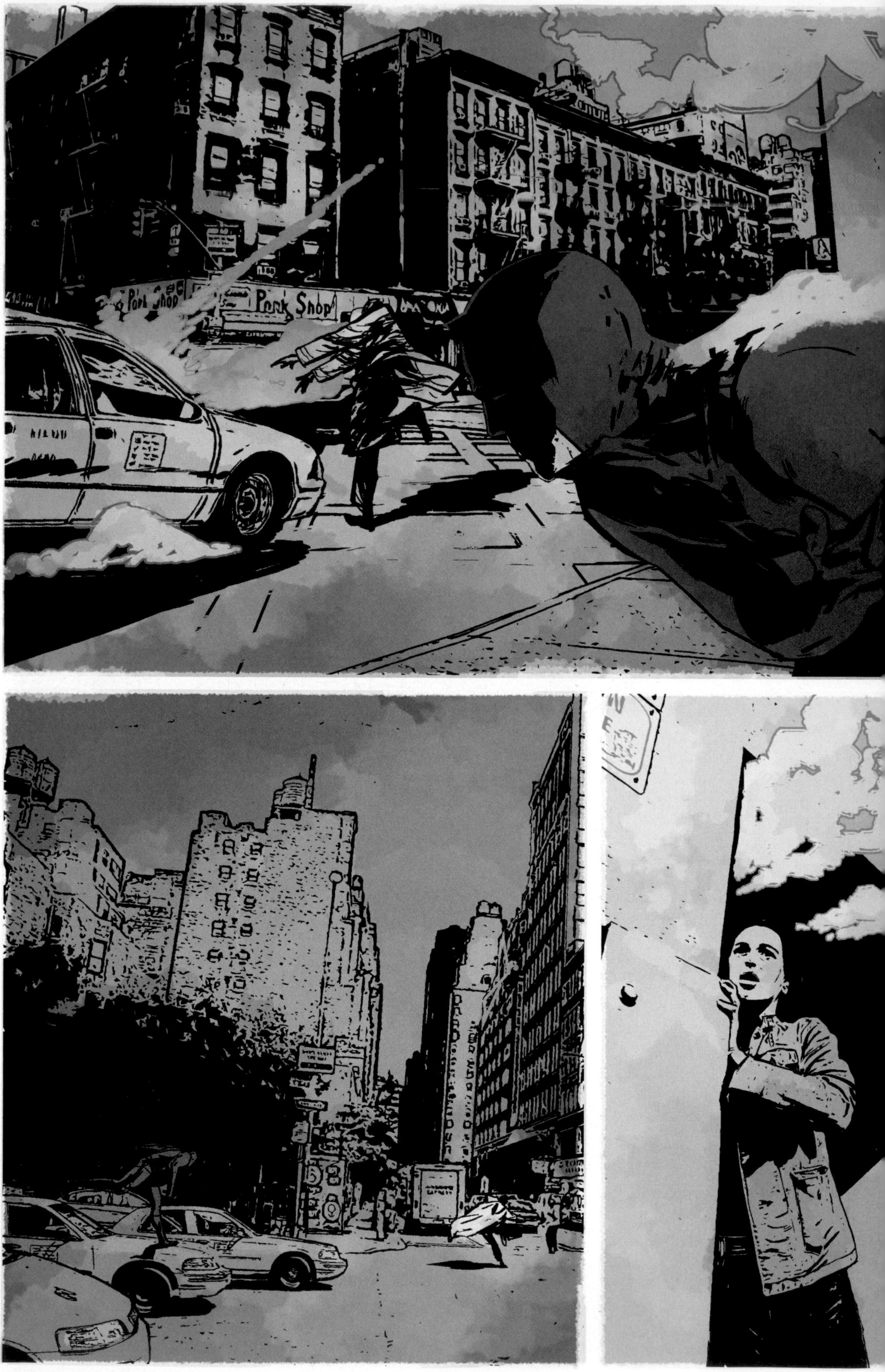
Pork Shop
Pork Shop

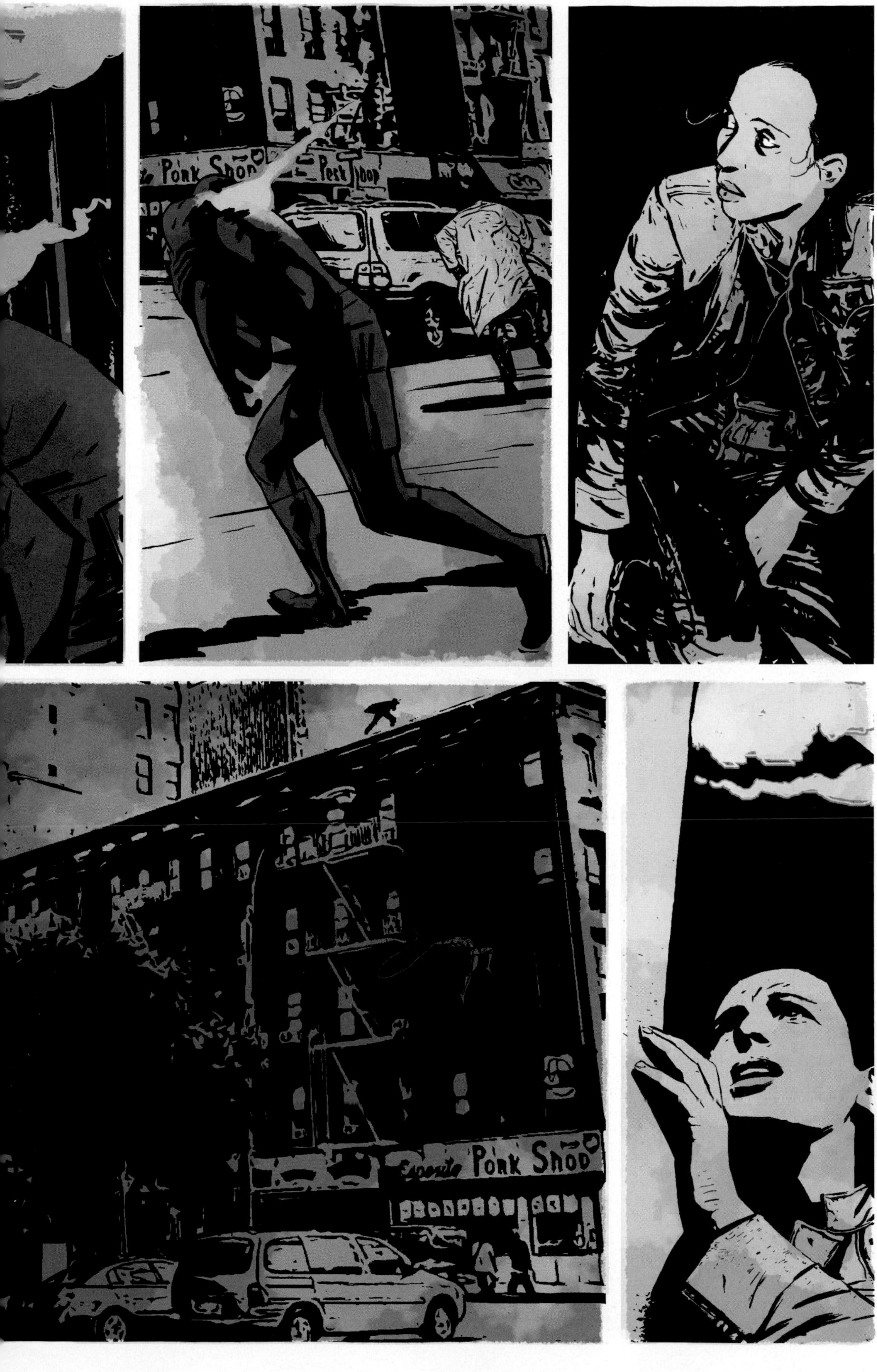

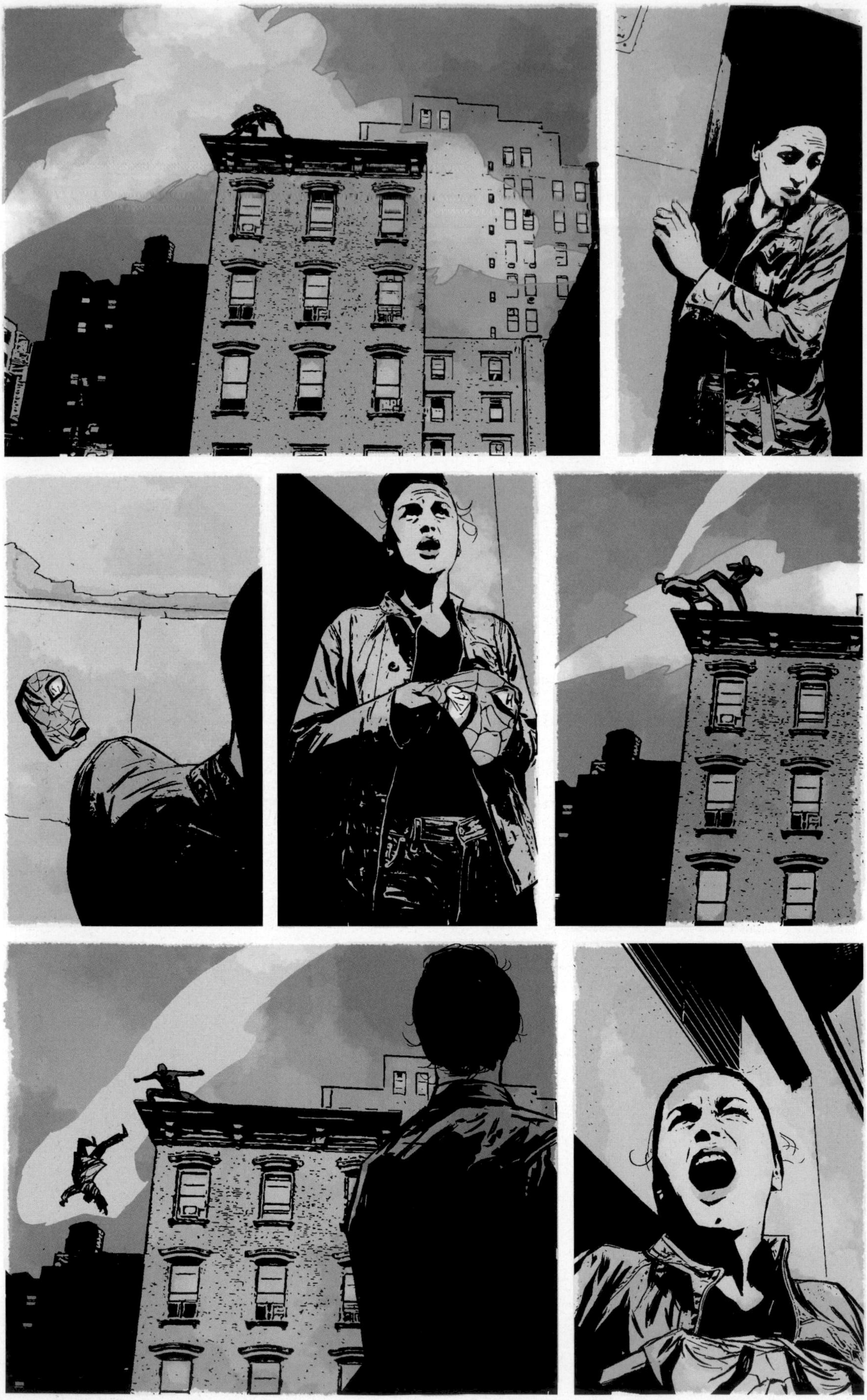

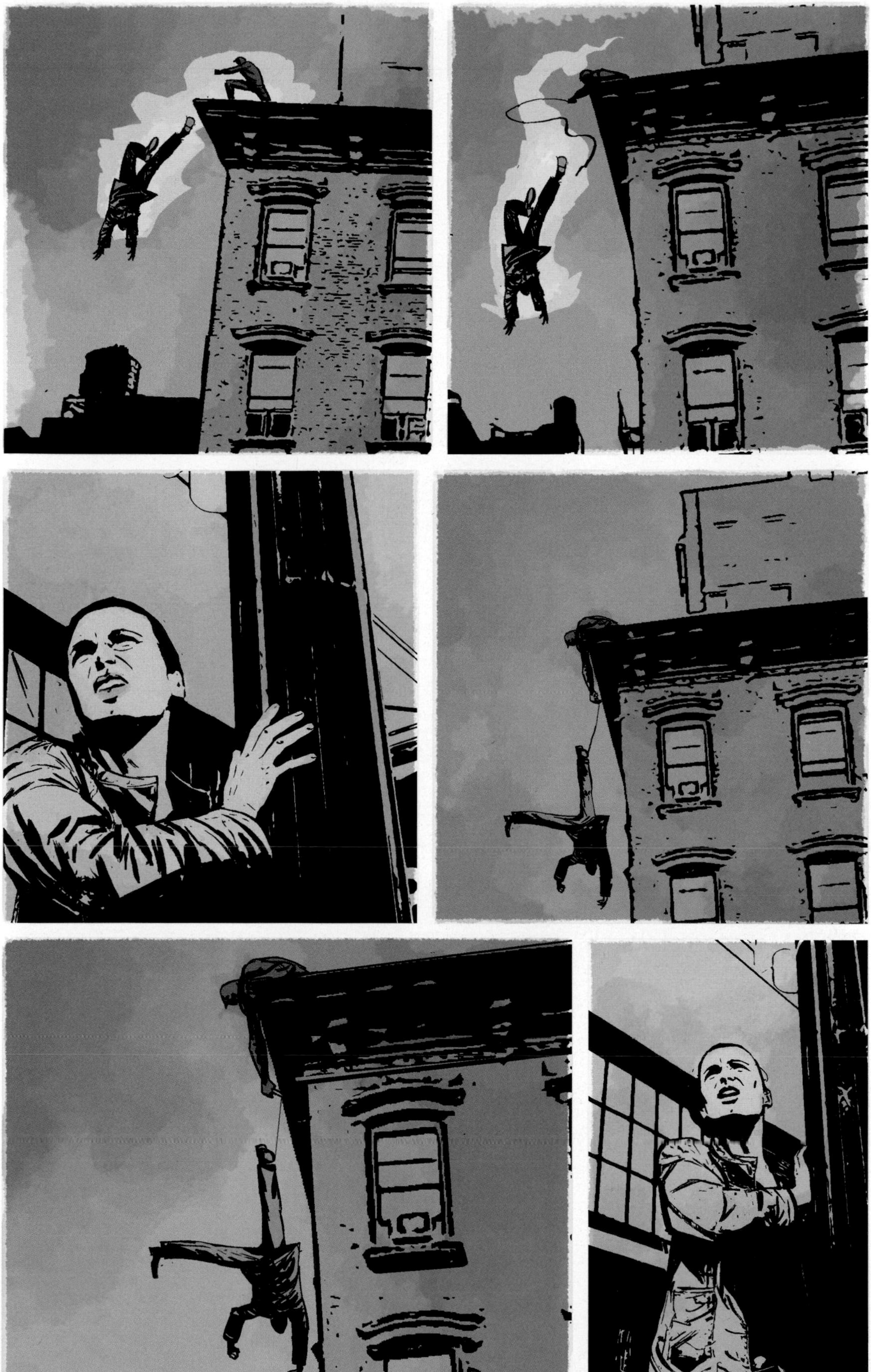

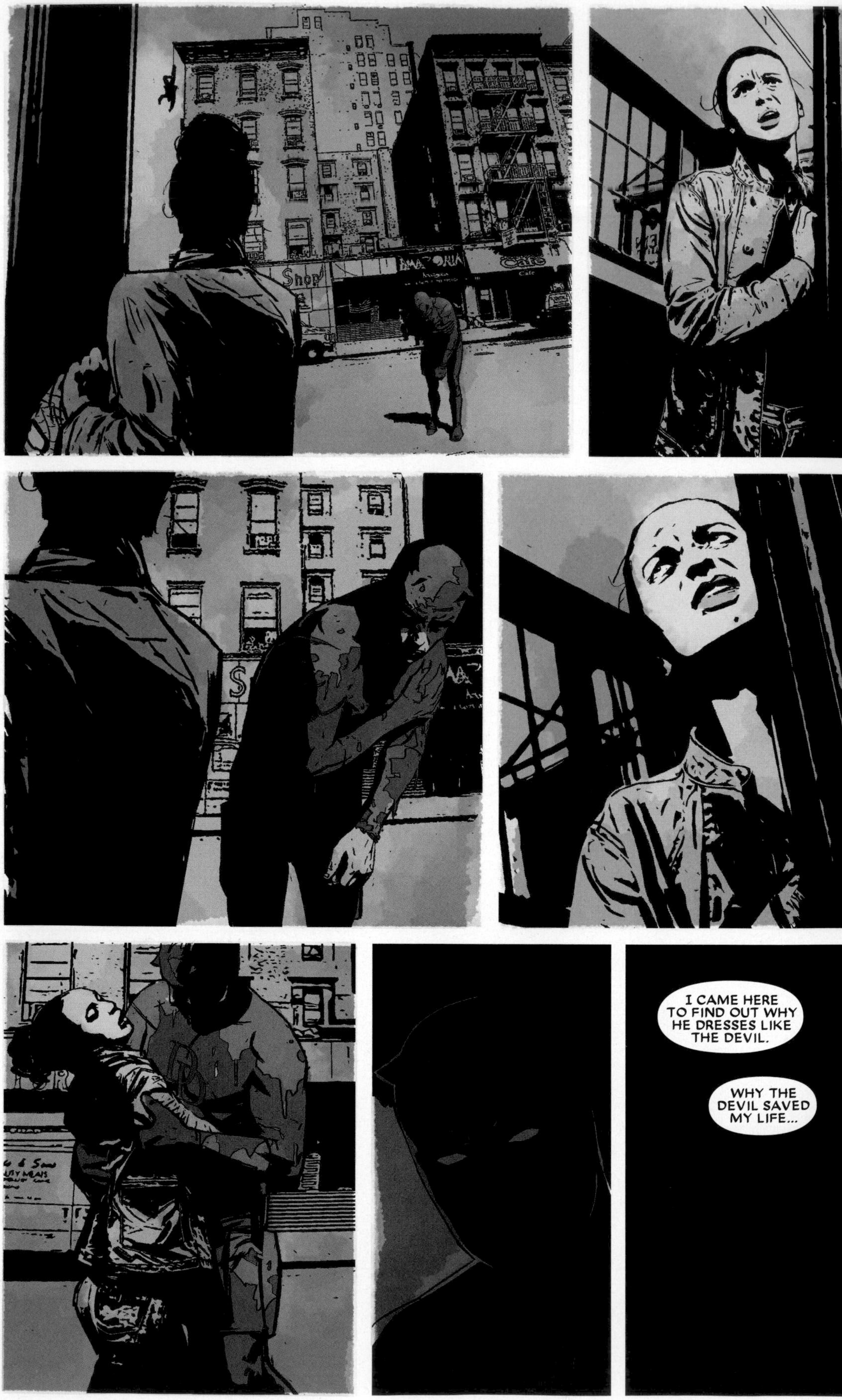
Shop
Cafe
I CAME HERE TO FIND OUT WHY HE DRESSES LIKE THE DEVIL.
WHY THE DEVIL SAVED MY LIFE...

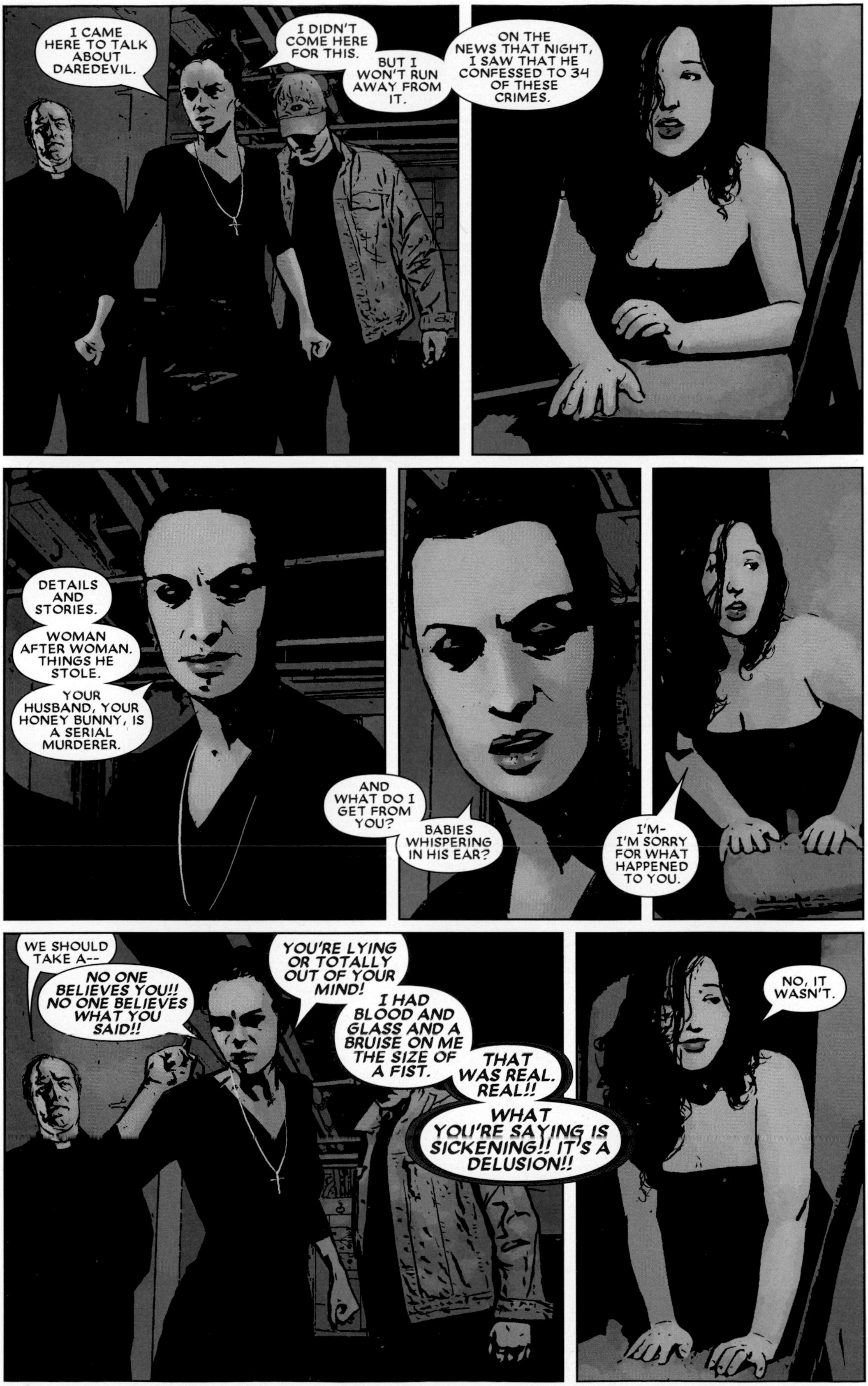
I CAME HERE TO TALK ABOUT DAREDEVIL.
I DIDN'T COME HERE FOR THIS.
BUT I WON'T RUN AWAY FROM IT.
ON THE NEWS THAT NIGHT, I SAW THAT HE CONFESSED TO 34 OF THESE CRIMES.
DETAILS AND STORIES.
WOMAN AFTER WOMAN. THINGS HE STOLE.
YOUR HUSBAND, YOUR HONEY BUNNY, IS A SERIAL MURDERER.
AND WHAT DO I GET FROM YOU?
BABIES WHISPERING IN HIS EAR?
I'M- I'M SORRY FOR WHAT HAPPENED TO YOU.
WE SHOULD TAKE A--
NO ONE BELIEVES YOU!! NO ONE BELIEVES WHAT YOU SAID!!
YOU'RE LYING OR TOTALLY OUT OF YOUR MIND!
I HAD BLOOD AND GLASS AND A BRUISE ON ME THE SIZE OF A FIST.
THAT WAS REAL. REAL!!
WHAT YOU'RE SAYING IS SICKENING!! IT'S A DELUSION!!
NO, IT WASN'T.

UM, I DON'T EVEN KNOW WHAT SHE SAID.

I DON'T THINK WE SHOULD CONTINUE THIS--

WHAT DID SHE SAY? A DEMON? IS THAT WHAT YOU SAID?

I DON'T-- THIS ISN'T THE DIRECTION I WANTED TO GO WITH THIS GROUP.

THIS ISN'T THE POINT OF THE--

FATHER?

I THINK WE SHOULD ALL LEAVE.

THEN LEAVE.

WE GOT MUTANTS AND ALIENS ON THE 11 O'CLOCK NEWS-- LET THE FATHER TALK.

THIS IS A CHURCH!

FATHER

FATHER, IF YOU DON'T MIND I'D LIKE.

I DIDN'T HU YOU--

DEMONS?

CAN WE ST BACK FOR A ND?

LET'S RESPECT THE FATHER'S WISHES.

I HAVE NO IDEA WHAT IS OING ON AND--

I'M MORE THAN A LITTLE--

DID IT LOOK ANYTHING LIKE THIS?

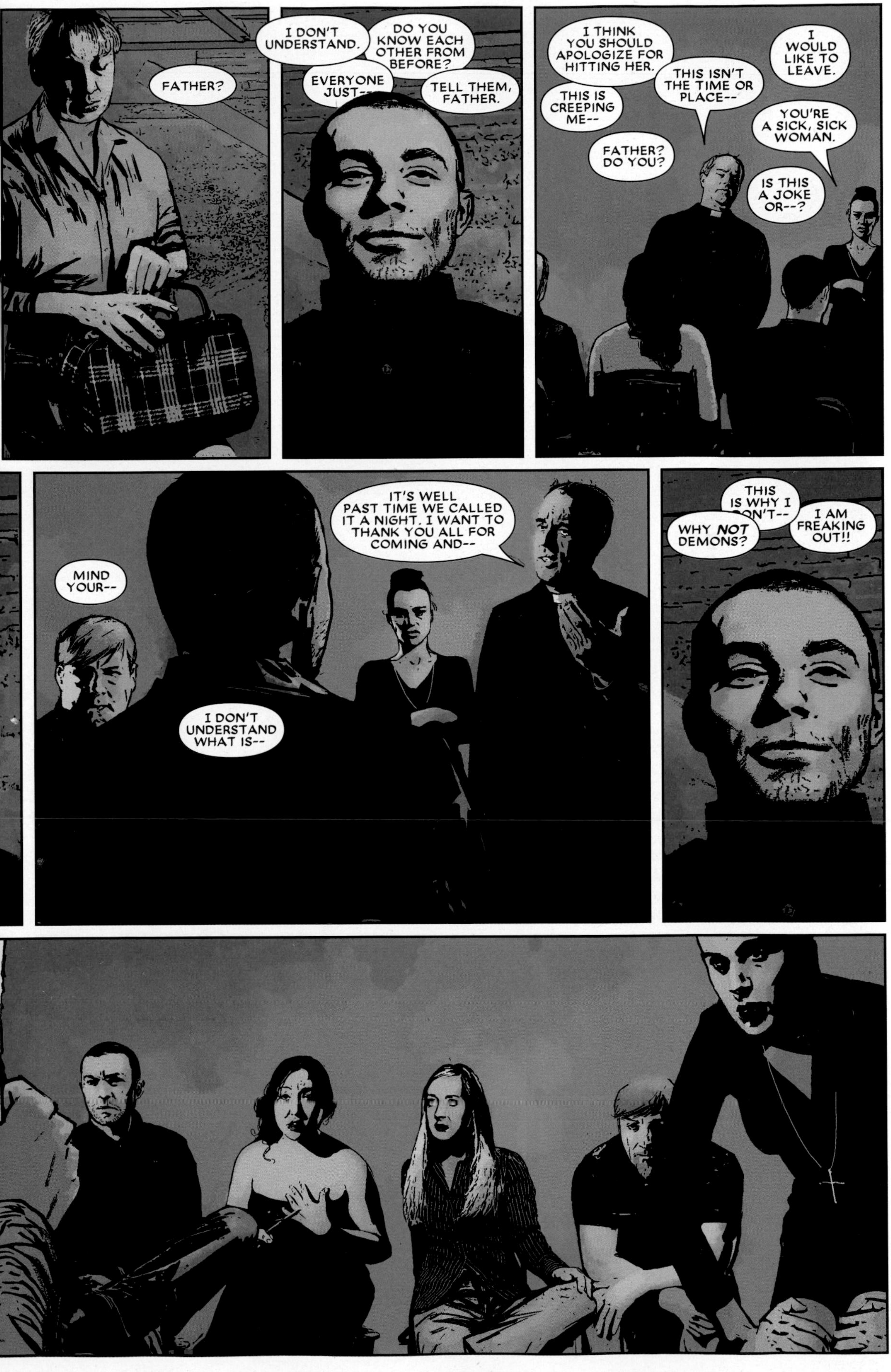
FATHER?
I DON'T UNDERSTAND.
DO YOU KNOW EACH OTHER FROM BEFORE?
EVERYONE JUST--
TELL THEM, FATHER.
I THINK YOU SHOULD APOLOGIZE FOR HITTING HER.
THIS ISN'T THE TIME OR PLACE--
I WOULD LIKE TO LEAVE.
THIS IS CREEPING ME--
YOU'RE A SICK, SICK WOMAN.
FATHER? DO YOU?
IS THIS A JOKE OR--?
IT'S WELL PAST TIME WE CALLED IT A NIGHT. I WANT TO THANK YOU ALL FOR COMING AND--
MIND YOUR--
I DON'T UNDERSTAND WHAT IS--
THIS IS WHY I DON'T--
WHY NOT DEMONS?
I AM FREAKING OUT!!

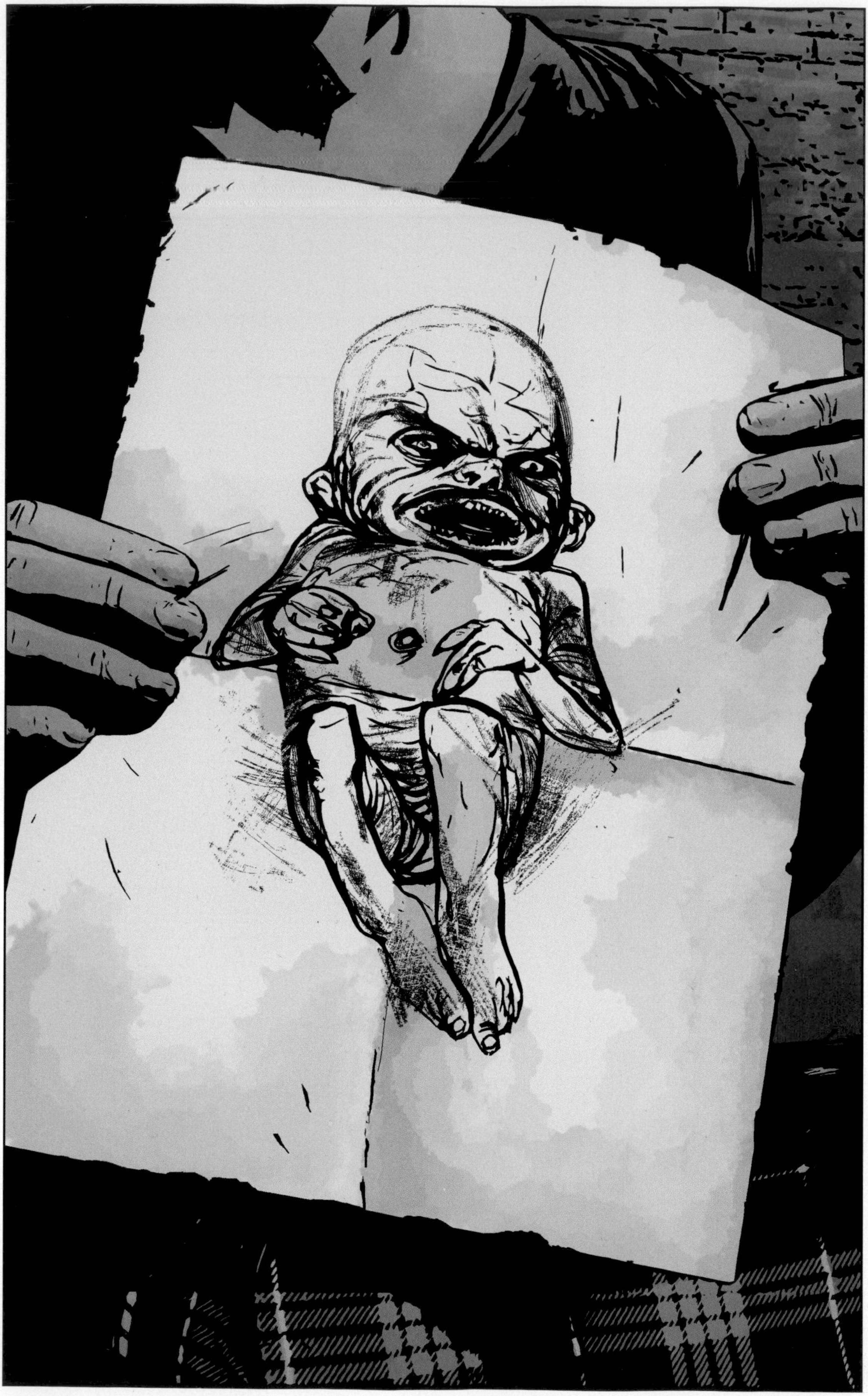

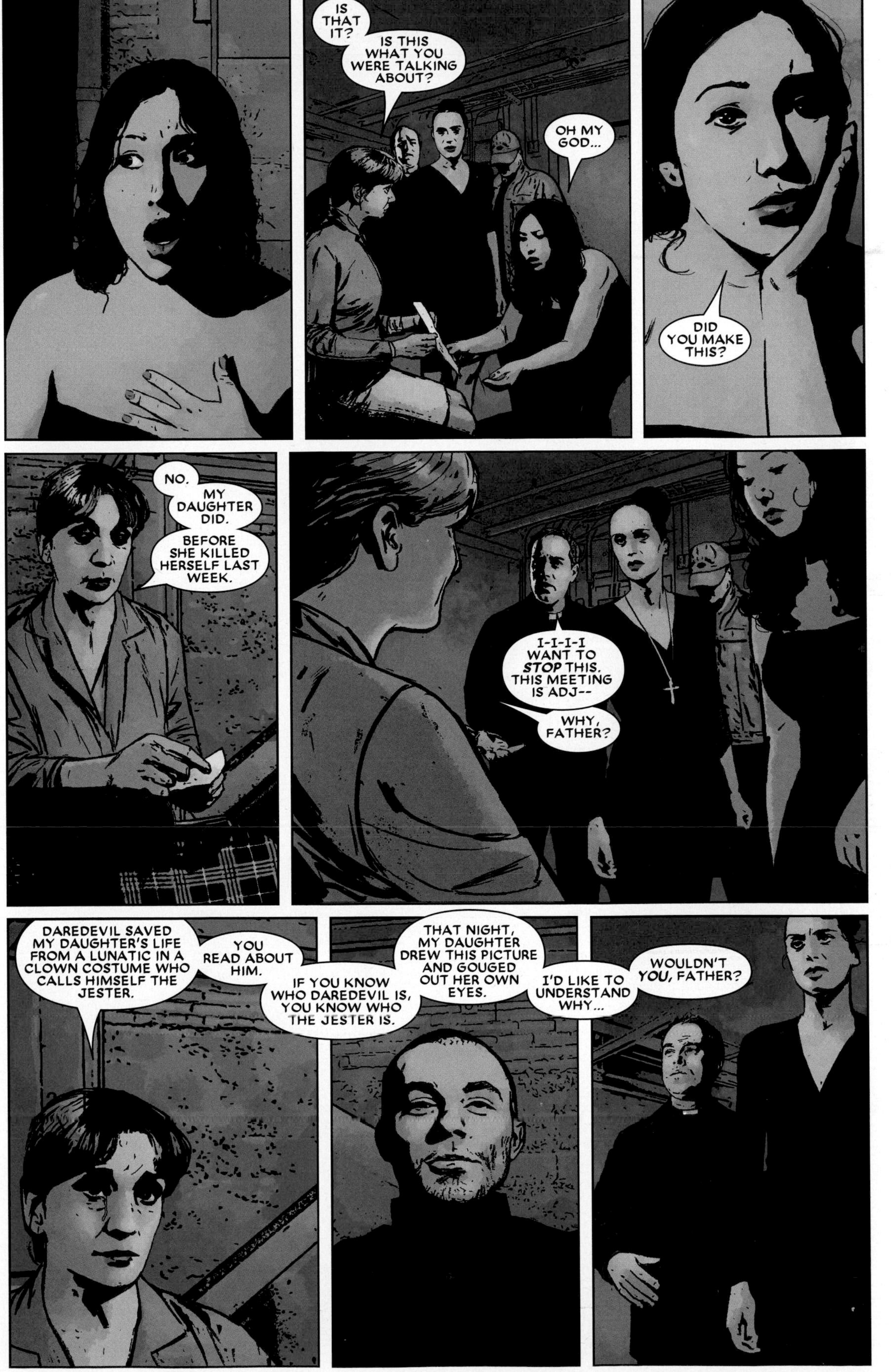
IS THAT IT?
IS THIS WHAT YOU WERE TALKING ABOUT?
OH MY GOD...
DID YOU MAKE THIS?
NO.
MY DAUGHTER DID.
BEFORE SHE KILLED HERSELF LAST WEEK.
I-I-I-I WANT TO STOP THIS. THIS MEETING IS ADJ--
WHY, FATHER?
DAREDEVIL SAVED MY DAUGHTER'S LIFE FROM A LUNATIC IN A CLOWN COSTUME WHO CALLS HIMSELF THE JESTER.
YOU READ ABOUT HIM.
IF YOU KNOW WHO DAREDEVIL IS, YOU KNOW WHO THE JESTER IS.
THAT NIGHT, MY DAUGHTER DREW THIS PICTURE AND GOUGED OUT HER OWN EYES.
I'D LIKE TO UNDERSTAND WHY...
WOULDN'T YOU, FATHER?

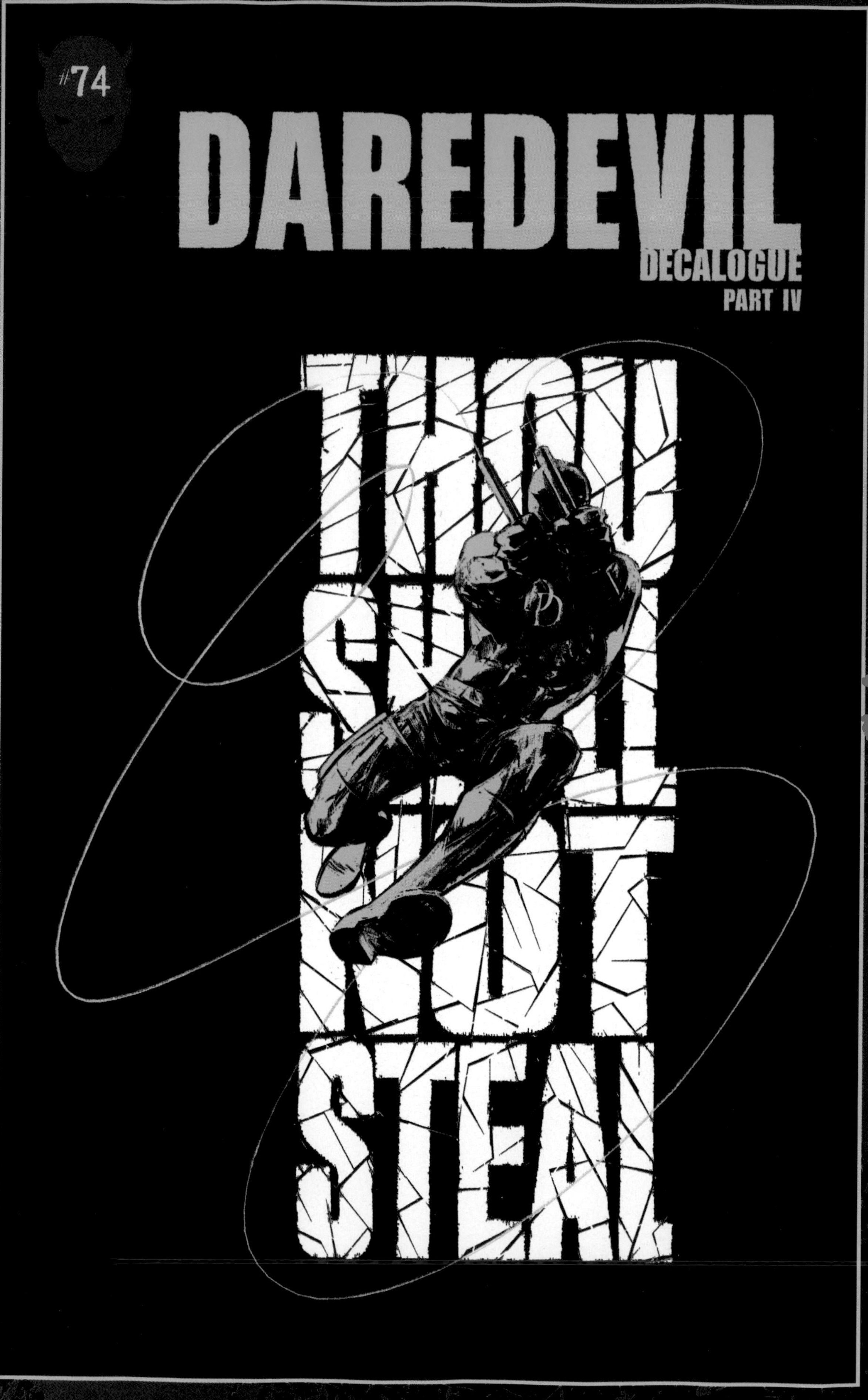
#74
DAREDEVIL
DECALOGUE
PART IV
THOU SHALT NOT STEAL

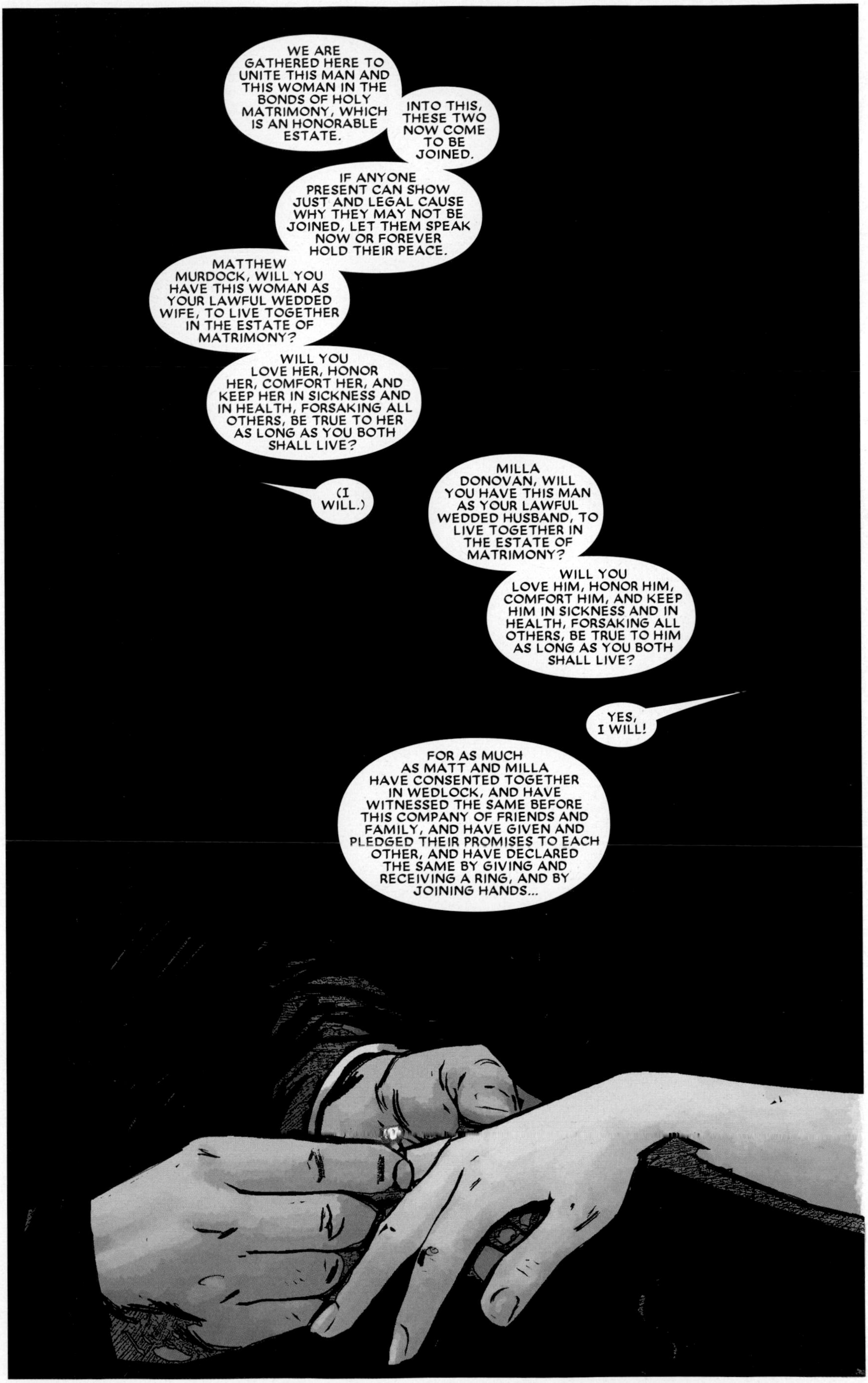
WE ARE GATHERED HERE TO UNITE THIS MAN AND THIS WOMAN IN THE BONDS OF HOLY MATRIMONY, WHICH IS AN HONORABLE ESTATE.
INTO THIS, THESE TWO NOW COME TO BE JOINED.
IF ANYONE PRESENT CAN SHOW JUST AND LEGAL CAUSE WHY THEY MAY NOT BE JOINED, LET THEM SPEAK NOW OR FOREVER HOLD THEIR PEACE.
MATTHEW MURDOCK, WILL YOU HAVE THIS WOMAN AS YOUR LAWFUL WEDDED WIFE, TO LIVE TOGETHER IN THE ESTATE OF MATRIMONY?
WILL YOU LOVE HER, HONOR HER, COMFORT HER, AND KEEP HER IN SICKNESS AND IN HEALTH, FORSAKING ALL OTHERS, BE TRUE TO HER AS LONG AS YOU BOTH SHALL LIVE?
(I WILL.)
MILLA DONOVAN, WILL YOU HAVE THIS MAN AS YOUR LAWFUL WEDDED HUSBAND, TO LIVE TOGETHER IN THE ESTATE OF MATRIMONY?
WILL YOU LOVE HIM, HONOR HIM, COMFORT HIM, AND KEEP HIM IN SICKNESS AND IN HEALTH, FORSAKING ALL OTHERS, BE TRUE TO HIM AS LONG AS YOU BOTH SHALL LIVE?
YES, I WILL!
FOR AS MUCH AS MATT AND MILLA HAVE CONSENTED TOGETHER IN WEDLOCK, AND HAVE WITNESSED THE SAME BEFORE THIS COMPANY OF FRIENDS AND FAMILY, AND HAVE GIVEN AND PLEDGED THEIR PROMISES TO EACH OTHER, AND HAVE DECLARED THE SAME BY GIVING AND RECEIVING A RING, AND BY JOINING HANDS...

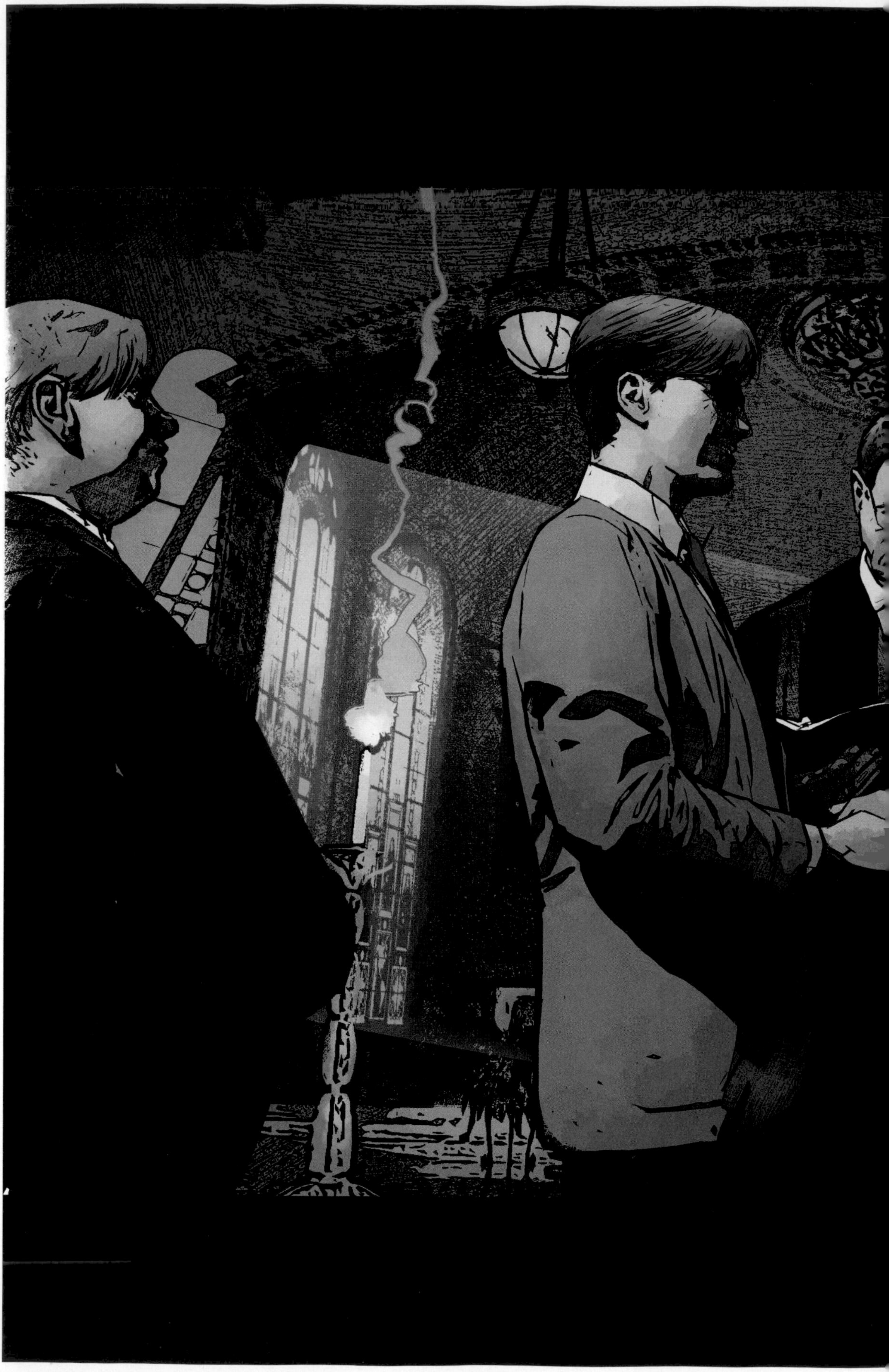

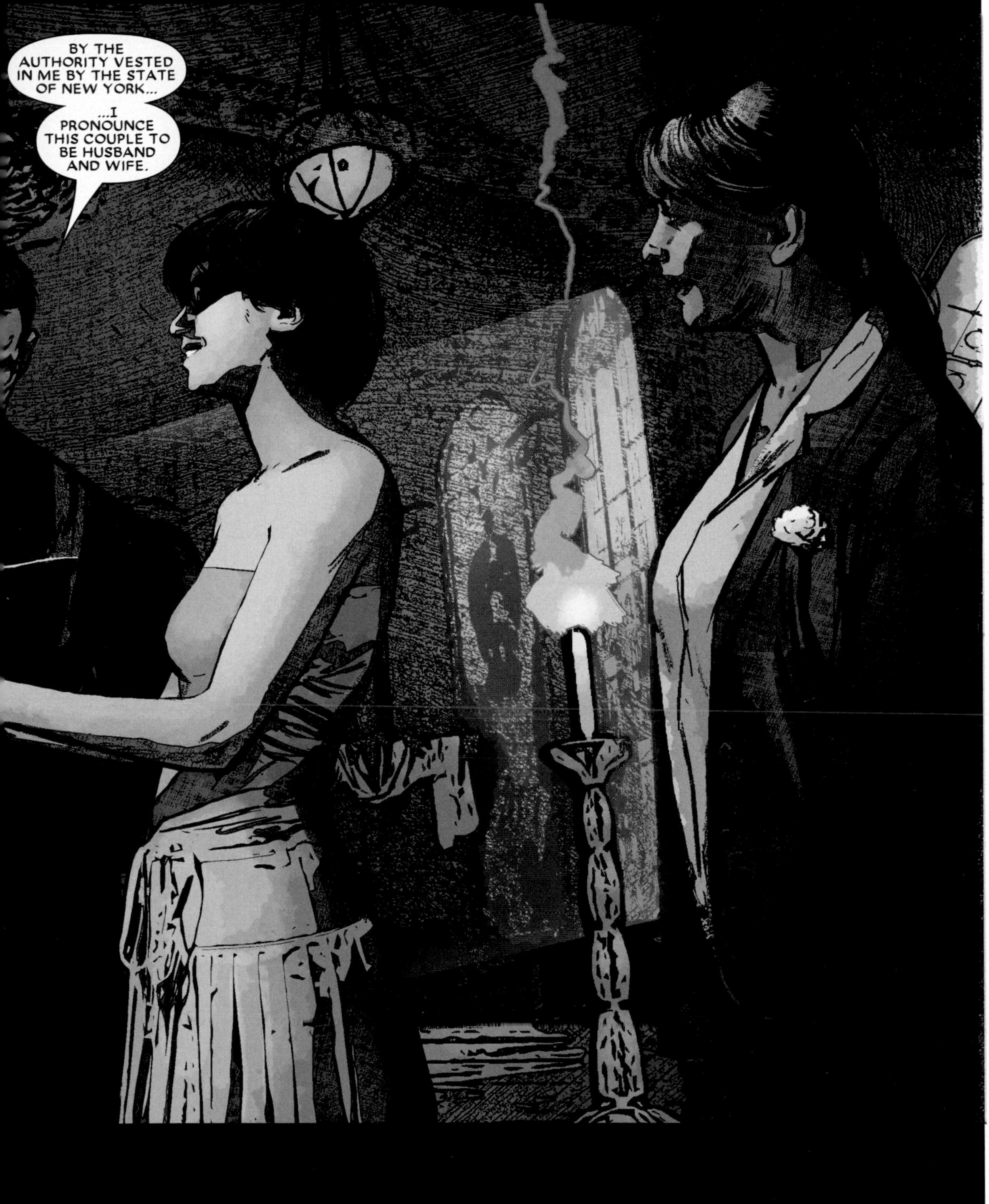
BY THE AUTHORITY VESTED IN ME BY THE STATE OF NEW YORK...
...I PRONOUNCE THIS COUPLE TO BE HUSBAND AND WIFE.

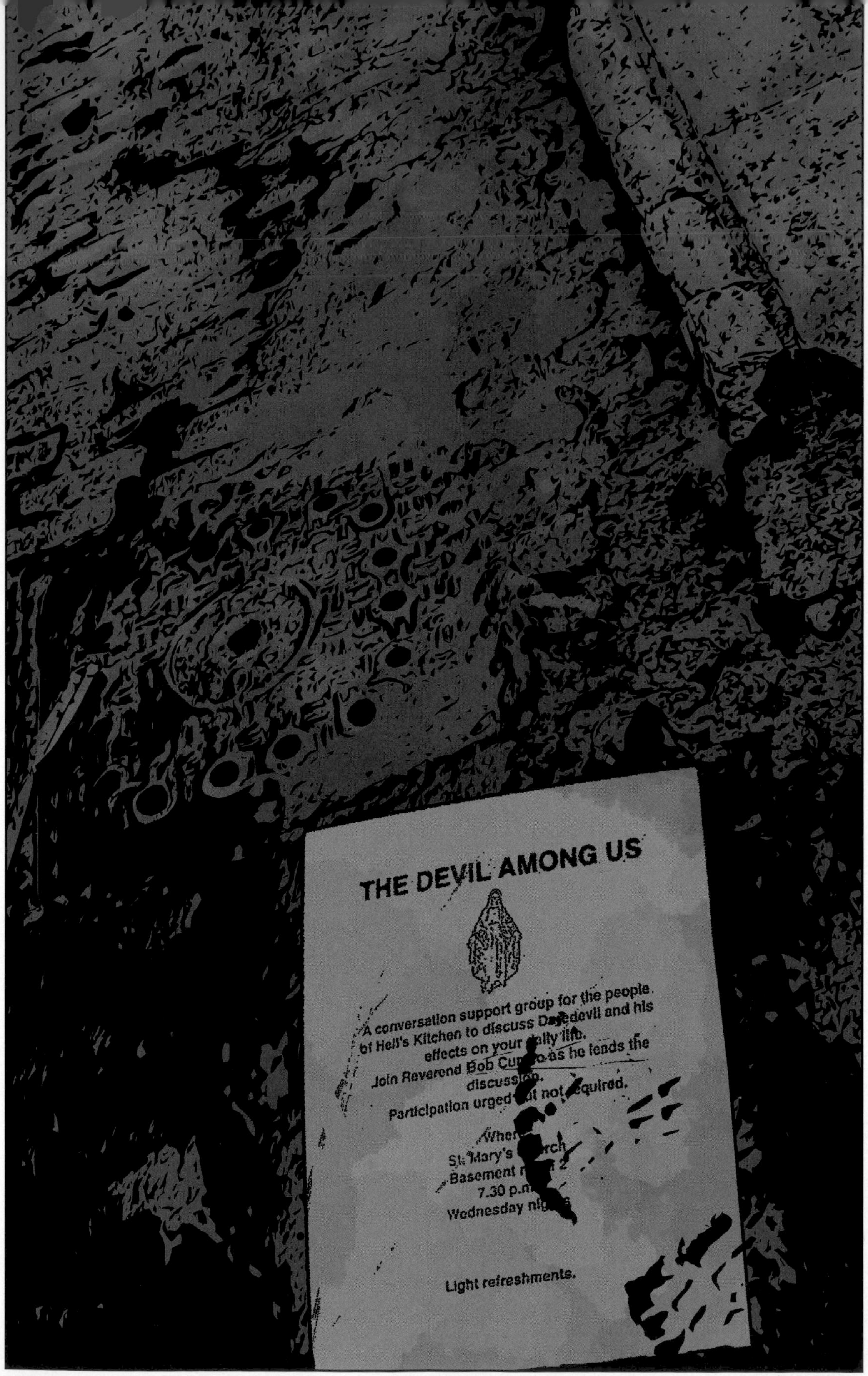
THE DEVIL AMONG US
A conversation support group for the people of Hell's Kitchen to discuss
effects on your
Join Reverend Bob
as he leads the
Participation urged
When
St. Mary's
Basement
7.30 p.m.
Wednesday
Light refreshments.

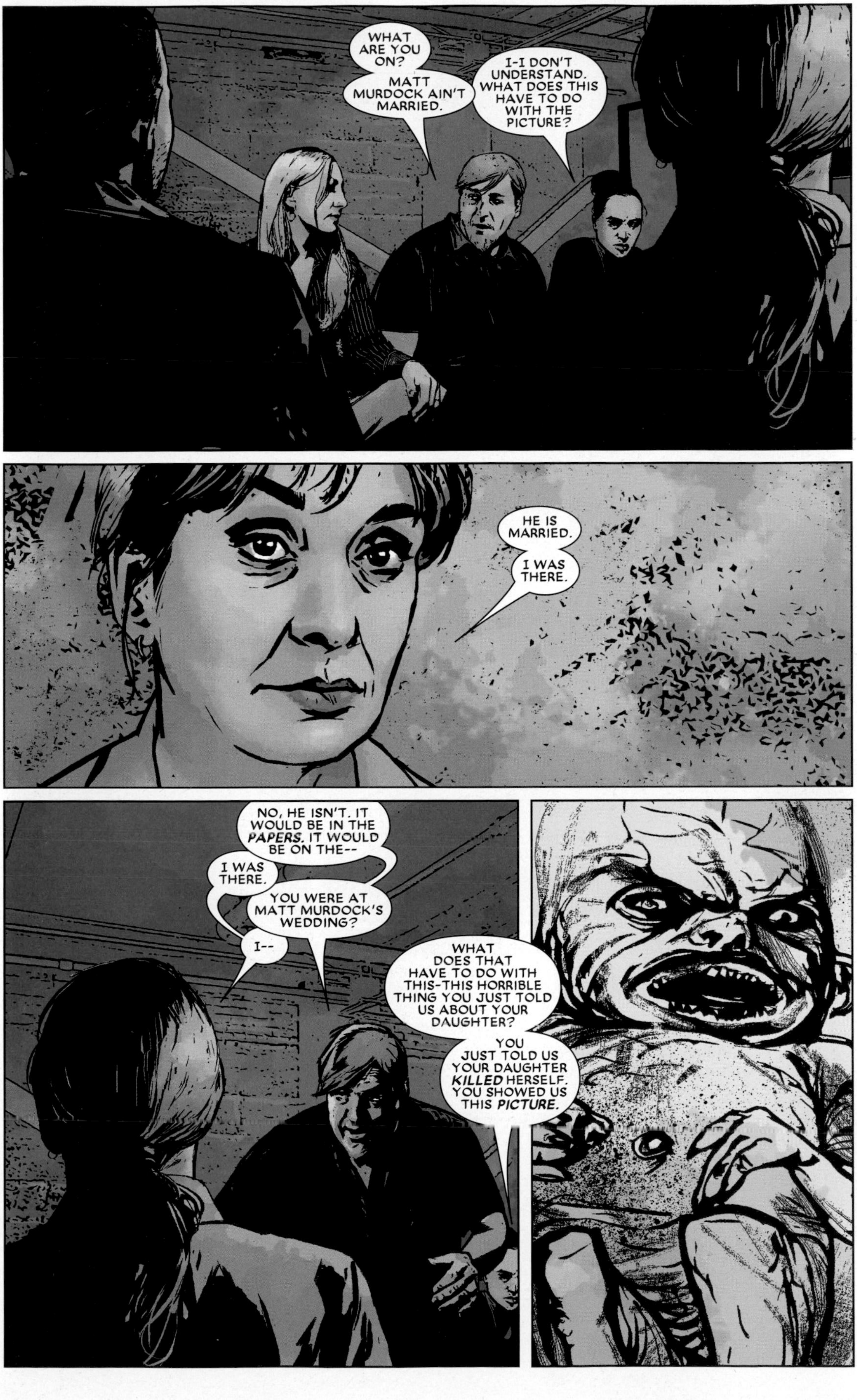
WHAT ARE YOU ON?
MATT MURDOCK AIN'T MARRIED.
I-I DON'T UNDERSTAND. WHAT DOES THIS HAVE TO DO WITH THE PICTURE?
HE IS MARRIED.
I WAS THERE.
NO, HE ISN'T. IT WOULD BE IN THE *PAPERS*. IT WOULD BE ON THE--
I WAS THERE.
YOU WERE AT MATT MURDOCK'S WEDDING?
I--
WHAT DOES THAT HAVE TO DO WITH THIS-THIS HORRIBLE THING YOU JUST TOLD US ABOUT YOUR DAUGHTER?
YOU JUST TOLD US YOUR DAUGHTER *KILLED* HERSELF. YOU SHOWED US THIS *PICTURE*.

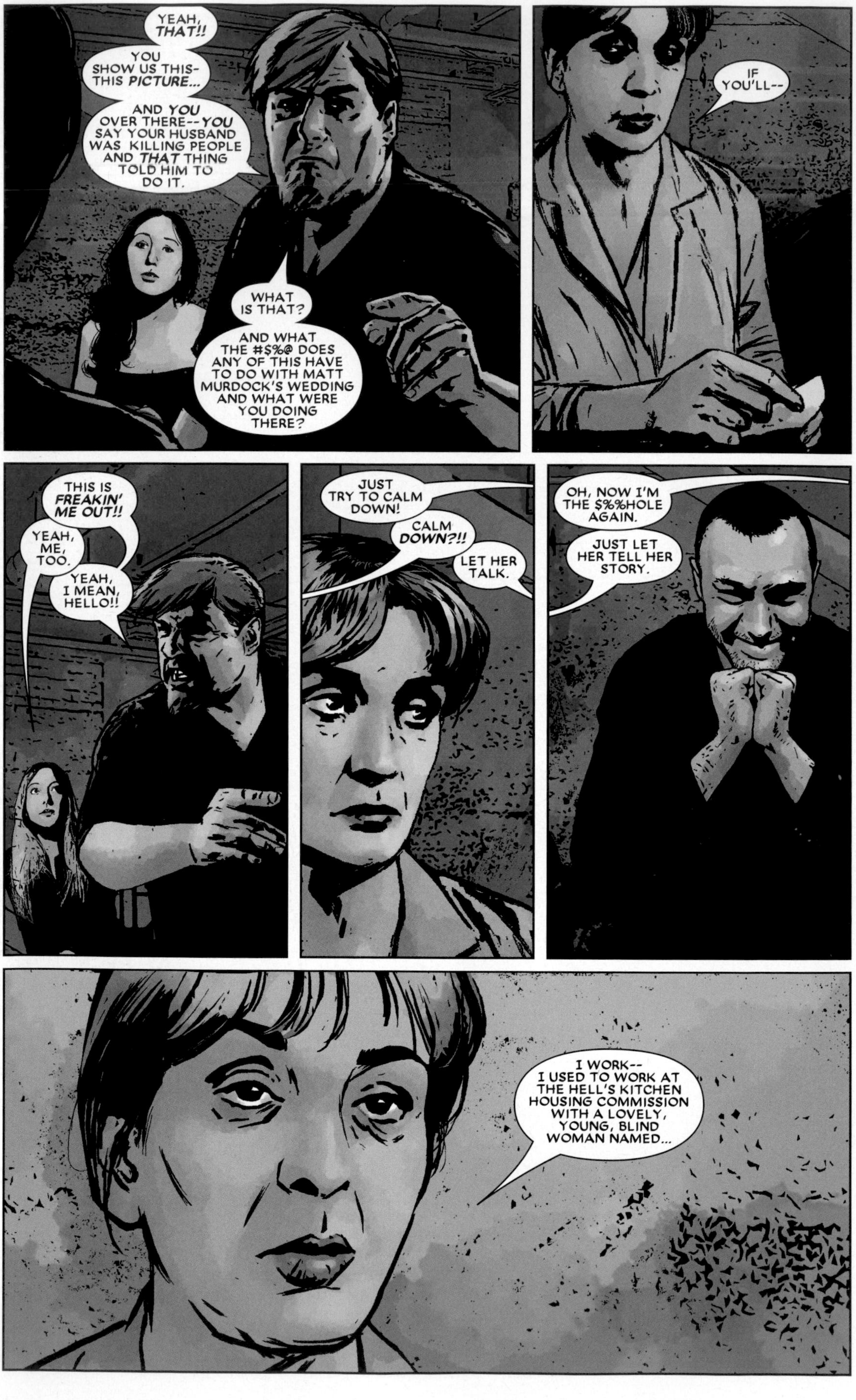
YEAH, *THAT!!*
YOU SHOW US THIS- THIS *PICTURE...*
AND *YOU* OVER THERE--*YOU* SAY YOUR HUSBAND WAS KILLING PEOPLE AND *THAT* THING TOLD HIM TO DO IT.
WHAT IS THAT?
AND WHAT THE #$%@ DOES ANY OF THIS HAVE TO DO WITH MATT MURDOCK'S WEDDING AND WHAT WERE YOU DOING THERE?
IF YOU'LL--
THIS IS *FREAKIN' ME OUT!!*
YEAH, ME, TOO.
YEAH, I MEAN, HELLO!!
JUST TRY TO CALM DOWN!
CALM *DOWN?!!*
LET HER TALK.
OH, NOW I'M THE $%%HOLE AGAIN.
JUST LET HER TELL HER STORY.
I WORK-- I USED TO WORK AT THE HELL'S KITCHEN HOUSING COMMISSION WITH A LOVELY, YOUNG, BLIND WOMAN NAMED...

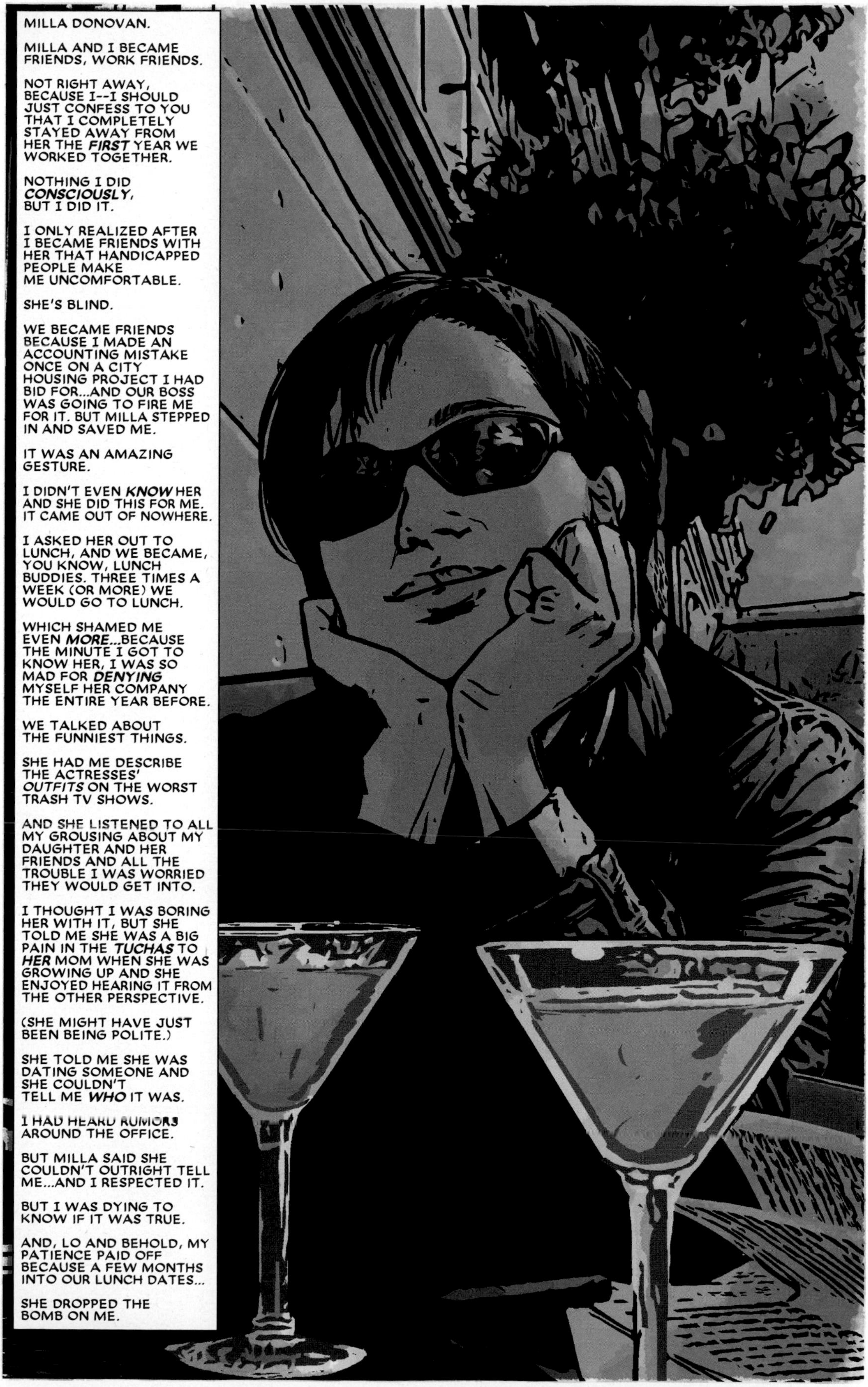
MILLA DONOVAN.
MILLA AND I BECAME FRIENDS, WORK FRIENDS.
NOT RIGHT AWAY, BECAUSE I--I SHOULD JUST CONFESS TO YOU THAT I COMPLETELY STAYED AWAY FROM HER THE *FIRST* YEAR WE WORKED TOGETHER.
NOTHING I DID *CONSCIOUSLY*, BUT I DID IT.
I ONLY REALIZED AFTER I BECAME FRIENDS WITH HER THAT HANDICAPPED PEOPLE MAKE ME UNCOMFORTABLE.
SHE'S BLIND.
WE BECAME FRIENDS BECAUSE I MADE AN ACCOUNTING MISTAKE ONCE ON A CITY HOUSING PROJECT I HAD BID FOR...AND OUR BOSS WAS GOING TO FIRE ME FOR IT. BUT MILLA STEPPED IN AND SAVED ME.
IT WAS AN AMAZING GESTURE.
I DIDN'T EVEN *KNOW* HER AND SHE DID THIS FOR ME. IT CAME OUT OF NOWHERE.
I ASKED HER OUT TO LUNCH, AND WE BECAME, YOU KNOW, LUNCH BUDDIES. THREE TIMES A WEEK (OR MORE) WE WOULD GO TO LUNCH.
WHICH SHAMED ME EVEN *MORE*...BECAUSE THE MINUTE I GOT TO KNOW HER, I WAS SO MAD FOR *DENYING* MYSELF HER COMPANY THE ENTIRE YEAR BEFORE.
WE TALKED ABOUT THE FUNNIEST THINGS.
SHE HAD ME DESCRIBE THE ACTRESSES' *OUTFITS* ON THE WORST TRASH TV SHOWS.
AND SHE LISTENED TO ALL MY GROUSING ABOUT MY DAUGHTER AND HER FRIENDS AND ALL THE TROUBLE I WAS WORRIED THEY WOULD GET INTO.
I THOUGHT I WAS BORING HER WITH IT, BUT SHE TOLD ME SHE WAS A BIG PAIN IN THE *TUCHAS* TO *HER* MOM WHEN SHE WAS GROWING UP AND SHE ENJOYED HEARING IT FROM THE OTHER PERSPECTIVE.
(SHE MIGHT HAVE JUST BEEN BEING POLITE.)
SHE TOLD ME SHE WAS DATING SOMEONE AND SHE COULDN'T TELL ME *WHO* IT WAS.
I HAD HEARD RUMORS AROUND THE OFFICE.
BUT MILLA SAID SHE COULDN'T OUTRIGHT TELL ME...AND I RESPECTED IT.
BUT I WAS DYING TO KNOW IF IT WAS TRUE.
AND, LO AND BEHOLD, MY PATIENCE PAID OFF BECAUSE A FEW MONTHS INTO OUR LUNCH DATES...
SHE DROPPED THE BOMB ON ME.

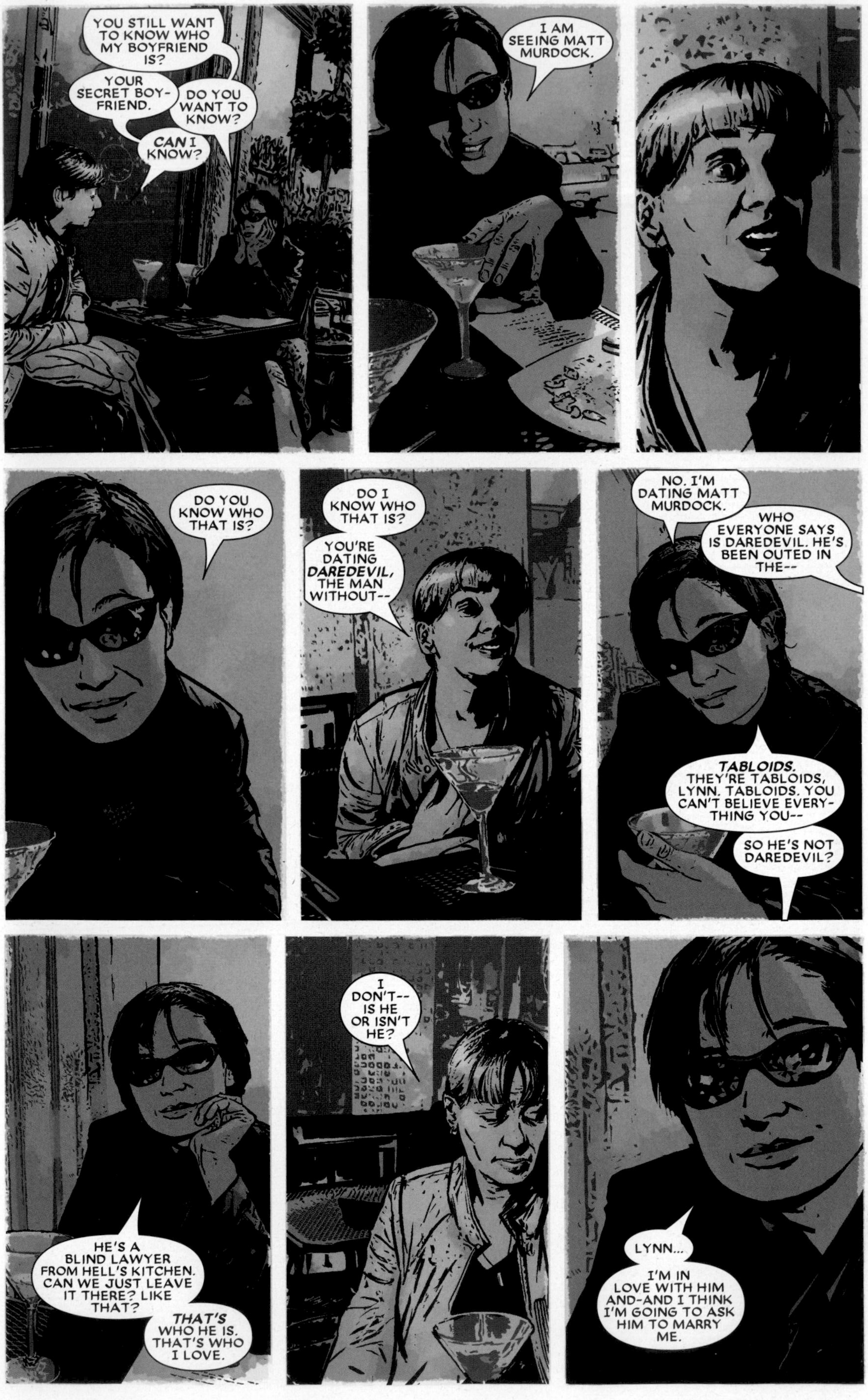

YOU STILL WANT TO KNOW WHO MY BOYFRIEND IS?
YOUR SECRET BOY-FRIEND.
DO YOU WANT TO KNOW?
CAN I KNOW?
I AM SEEING MATT MURDOCK.
DO YOU KNOW WHO THAT IS?
DO I KNOW WHO THAT IS?
YOU'RE DATING *DAREDEVIL,* THE MAN WITHOUT--
NO. I'M DATING MATT MURDOCK.
WHO EVERYONE SAYS IS DAREDEVIL. HE'S BEEN OUTED IN THE--
TABLOIDS. THEY'RE TABLOIDS, LYNN. TABLOIDS. YOU CAN'T BELIEVE EVERY-THING YOU--
SO HE'S NOT DAREDEVIL?
HE'S A BLIND LAWYER FROM HELL'S KITCHEN. CAN WE JUST LEAVE IT THERE? LIKE THAT?
THAT'S WHO HE IS. THAT'S WHO I LOVE.
I DON'T-- IS HE OR ISN'T HE?
LYNN...
I'M IN LOVE WITH HIM AND-AND I THINK I'M GOING TO ASK HIM TO MARRY ME.

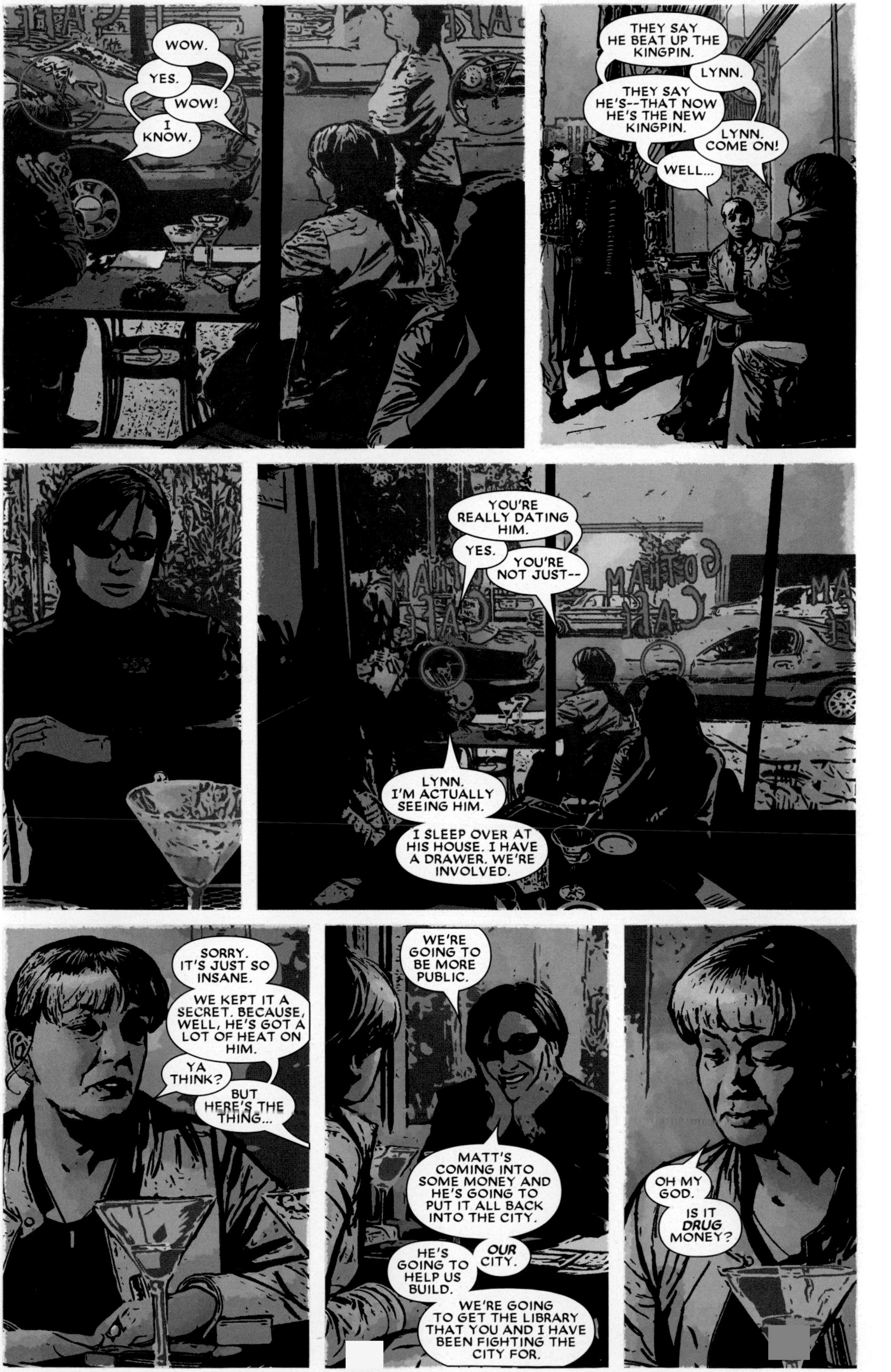
WOW.
YES.
WOW!
I KNOW.
THEY SAY HE BEAT UP THE KINGPIN.
LYNN.
THEY SAY HE'S--THAT NOW HE'S THE NEW KINGPIN.
LYNN. COME ON!
WELL...
YOU'RE REALLY DATING HIM.
YES.
YOU'RE NOT JUST--
LYNN. I'M ACTUALLY SEEING HIM.
I SLEEP OVER AT HIS HOUSE. I HAVE A DRAWER. WE'RE INVOLVED.
SORRY. IT'S JUST SO INSANE.
WE KEPT IT A SECRET. BECAUSE, WELL, HE'S GOT A LOT OF HEAT ON HIM.
YA THINK?
BUT HERE'S THE THING...
WE'RE GOING TO BE MORE PUBLIC.
MATT'S COMING INTO SOME MONEY AND HE'S GOING TO PUT IT ALL BACK INTO THE CITY.
OUR CITY.
HE'S GOING TO HELP US BUILD.
WE'RE GOING TO GET THE LIBRARY THAT YOU AND I HAVE BEEN FIGHTING THE CITY FOR.
OH MY GOD.
IS IT *DRUG* MONEY?

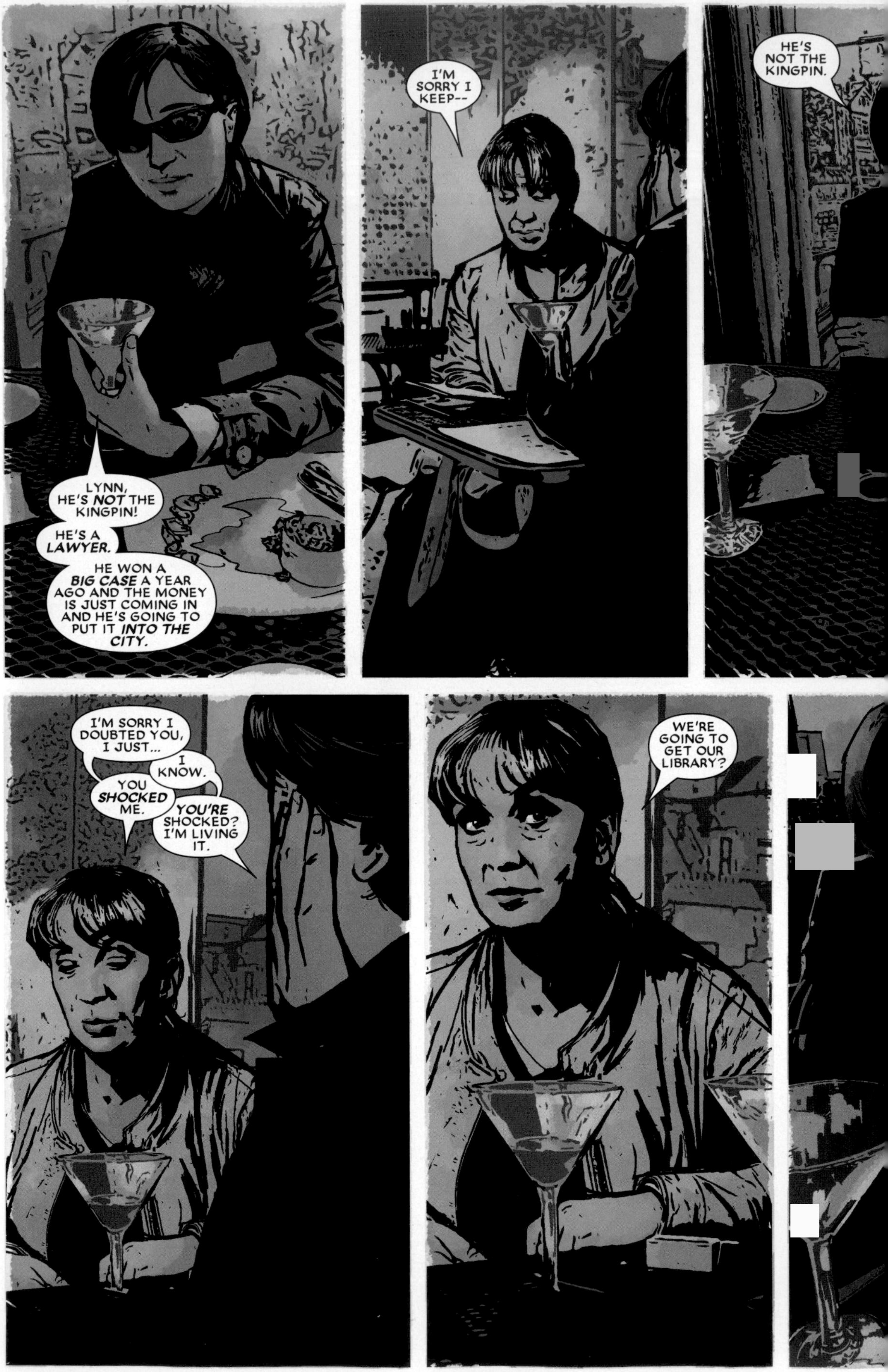
LYNN, HE'S NOT THE KINGPIN!
HE'S A LAWYER.
HE WON A BIG CASE A YEAR AGO AND THE MONEY IS JUST COMING IN AND HE'S GOING TO PUT IT INTO THE CITY.
I'M SORRY I KEEP--
HE'S NOT THE KINGPIN.
I'M SORRY I DOUBTED YOU, I JUST...
I KNOW.
YOU SHOCKED ME.
YOU'RE SHOCKED? I'M LIVING IT.
WE'RE GOING TO GET OUR LIBRARY?

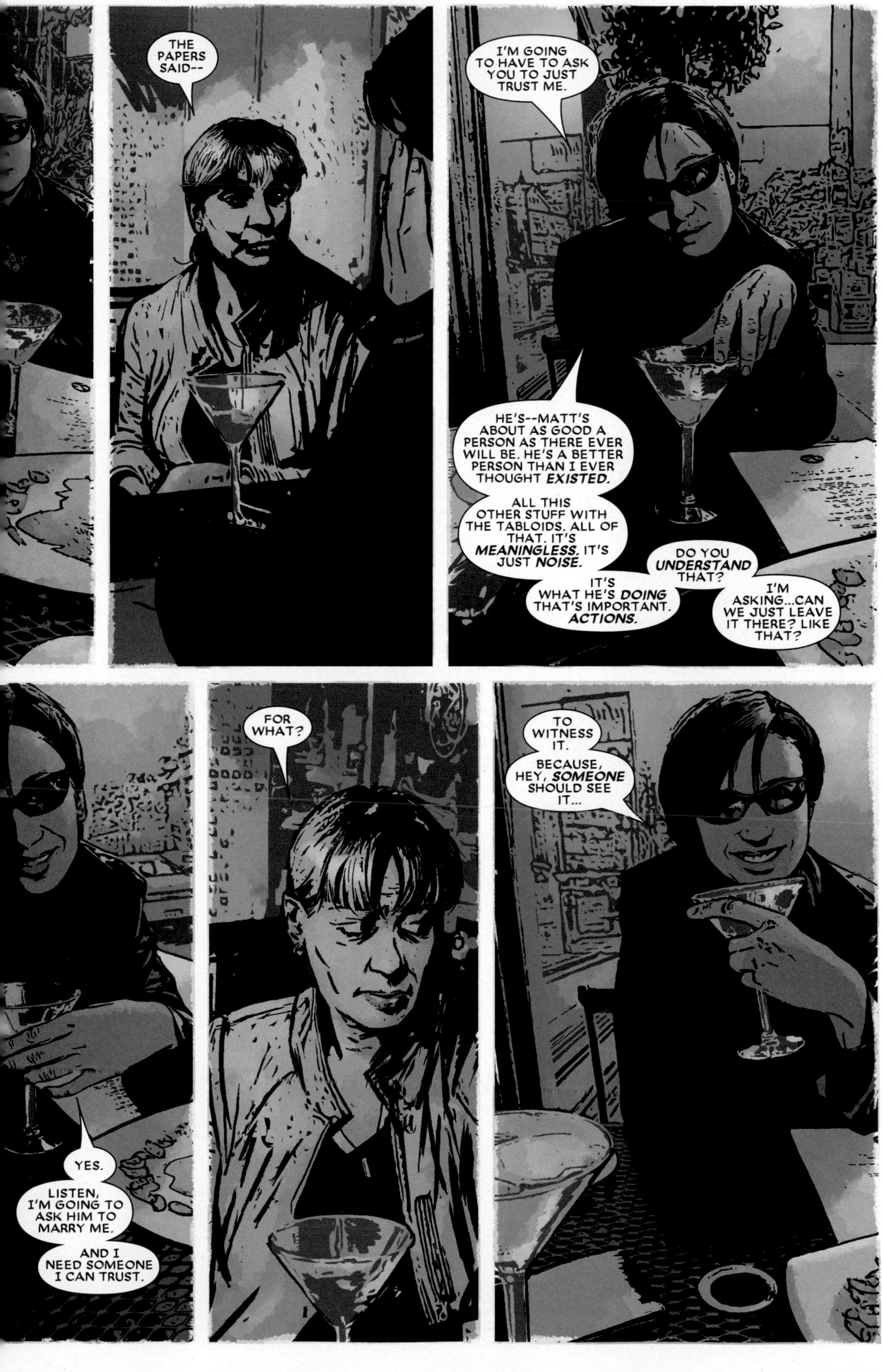
THE PAPERS SAID--
I'M GOING TO HAVE TO ASK YOU TO JUST TRUST ME.
HE'S--MATT'S ABOUT AS GOOD A PERSON AS THERE EVER WILL BE. HE'S A BETTER PERSON THAN I EVER THOUGHT *EXISTED.*
ALL THIS OTHER STUFF WITH THE TABLOIDS. ALL OF THAT. IT'S *MEANINGLESS.* IT'S JUST *NOISE.*
IT'S WHAT HE'S *DOING* THAT'S IMPORTANT. *ACTIONS.*
DO YOU *UNDERSTAND* THAT?
I'M ASKING...CAN WE JUST LEAVE IT THERE? LIKE THAT?
YES.
LISTEN, I'M GOING TO ASK HIM TO MARRY ME.
AND I NEED SOMEONE I CAN TRUST.
FOR WHAT?
TO WITNESS IT.
BECAUSE, HEY, *SOMEONE* SHOULD SEE IT...

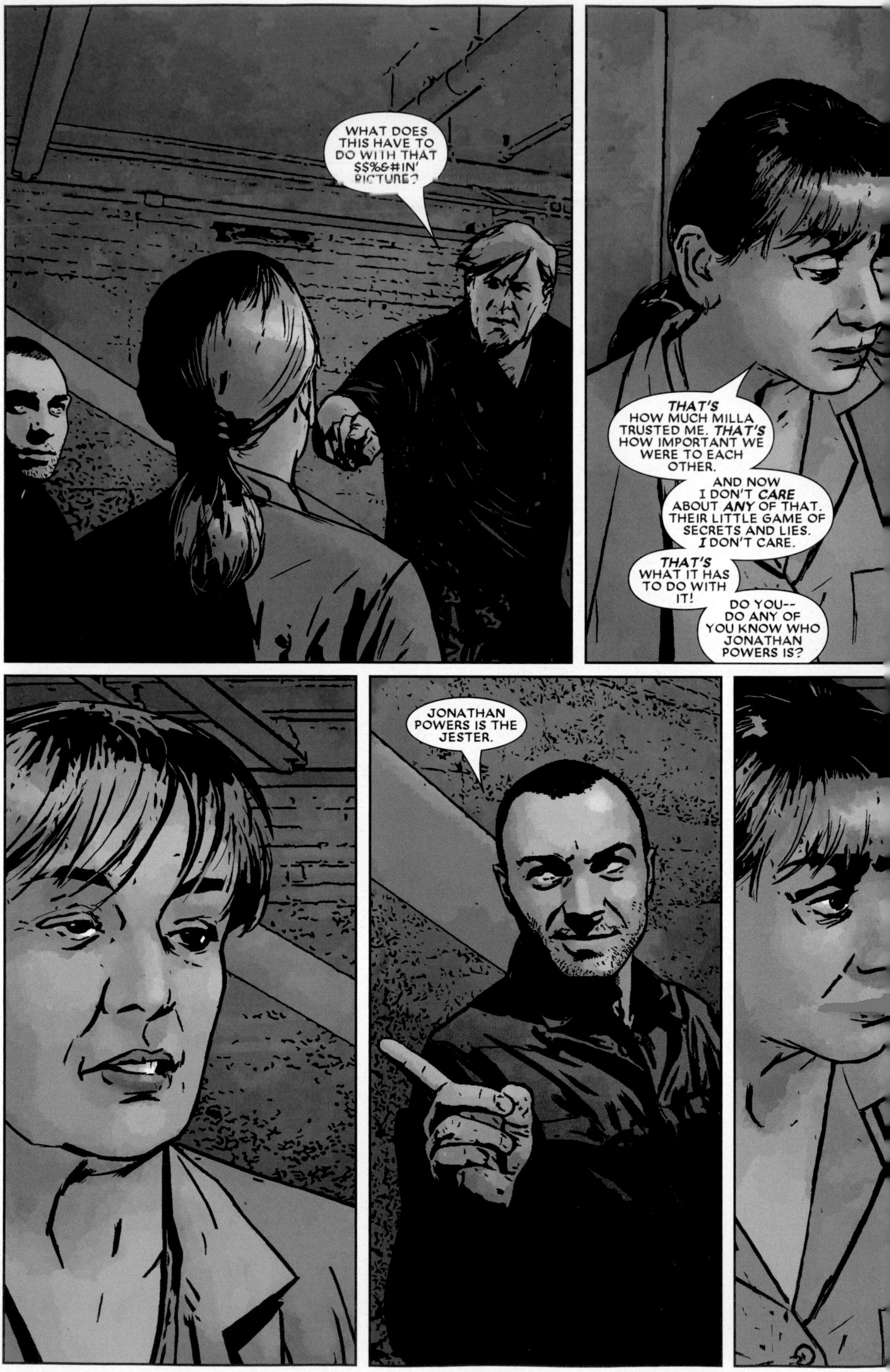
WHAT DOES THIS HAVE TO DO WITH THAT $$%&#IN' PICTURE?
THAT'S HOW MUCH MILLA TRUSTED ME. THAT'S HOW IMPORTANT WE WERE TO EACH OTHER.
AND NOW I DON'T CARE ABOUT ANY OF THAT. THEIR LITTLE GAME OF SECRETS AND LIES. I DON'T CARE.
THAT'S WHAT IT HAS TO DO WITH IT!
DO YOU-- DO ANY OF YOU KNOW WHO JONATHAN POWERS IS?
JONATHAN POWERS IS THE JESTER.

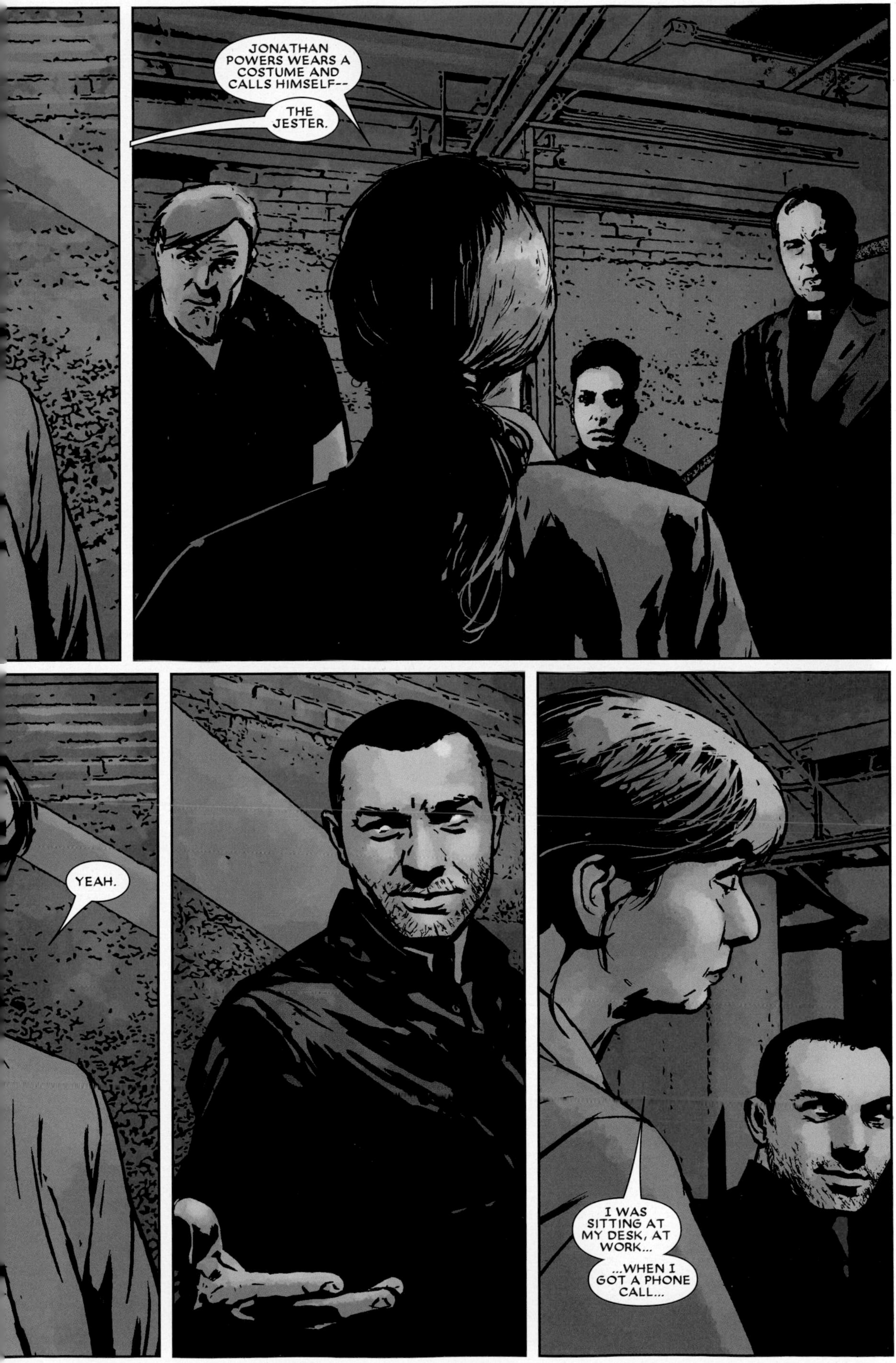
JONATHAN POWERS WEARS A COSTUME AND CALLS HIMSELF--
THE JESTER.
YEAH.
I WAS SITTING AT MY DESK, AT WORK...
...WHEN I GOT A PHONE CALL...

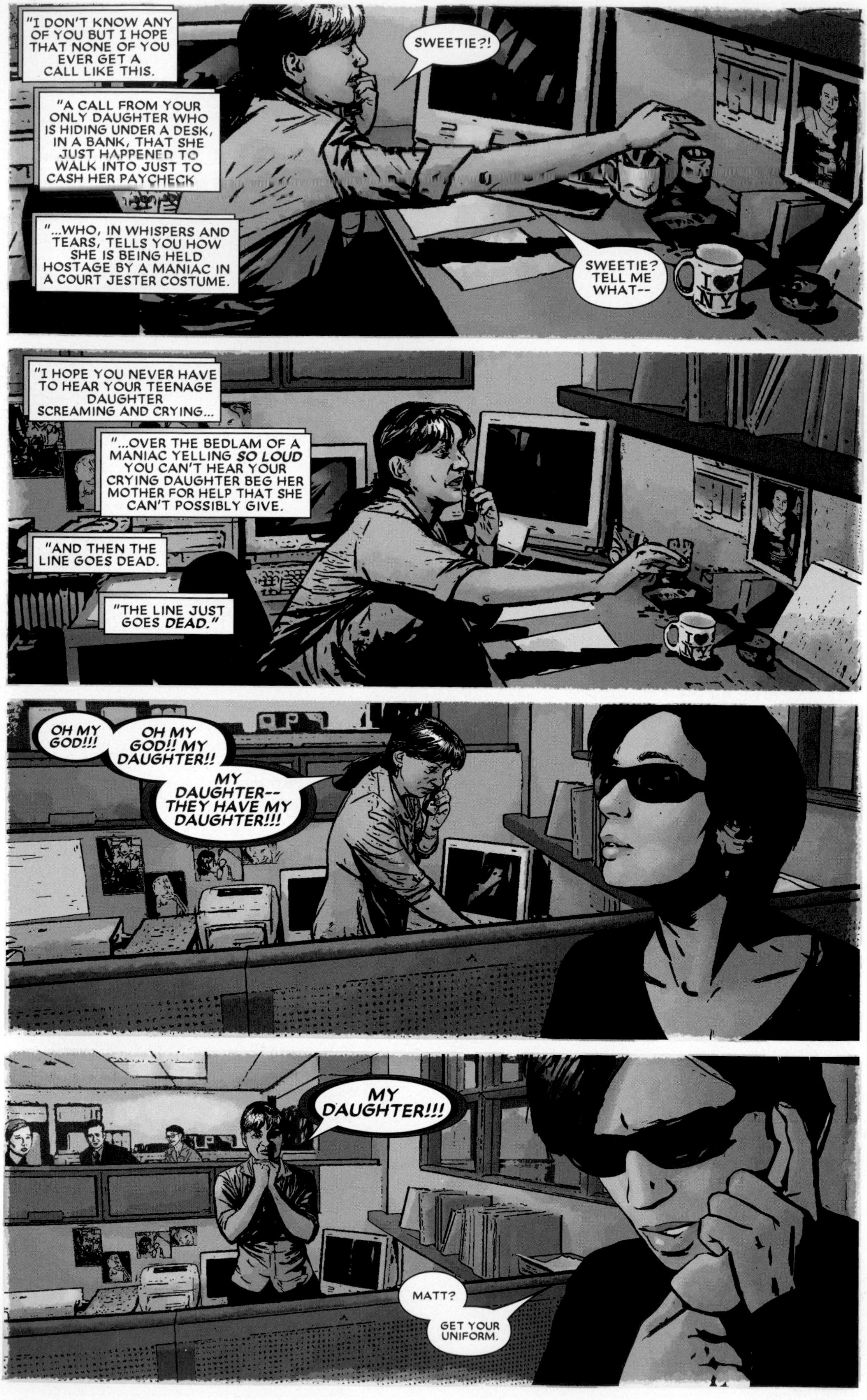
"I DON'T KNOW ANY OF YOU BUT I HOPE THAT NONE OF YOU EVER GET A CALL LIKE THIS.
SWEETIE?!
"A CALL FROM YOUR ONLY DAUGHTER WHO IS HIDING UNDER A DESK, IN A BANK, THAT SHE JUST HAPPENED TO WALK INTO JUST TO CASH HER PAYCHECK
"...WHO, IN WHISPERS AND TEARS, TELLS YOU HOW SHE IS BEING HELD HOSTAGE BY A MANIAC IN A COURT JESTER COSTUME.
SWEETIE? TELL ME WHAT--
"I HOPE YOU NEVER HAVE TO HEAR YOUR TEENAGE DAUGHTER SCREAMING AND CRYING...
"...OVER THE BEDLAM OF A MANIAC YELLING *SO LOUD* YOU CAN'T HEAR YOUR CRYING DAUGHTER BEG HER MOTHER FOR HELP THAT SHE CAN'T POSSIBLY GIVE.
"AND THEN THE LINE GOES DEAD.
"THE LINE JUST GOES *DEAD.*"
OH MY GOD!!!
OH MY GOD!! MY DAUGHTER!!
MY DAUGHTER-- THEY HAVE MY DAUGHTER!!!
MY DAUGHTER!!!
MATT?
GET YOUR UNIFORM.

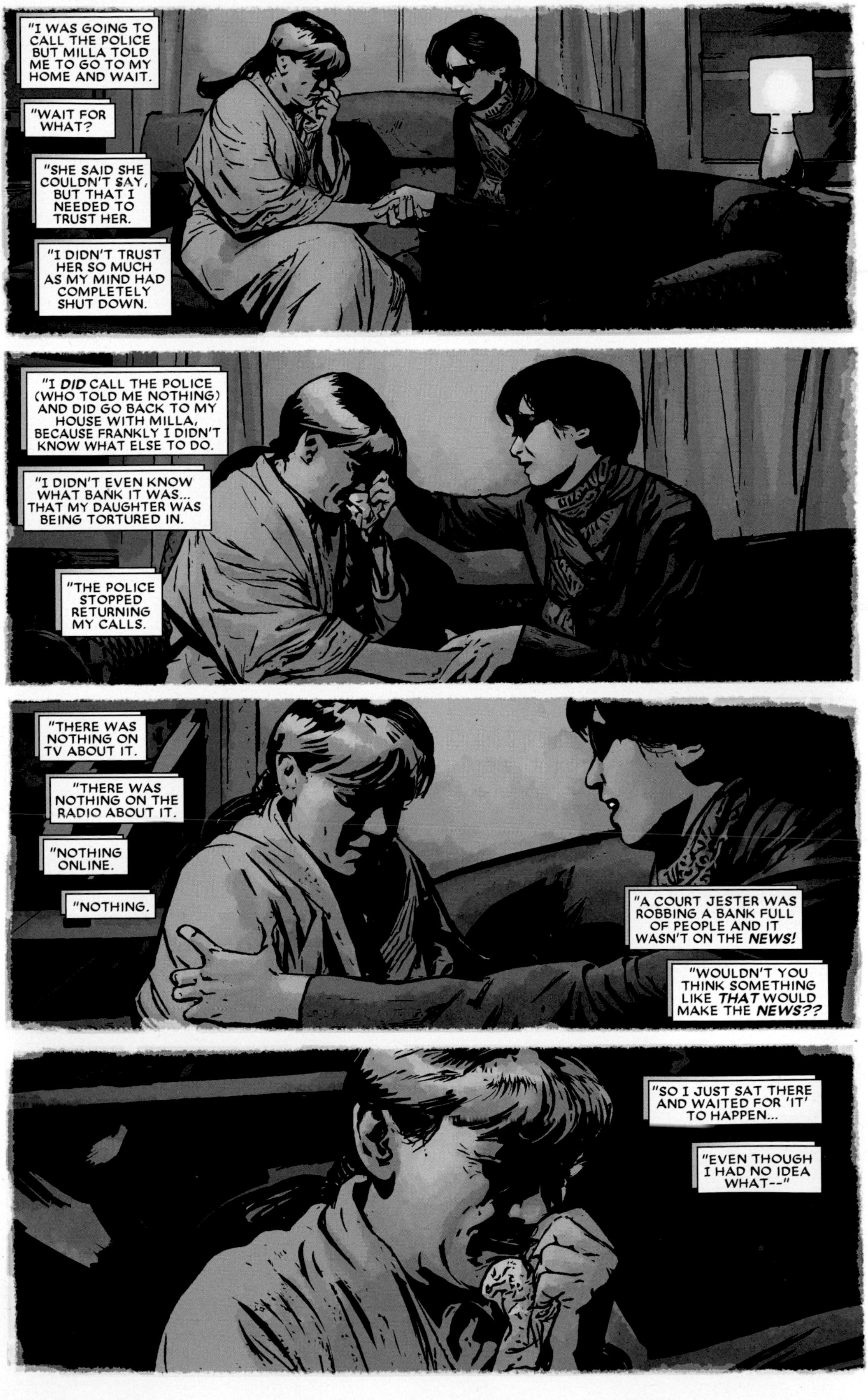
"I WAS GOING TO CALL THE POLICE BUT MILLA TOLD ME TO GO TO MY HOME AND WAIT.
"WAIT FOR WHAT?
"SHE SAID SHE COULDN'T SAY, BUT THAT I NEEDED TO TRUST HER.
"I DIDN'T TRUST HER SO MUCH AS MY MIND HAD COMPLETELY SHUT DOWN.
"I DID CALL THE POLICE (WHO TOLD ME NOTHING) AND DID GO BACK TO MY HOUSE WITH MILLA, BECAUSE FRANKLY I DIDN'T KNOW WHAT ELSE TO DO.
"I DIDN'T EVEN KNOW WHAT BANK IT WAS... THAT MY DAUGHTER WAS BEING TORTURED IN.
"THE POLICE STOPPED RETURNING MY CALLS.
"THERE WAS NOTHING ON TV ABOUT IT.
"THERE WAS NOTHING ON THE RADIO ABOUT IT.
"NOTHING ONLINE.
"NOTHING.
"A COURT JESTER WAS ROBBING A BANK FULL OF PEOPLE AND IT WASN'T ON THE NEWS!
"WOULDN'T YOU THINK SOMETHING LIKE THAT WOULD MAKE THE NEWS??
"SO I JUST SAT THERE AND WAITED FOR 'IT' TO HAPPEN...
"EVEN THOUGH I HAD NO IDEA WHAT--"

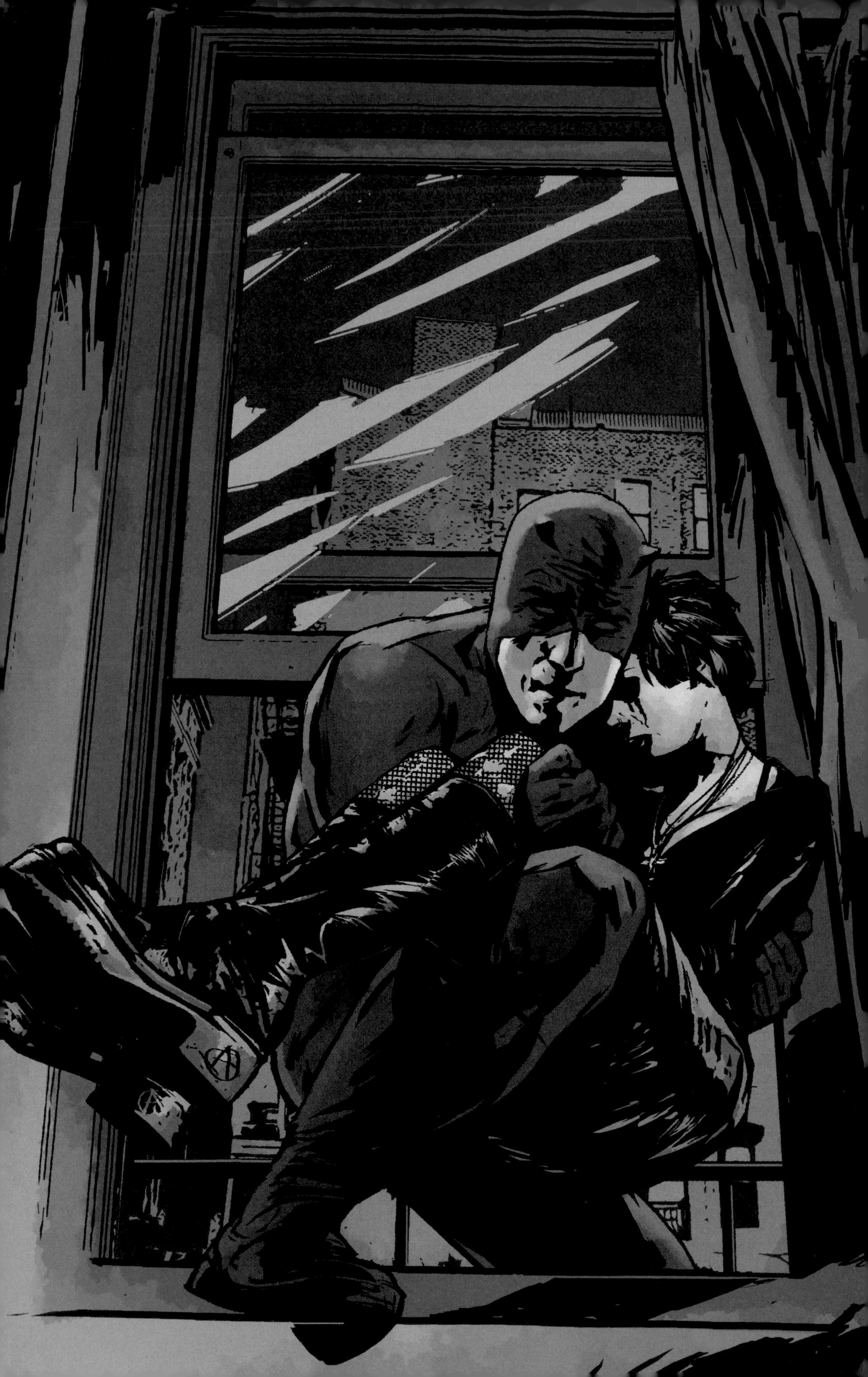

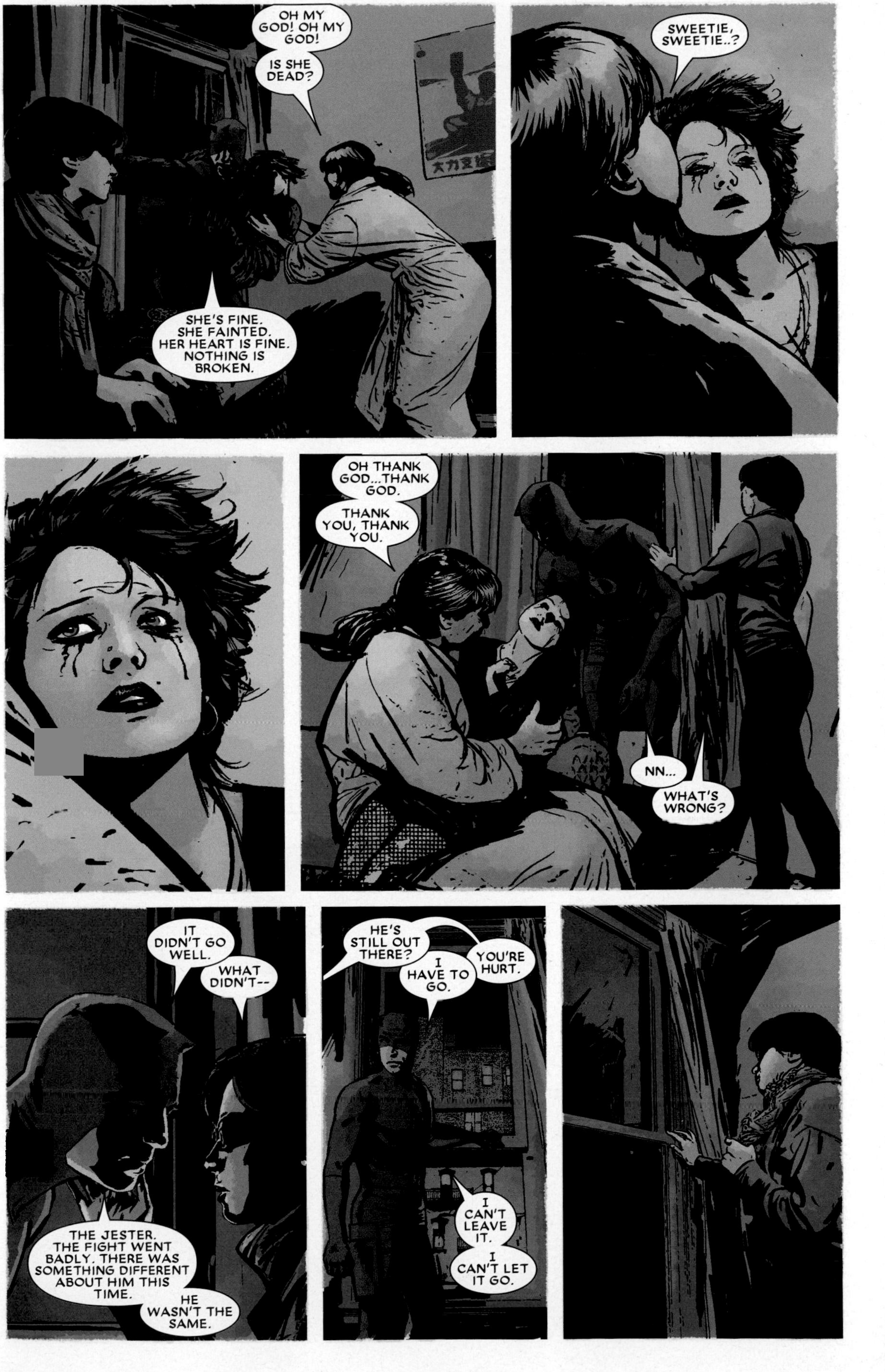
OH MY GOD! OH MY GOD!
IS SHE DEAD?
SHE'S FINE. SHE FAINTED. HER HEART IS FINE. NOTHING IS BROKEN.
SWEETIE, SWEETIE..?
OH THANK GOD...THANK GOD.
THANK YOU, THANK YOU.
NN...
WHAT'S WRONG?
IT DIDN'T GO WELL.
WHAT DIDN'T--
THE JESTER. THE FIGHT WENT BADLY. THERE WAS SOMETHING DIFFERENT ABOUT HIM THIS TIME.
HE WASN'T THE SAME.
HE'S STILL OUT THERE?
YOU'RE HURT.
I HAVE TO GO.
I CAN'T LEAVE IT.
I CAN'T LET IT GO.

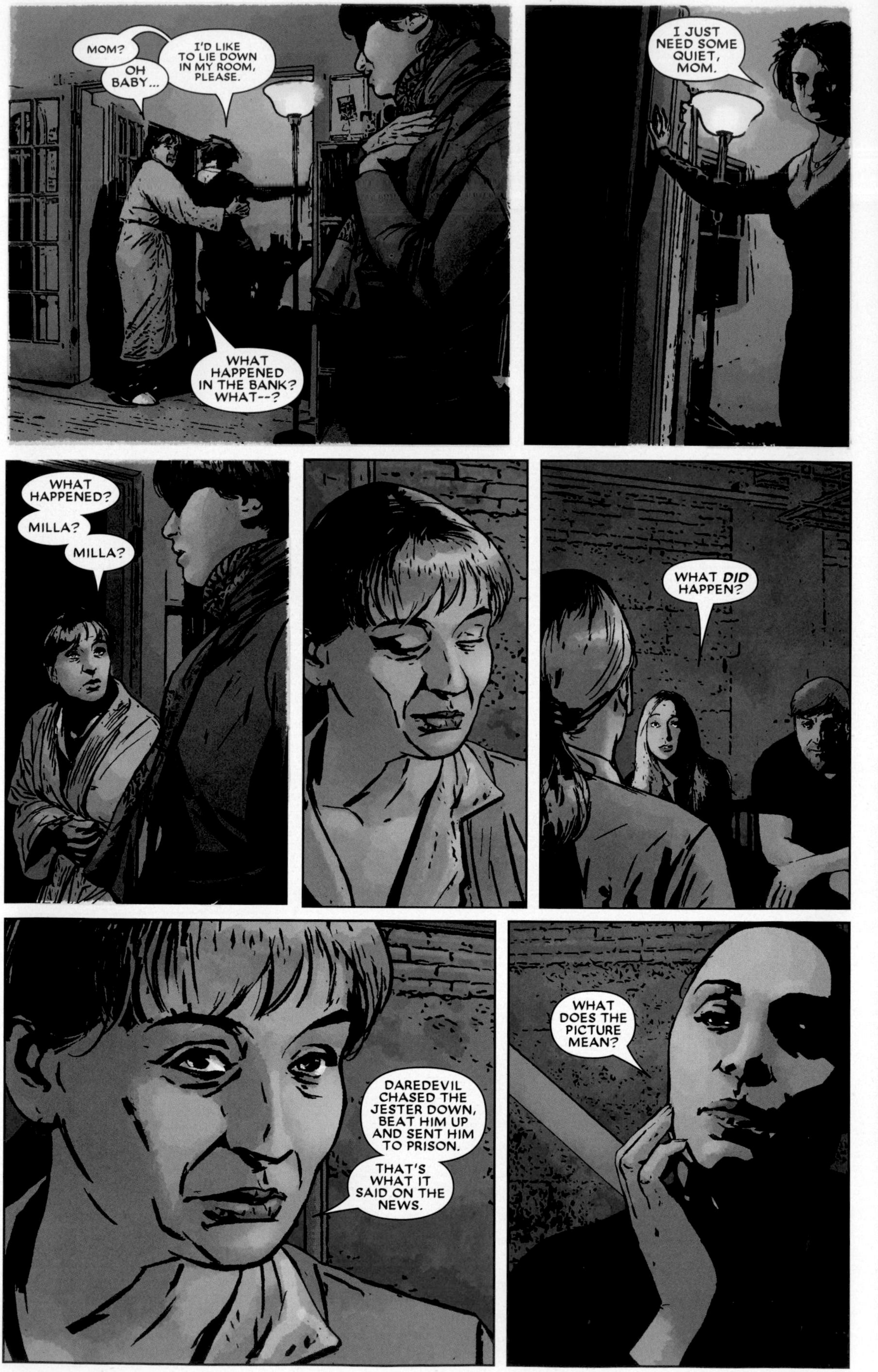

MOM?
OH BABY...
I'D LIKE TO LIE DOWN IN MY ROOM, PLEASE.
WHAT HAPPENED IN THE BANK? WHAT--?
I JUST NEED SOME QUIET, MOM.
WHAT HAPPENED?
MILLA?
MILLA?
WHAT DID HAPPEN?
DAREDEVIL CHASED THE JESTER DOWN, BEAT HIM UP AND SENT HIM TO PRISON.
THAT'S WHAT IT SAID ON THE NEWS.
WHAT DOES THE PICTURE MEAN?

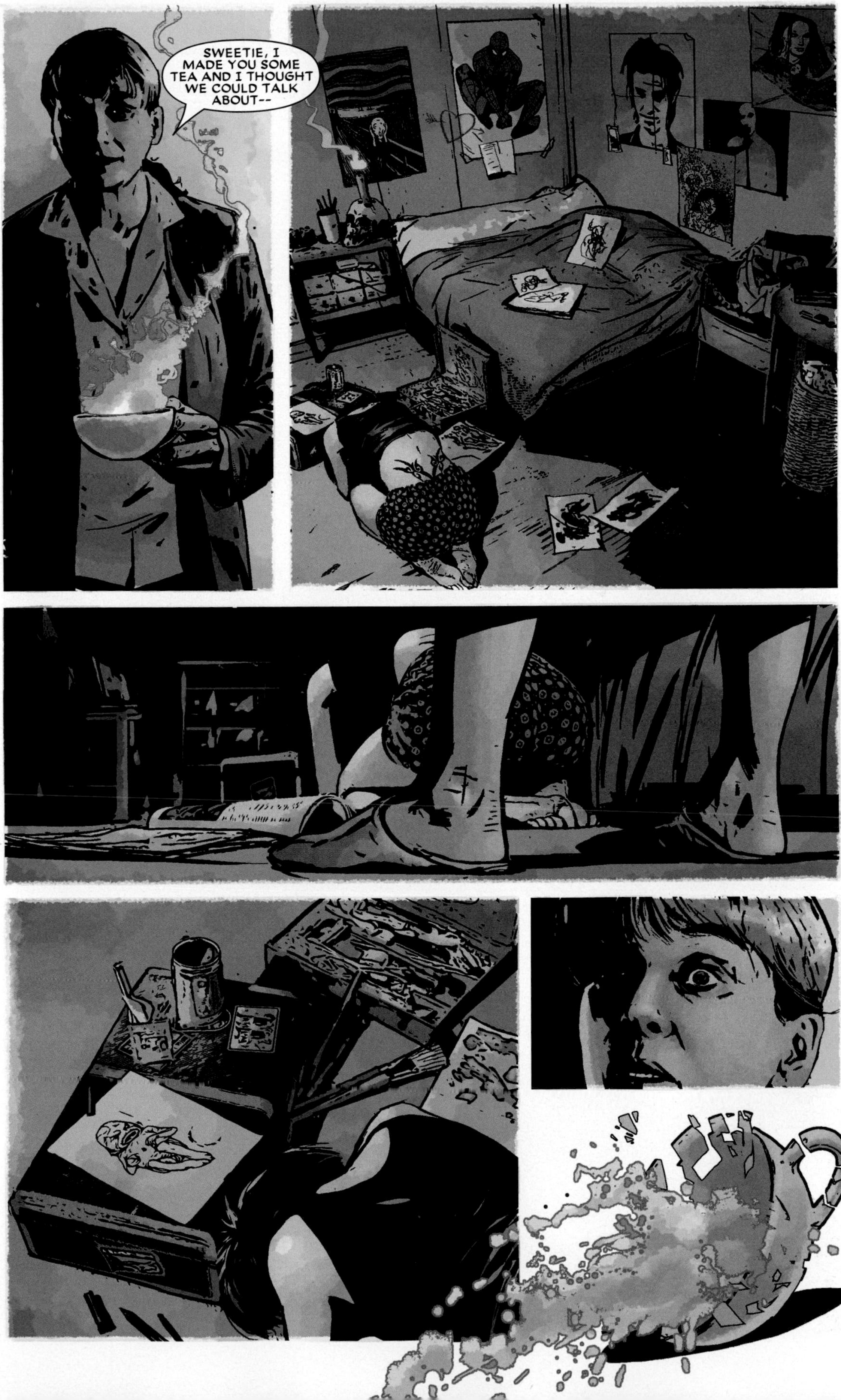
SWEETIE, I MADE YOU SOME TEA AND I THOUGHT WE COULD TALK ABOUT--

FOR WHAT HE DID THAT NIGHT THAT WOULD MAKE A NORMAL LITTLE GIRL CUT OUT HER OWN EYES AND SLIT HER OWN WRISTS.

AND LEAVE *THIS* AS HER NOTE.

I KNOW HE "SAVED" HER. I KNOW.

BUT *THIS*. THIS IS ALL I AM LEFT WITH.

THIS WAS HER LAST THOUGHT.

HER GOODBYE.

THIS.

A DEVIL.

A BAD DRAWING OF DAREDEVIL.

FIRST I THOUGHT IT WAS A DRAWING OF MATT MURDOCK.

I THOUGHT I MIGHT HAVE TO KILL DAREDEVIL FOR WHAT HE HAD DONE TO MY DAUGHTER.

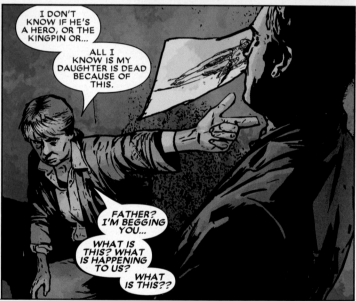

MY LIFE IS OVER...BECAUSE OF *THIS!!*

I DON'T KNOW IF HE'S A HERO, OR THE KINGPIN OR...

ALL I KNOW IS MY DAUGHTER IS DEAD BECAUSE OF THIS.

FATHER? I'M BEGGING YOU...

WHAT IS THIS? WHAT IS HAPPENING TO US?

WHAT IS THIS??

I CAME HERE TONIGHT, TO CHURCH, BECAUSE I DON'T KNOW WHERE ELSE TO GO.

I DON'T KNOW WHAT MATT MURDOCK IS AND I DON'T KNOW HOW HE DOES WHAT HE DOES!!

HEE HEEHEEHEE HEE...

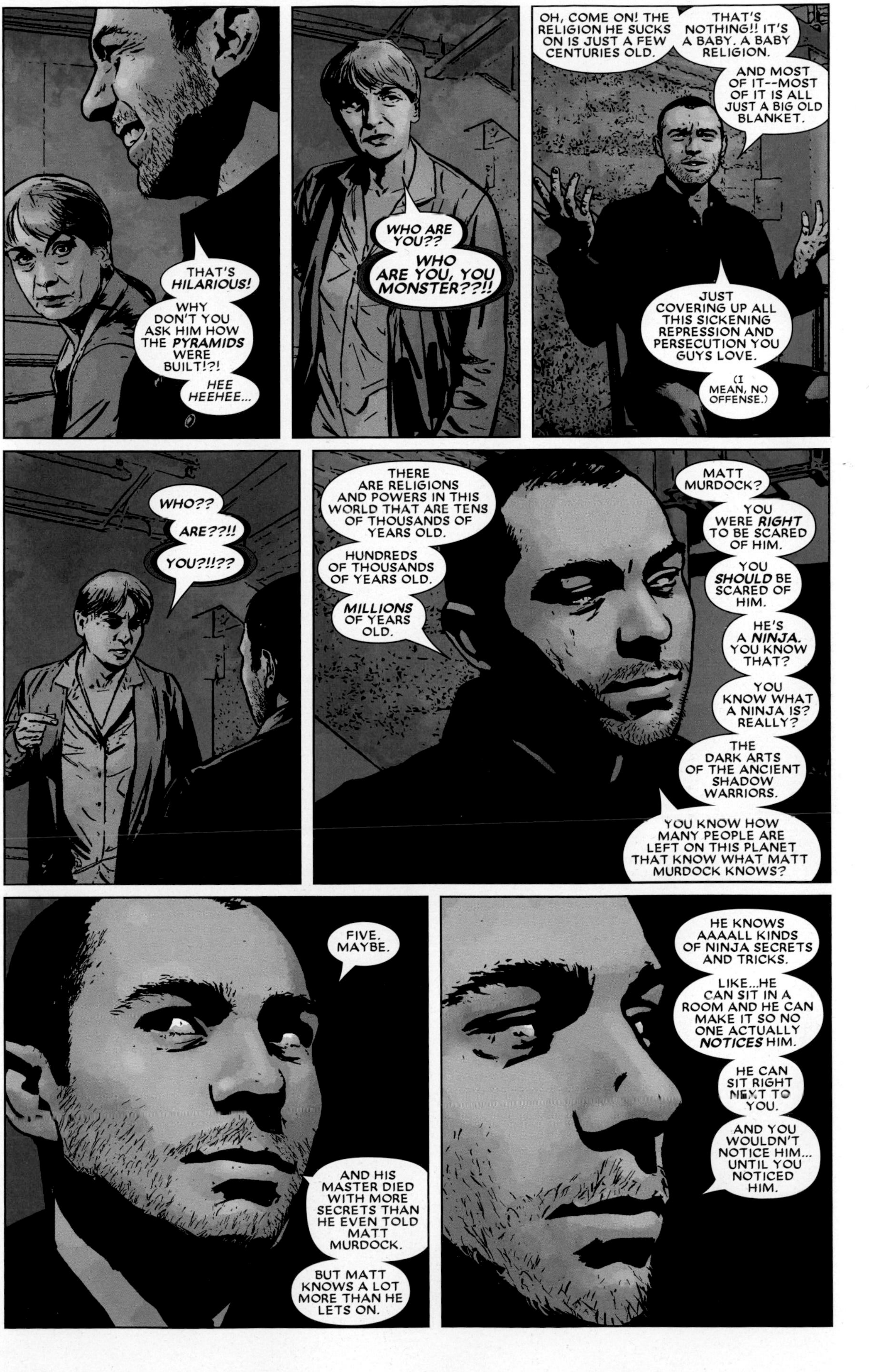
THAT'S HILARIOUS!
WHY DON'T YOU ASK HIM HOW THE PYRAMIDS WERE BUILT!?!
HEE HEEHEE...
WHO ARE YOU??
WHO ARE YOU, YOU MONSTER??!!
OH, COME ON! THE RELIGION HE SUCKS ON IS JUST A FEW CENTURIES OLD.
THAT'S NOTHING!! IT'S A BABY. A BABY RELIGION.
AND MOST OF IT--MOST OF IT IS ALL JUST A BIG OLD BLANKET.
JUST COVERING UP ALL THIS SICKENING REPRESSION AND PERSECUTION YOU GUYS LOVE.
(I MEAN, NO OFFENSE.)
WHO??
ARE??!!
YOU?!!??
THERE ARE RELIGIONS AND POWERS IN THIS WORLD THAT ARE TENS OF THOUSANDS OF YEARS OLD.
HUNDREDS OF THOUSANDS OF YEARS OLD.
MILLIONS OF YEARS OLD.
MATT MURDOCK?
YOU WERE RIGHT TO BE SCARED OF HIM.
YOU SHOULD BE SCARED OF HIM.
HE'S A NINJA. YOU KNOW THAT?
YOU KNOW WHAT A NINJA IS? REALLY?
THE DARK ARTS OF THE ANCIENT SHADOW WARRIORS.
YOU KNOW HOW MANY PEOPLE ARE LEFT ON THIS PLANET THAT KNOW WHAT MATT MURDOCK KNOWS?
FIVE. MAYBE.
AND HIS MASTER DIED WITH MORE SECRETS THAN HE EVEN TOLD MATT MURDOCK.
BUT MATT KNOWS A LOT MORE THAN HE LETS ON.
HE KNOWS AAAALL KINDS OF NINJA SECRETS AND TRICKS.
LIKE...HE CAN SIT IN A ROOM AND HE CAN MAKE IT SO NO ONE ACTUALLY NOTICES HIM.
HE CAN SIT RIGHT NEXT TO YOU.
AND YOU WOULDN'T NOTICE HIM... UNTIL YOU NOTICED HIM.

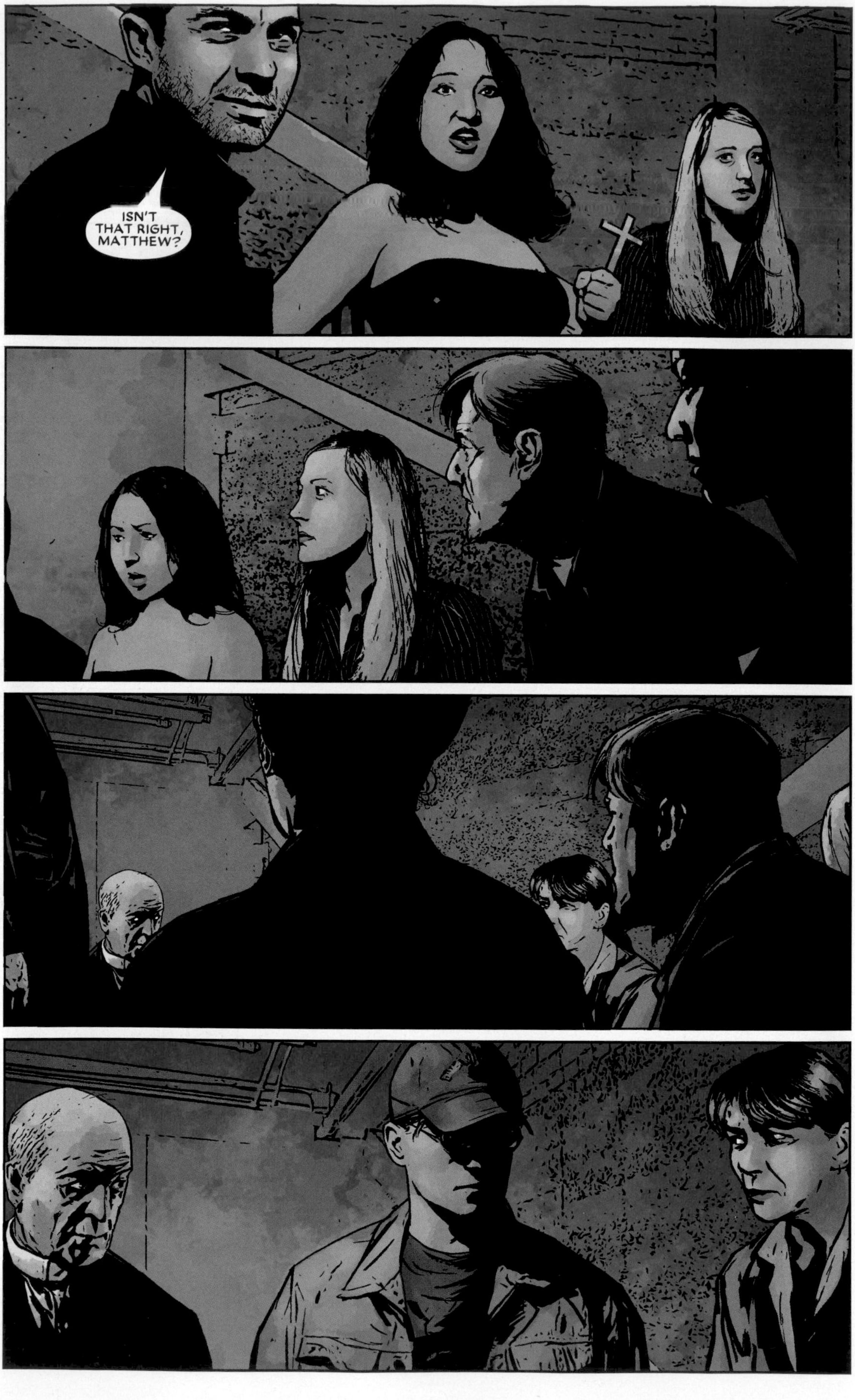
ISN'T THAT RIGHT, MATTHEW?

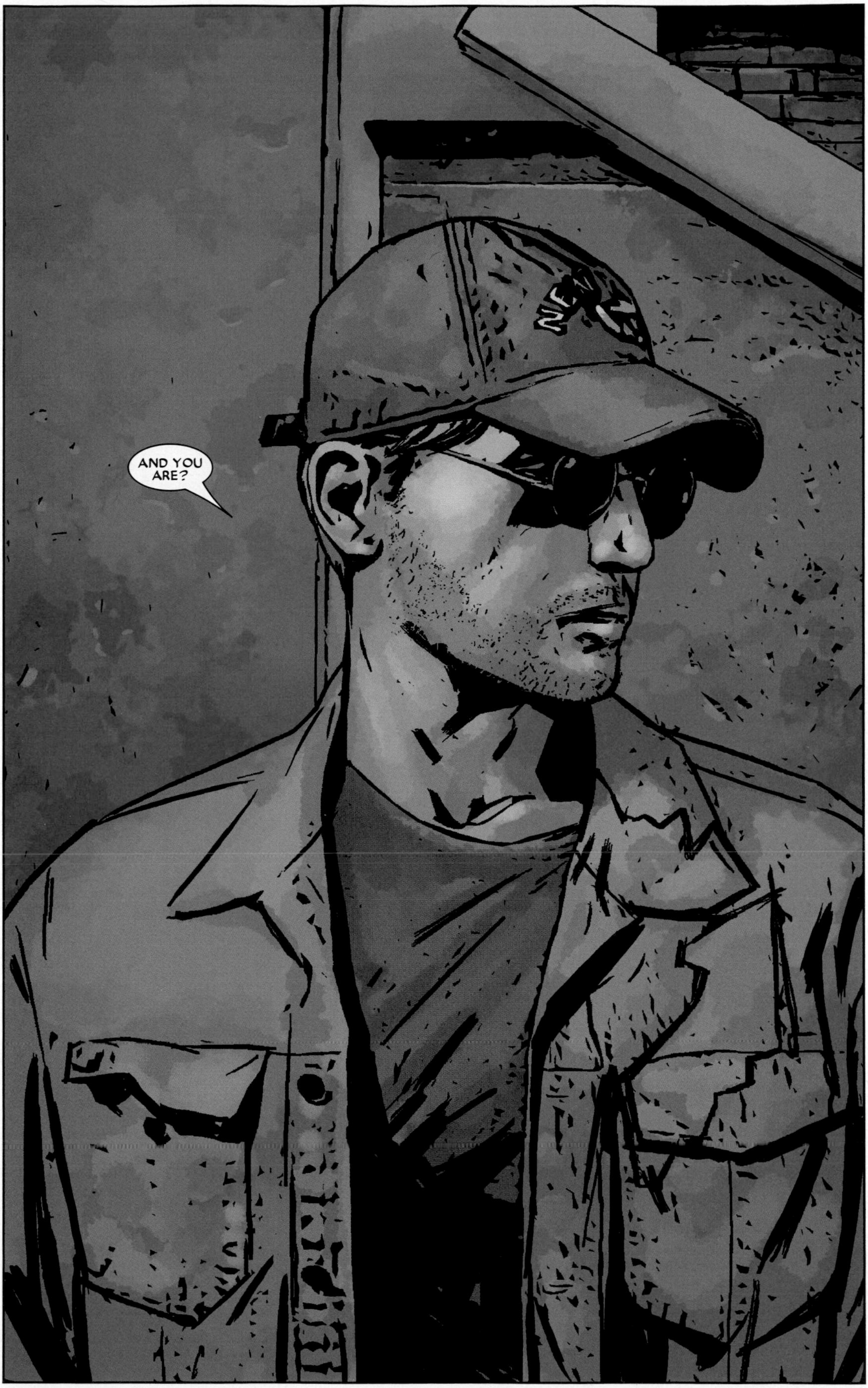
AND YOU ARE?

#75

DAREDEVIL

DECALOGUE
PART V

THOU SHALL NOT

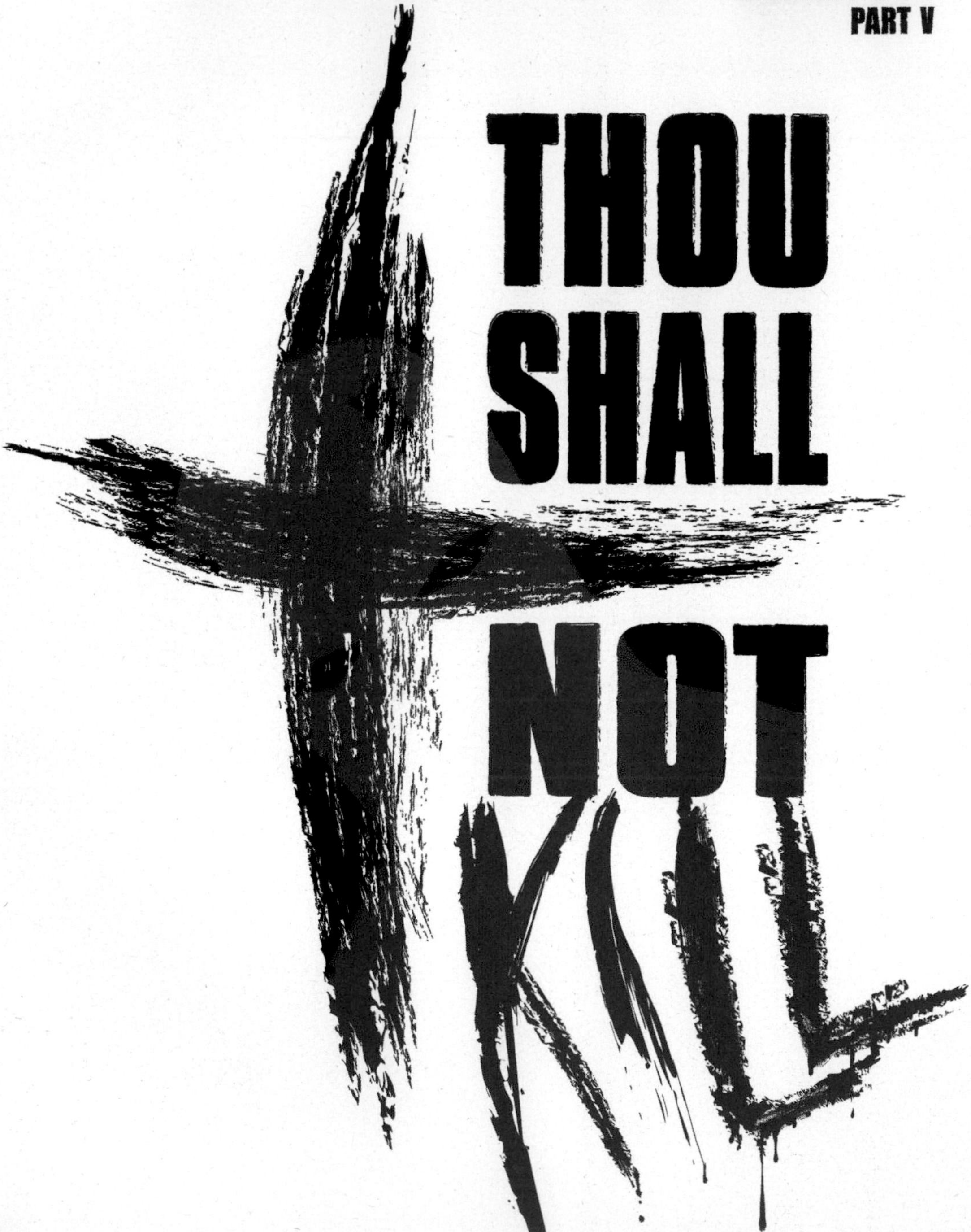

KILL

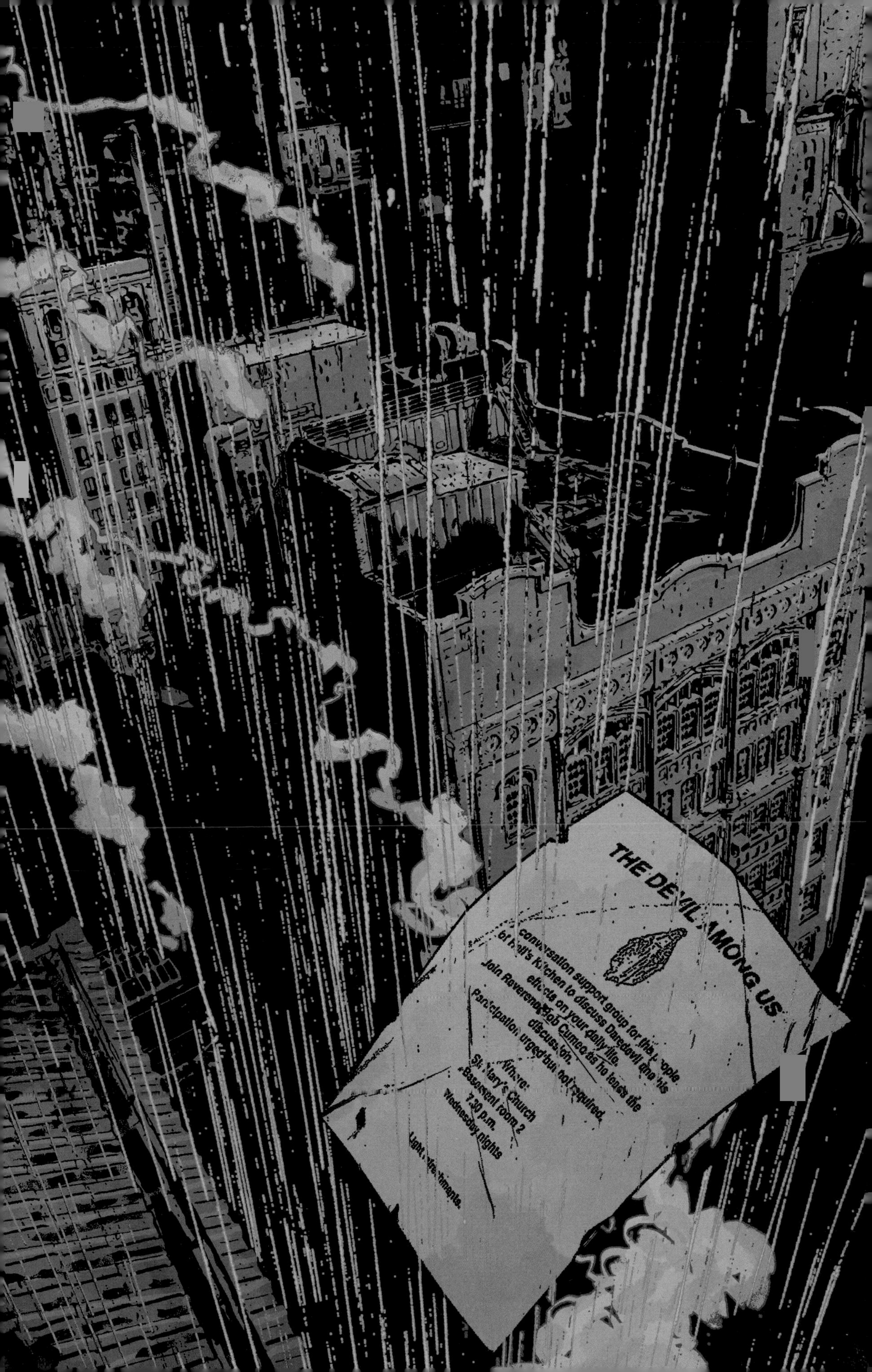
THE DEVIL AMONG US
conversation support group for the people
of hell's Kitchen to discuss Daredevil and his
effects on your daily life.
Join Reverend Bob Cumco as he leads the
discussion.
Participation urged but not required.
Where:
St. Mary's Church
Basement room 2
7:30 p.m.
Wednesday nights
Light refreshments.

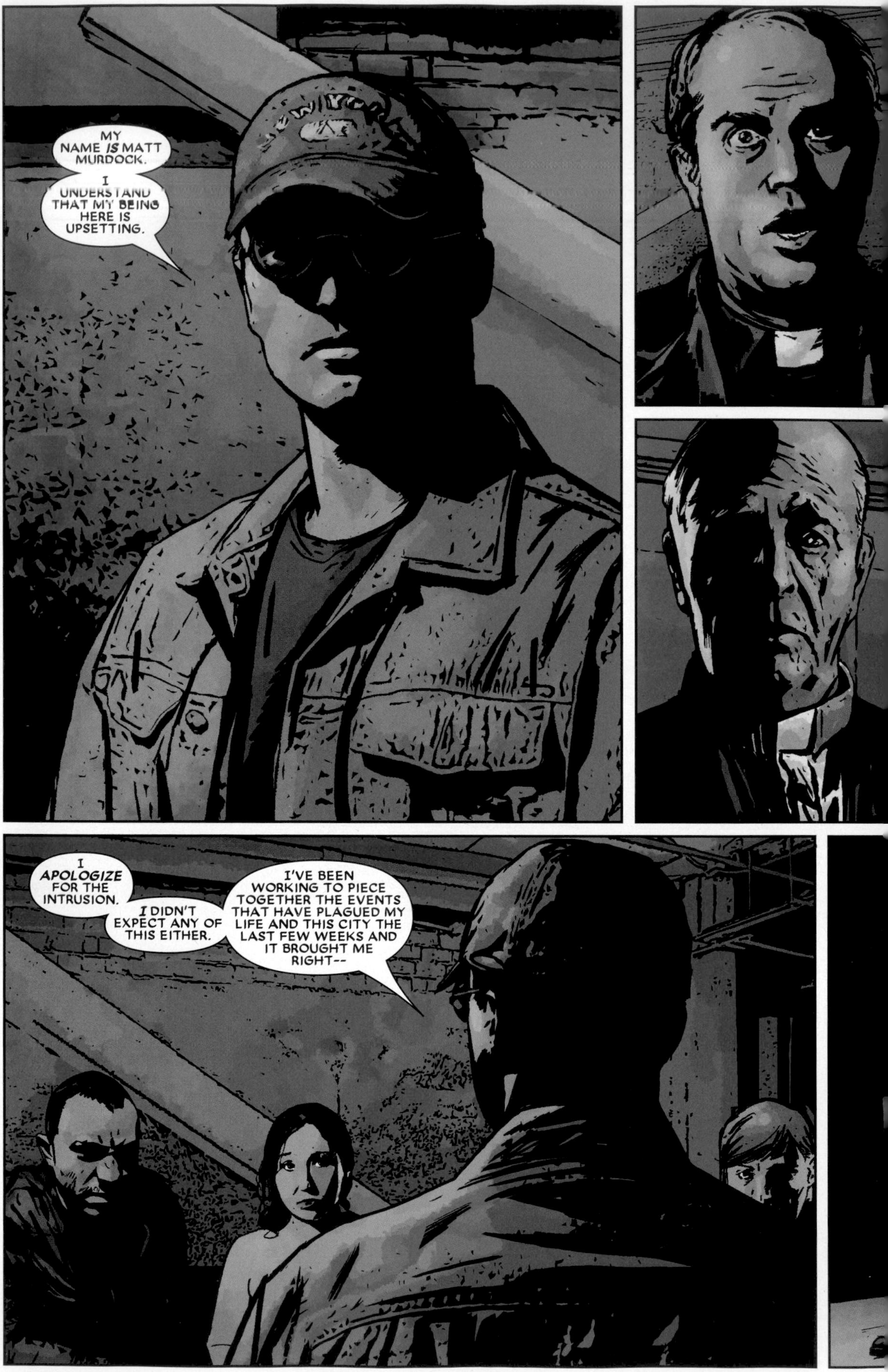
MY NAME *IS* MATT MURDOCK.
I UNDERSTAND THAT MY BEING HERE IS UPSETTING.
I *APOLOGIZE* FOR THE INTRUSION.
I DIDN'T EXPECT ANY OF THIS EITHER.
I'VE BEEN WORKING TO PIECE TOGETHER THE EVENTS THAT HAVE PLAGUED MY LIFE AND THIS CITY THE LAST FEW WEEKS AND IT BROUGHT ME RIGHT--

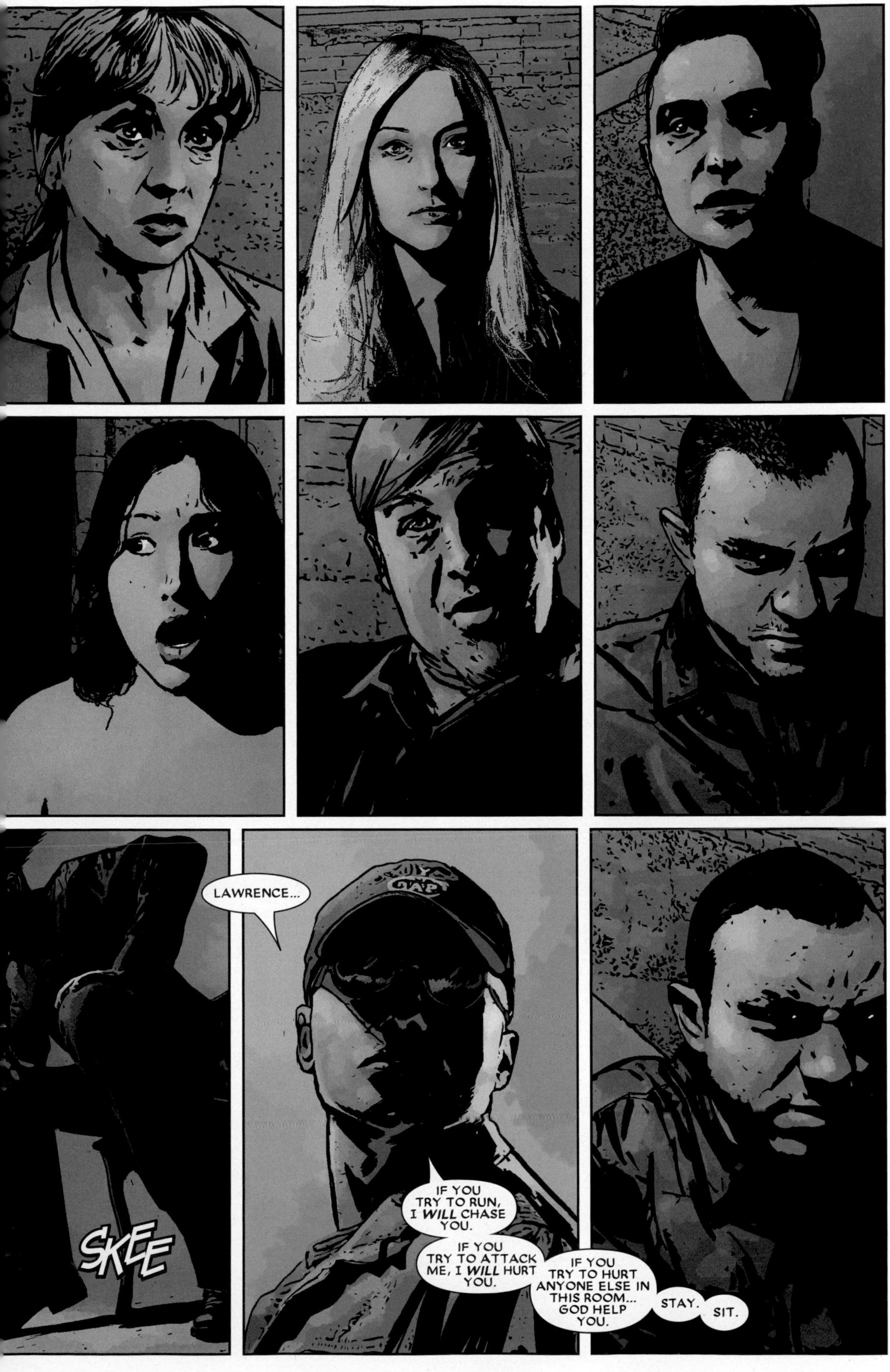
LAWRENCE...
SKEE
IF YOU TRY TO RUN, I WILL CHASE YOU.
IF YOU TRY TO ATTACK ME, I WILL HURT YOU.
IF YOU TRY TO HURT ANYONE ELSE IN THIS ROOM... GOD HELP YOU.
STAY.
SIT.

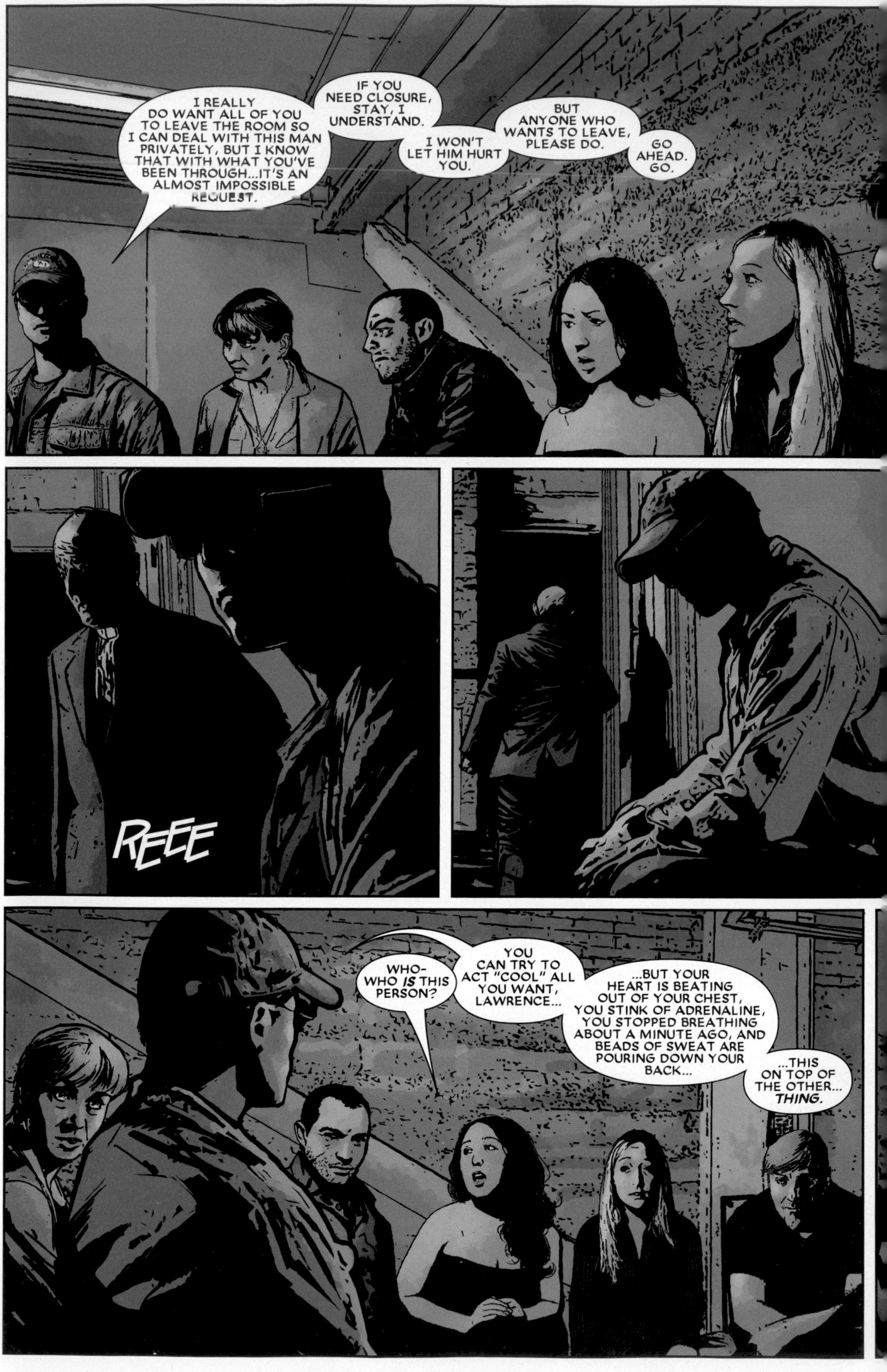

I REALLY DO WANT ALL OF YOU TO LEAVE THE ROOM SO I CAN DEAL WITH THIS MAN PRIVATELY, BUT I KNOW THAT WITH WHAT YOU'VE BEEN THROUGH...IT'S AN ALMOST IMPOSSIBLE REQUEST.
IF YOU NEED CLOSURE, STAY, I UNDERSTAND.
I WON'T LET HIM HURT YOU.
BUT ANYONE WHO WANTS TO LEAVE, PLEASE DO.
GO AHEAD. GO.
REEE
WHO-WHO *IS* THIS PERSON?
YOU CAN TRY TO ACT "COOL" ALL YOU WANT, LAWRENCE...
...BUT YOUR HEART IS BEATING OUT OF YOUR CHEST, YOU STINK OF ADRENALINE, YOU STOPPED BREATHING ABOUT A MINUTE AGO, AND BEADS OF SWEAT ARE POURING DOWN YOUR BACK...
...THIS ON TOP OF THE OTHER... *THING*.

WHAT IS GOING ON HERE?

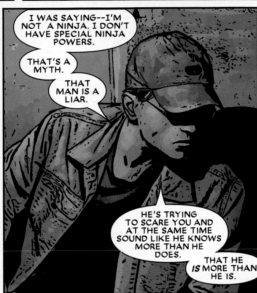

I WAS SAYING--I'M NOT A NINJA. I DON'T HAVE SPECIAL NINJA POWERS.

THAT'S A MYTH.

THAT MAN IS A LIAR.

HE'S TRYING TO SCARE YOU AND AT THE SAME TIME SOUND LIKE HE KNOWS MORE THAN HE DOES.

THAT HE *IS* MORE THAN HE IS.

I'M HERE BECAUSE I FOLLOWED *HIM* AND HE *BROUGHT* ME HERE.

YOUR BODY IS BETRAYING YOU.

MORE NOW THAN YOU ALREADY THOUGHT IT WAS.

YOU ARE MORE SCARED THAN ANYONE ELSE IN THIS ROOM AND YOU *SHOULD* BE.

WHO *IS* HE?

NOTICE HOW QUIET HE'S GOTTEN.

WHY WERE YOU FOLLOWING HIM?

I'LL TELL YOU.

YOU DESERVE TO KNOW THE TRUTH. YOU DESERVE *MORE* THAN THAT REALLY.

YOU'RE JUST PEOPLE TRYING TO LIVE YOUR LIVES AND LOOK WHAT YOU'VE HAD TO DEAL WITH.

AT FIRST, I THOUGHT THIS *WAS* ABOUT JONATHAN POWERS...

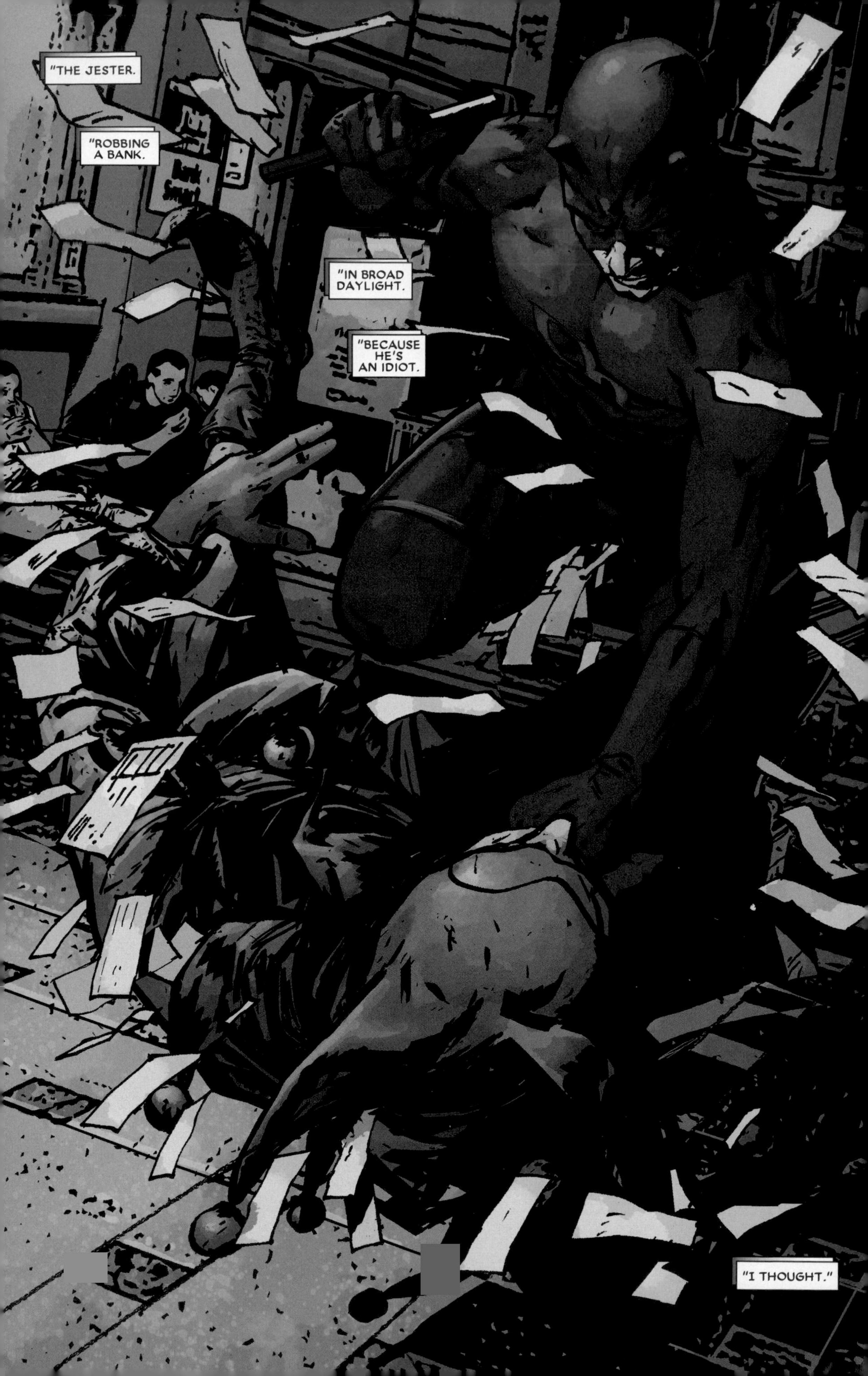
"THE JESTER.
"ROBBING A BANK.
"IN BROAD DAYLIGHT.
"BECAUSE HE'S AN IDIOT.
"I THOUGHT."

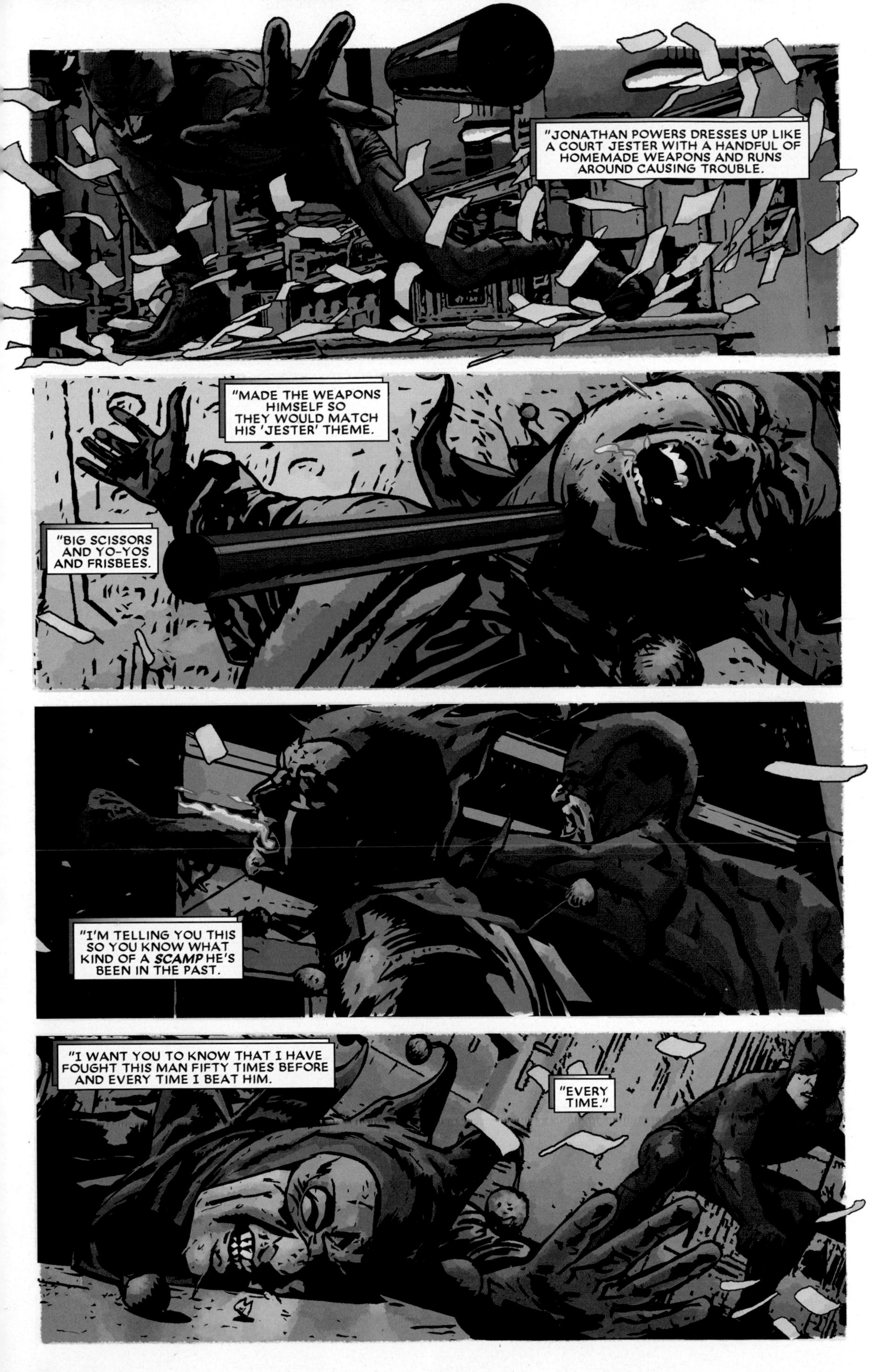
"JONATHAN POWERS DRESSES UP LIKE A COURT JESTER WITH A HANDFUL OF HOMEMADE WEAPONS AND RUNS AROUND CAUSING TROUBLE.
"MADE THE WEAPONS HIMSELF SO THEY WOULD MATCH HIS 'JESTER' THEME.
"BIG SCISSORS AND YO-YOS AND FRISBEES.
"I'M TELLING YOU THIS SO YOU KNOW WHAT KIND OF A SCAMP HE'S BEEN IN THE PAST.
"I WANT YOU TO KNOW THAT I HAVE FOUGHT THIS MAN FIFTY TIMES BEFORE AND EVERY TIME I BEAT HIM.
"EVERY TIME."

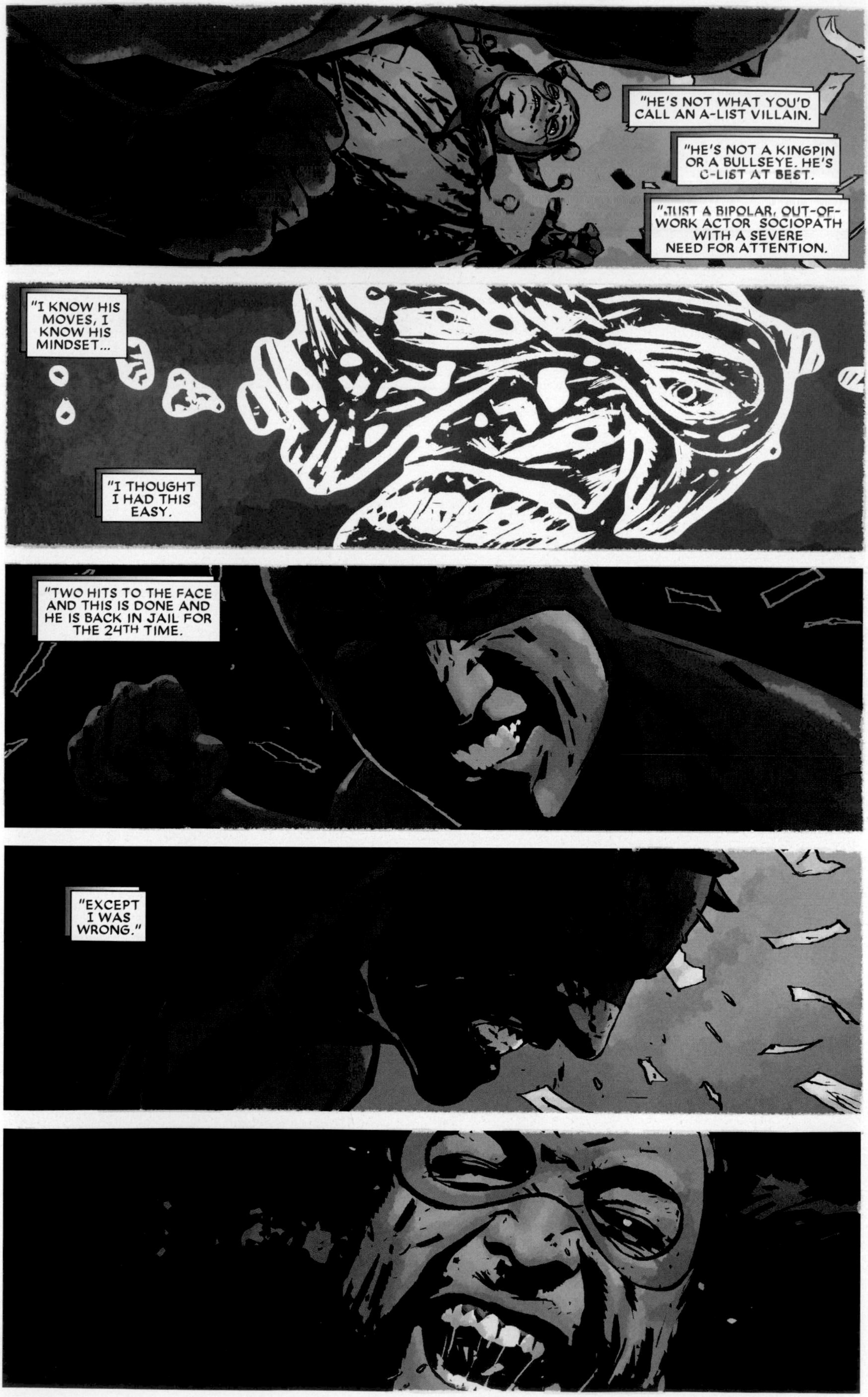
"HE'S NOT WHAT YOU'D CALL AN A-LIST VILLAIN.
"HE'S NOT A KINGPIN OR A BULLSEYE. HE'S C-LIST AT BEST.
"JUST A BIPOLAR, OUT-OF-WORK ACTOR SOCIOPATH WITH A SEVERE NEED FOR ATTENTION.
"I KNOW HIS MOVES, I KNOW HIS MINDSET...
"I THOUGHT I HAD THIS EASY.
"TWO HITS TO THE FACE AND THIS IS DONE AND HE IS BACK IN JAIL FOR THE 24TH TIME.
"EXCEPT I WAS WRONG."

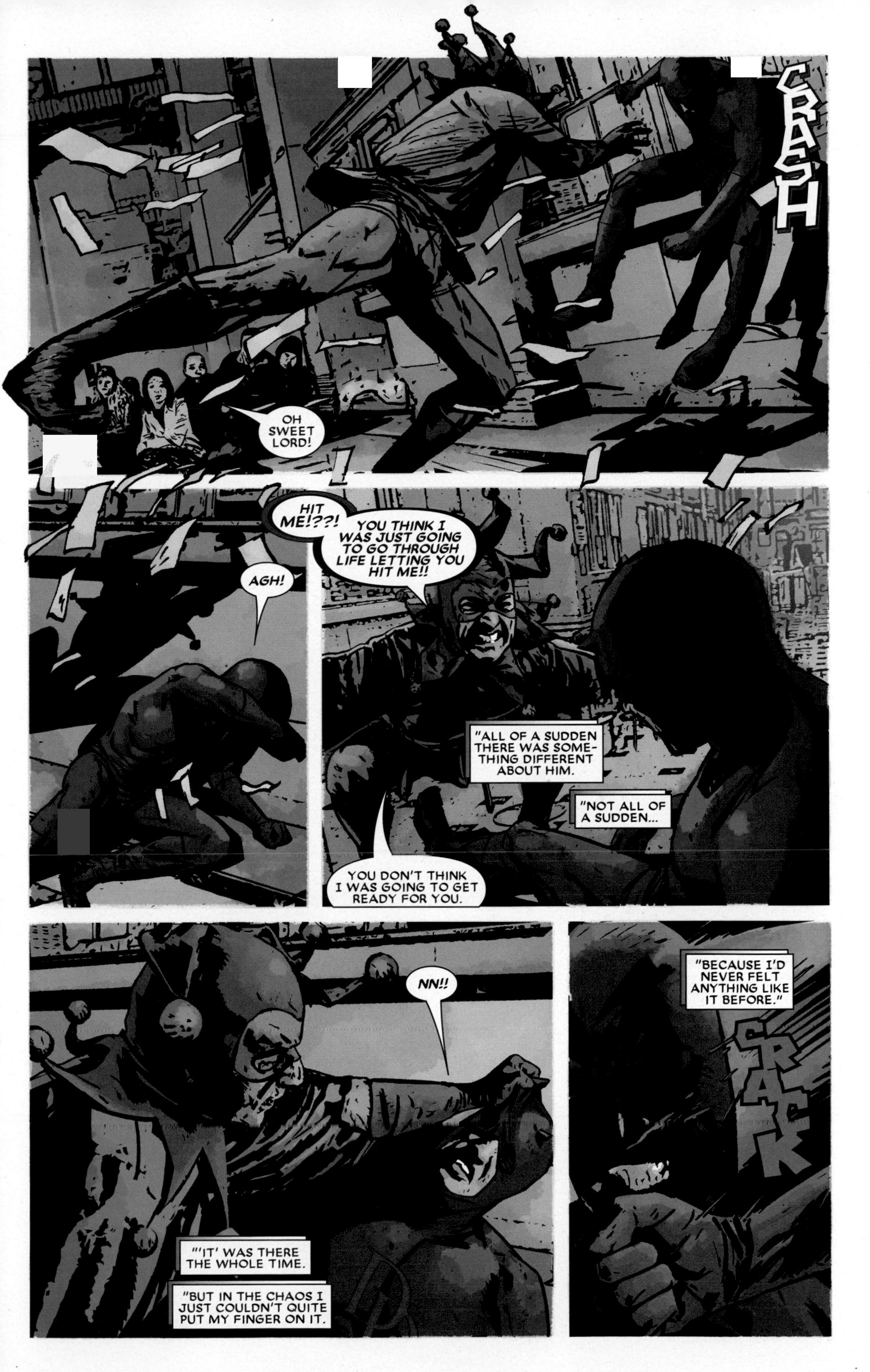

CRASH
OH SWEET LORD!
AGH!
HIT ME!??!
YOU THINK I WAS JUST GOING TO GO THROUGH LIFE LETTING YOU HIT ME!!
"ALL OF A SUDDEN THERE WAS SOME-THING DIFFERENT ABOUT HIM.
"NOT ALL OF A SUDDEN...
YOU DON'T THINK I WAS GOING TO GET READY FOR YOU.
NN!!
"'IT' WAS THERE THE WHOLE TIME.
"BUT IN THE CHAOS I JUST COULDN'T QUITE PUT MY FINGER ON IT.
"BECAUSE I'D NEVER FELT ANYTHING LIKE IT BEFORE."
CRACK

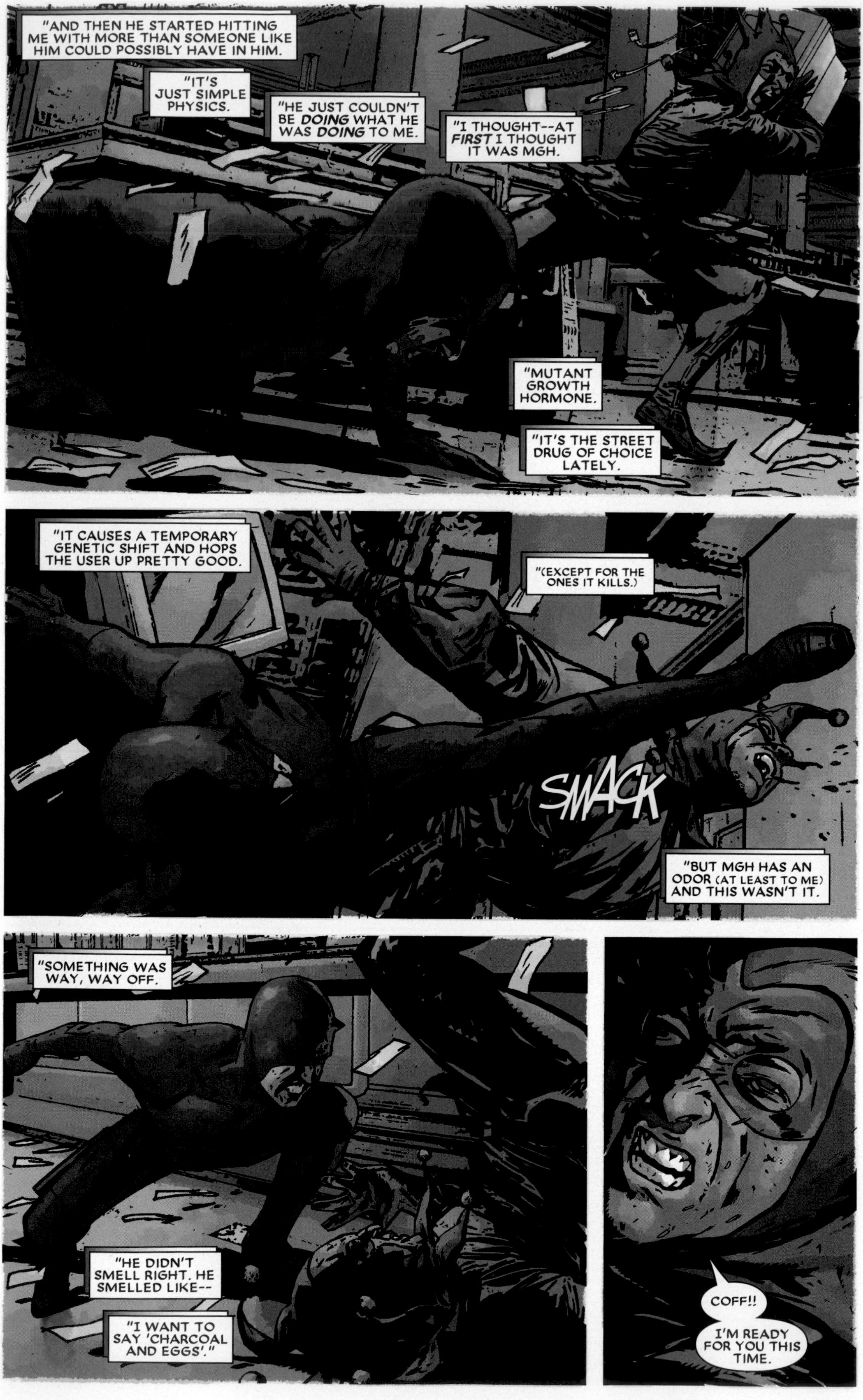
"AND THEN HE STARTED HITTING ME WITH MORE THAN SOMEONE LIKE HIM COULD POSSIBLY HAVE IN HIM.
"IT'S JUST SIMPLE PHYSICS.
"HE JUST COULDN'T BE DOING WHAT HE WAS DOING TO ME.
"I THOUGHT--AT FIRST I THOUGHT IT WAS MGH.
"MUTANT GROWTH HORMONE.
"IT'S THE STREET DRUG OF CHOICE LATELY.
"IT CAUSES A TEMPORARY GENETIC SHIFT AND HOPS THE USER UP PRETTY GOOD.
"(EXCEPT FOR THE ONES IT KILLS.)
SMACK
"BUT MGH HAS AN ODOR (AT LEAST TO ME) AND THIS WASN'T IT.
"SOMETHING WAS WAY, WAY OFF.
"HE DIDN'T SMELL RIGHT. HE SMELLED LIKE--
"I WANT TO SAY 'CHARCOAL AND EGGS'."
COFF!!
I'M READY FOR YOU THIS TIME.

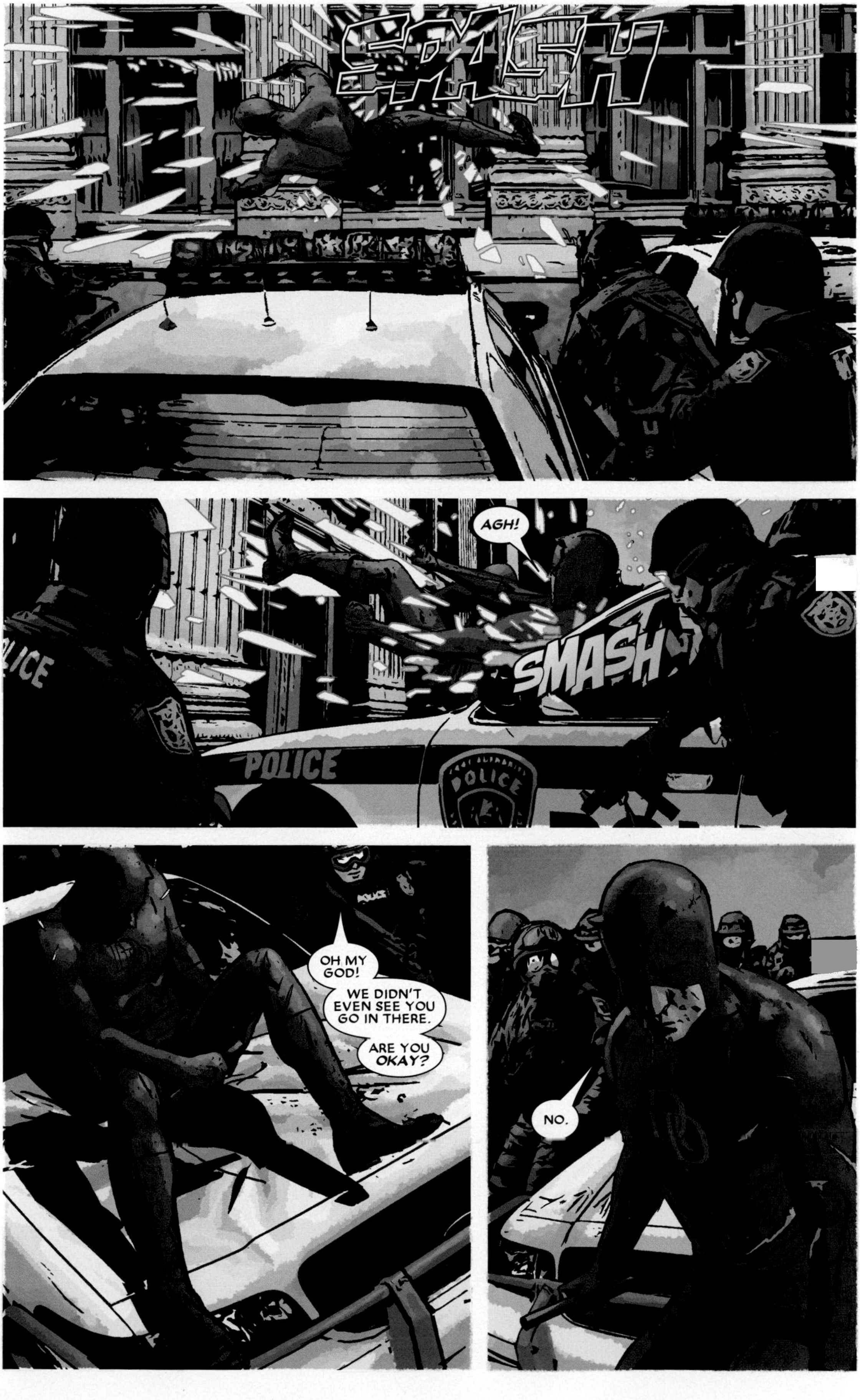
SMASH
AGH!
SMASH
POLICE
POLICE
OH MY GOD!
WE DIDN'T EVEN SEE YOU GO IN THERE.
ARE YOU OKAY?
NO.

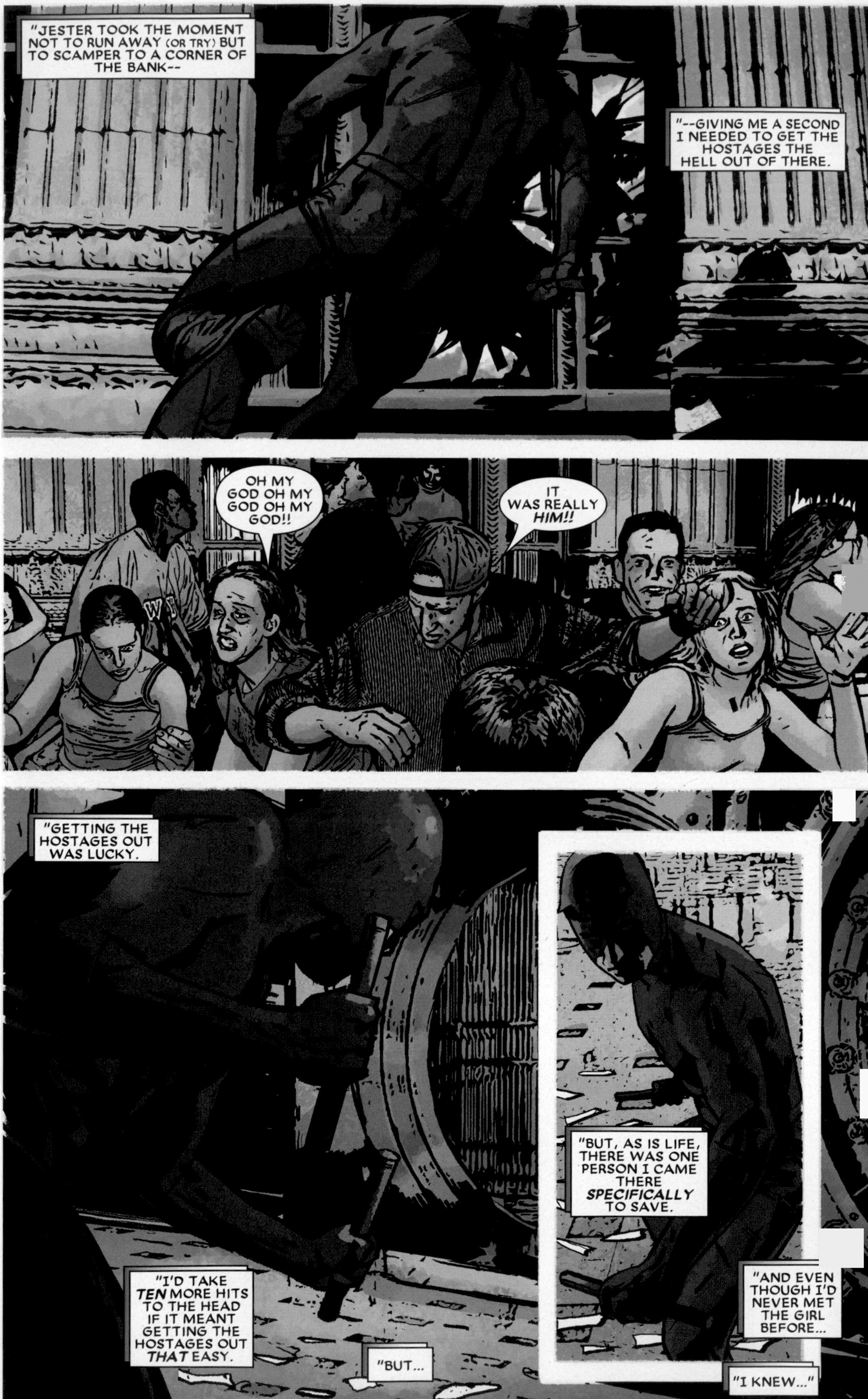
"JESTER TOOK THE MOMENT NOT TO RUN AWAY (OR TRY) BUT TO SCAMPER TO A CORNER OF THE BANK--
"--GIVING ME A SECOND I NEEDED TO GET THE HOSTAGES THE HELL OUT OF THERE.
OH MY GOD OH MY GOD OH MY GOD!!
IT WAS REALLY *HIM!!*
"GETTING THE HOSTAGES OUT WAS LUCKY.
"I'D TAKE *TEN* MORE HITS TO THE HEAD IF IT MEANT GETTING THE HOSTAGES OUT *THAT* EASY.
"BUT...
"BUT, AS IS LIFE, THERE WAS ONE PERSON I CAME THERE *SPECIFICALLY* TO SAVE.
"AND EVEN THOUGH I'D NEVER MET THE GIRL BEFORE...
"I KNEW..."

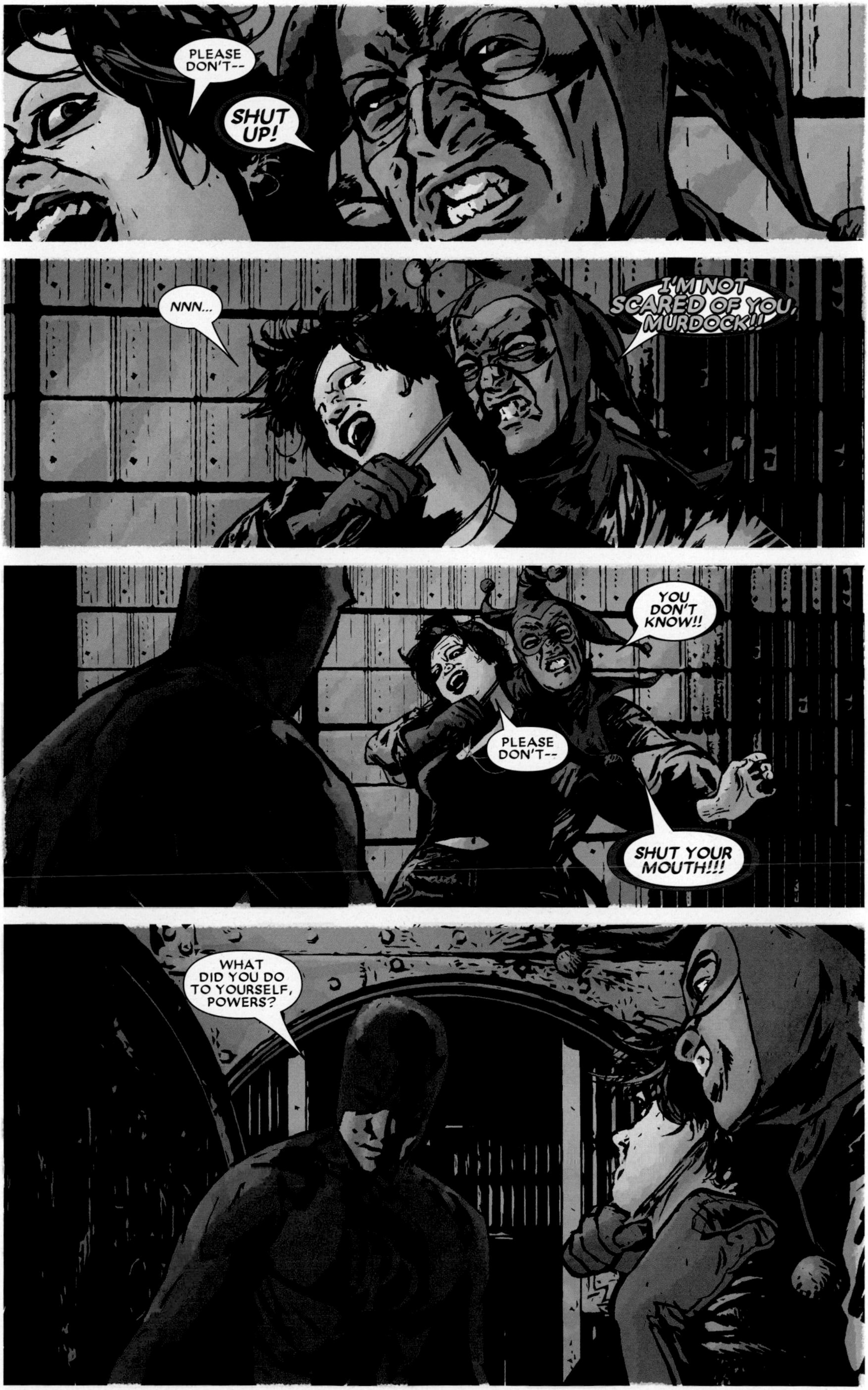
PLEASE DON'T--
SHUT UP!
NNN...
I'M NOT SCARED OF YOU, MURDOCK!!
YOU DON'T KNOW!!
PLEASE DON'T--
SHUT YOUR MOUTH!!!
WHAT DID YOU DO TO YOURSELF, POWERS?

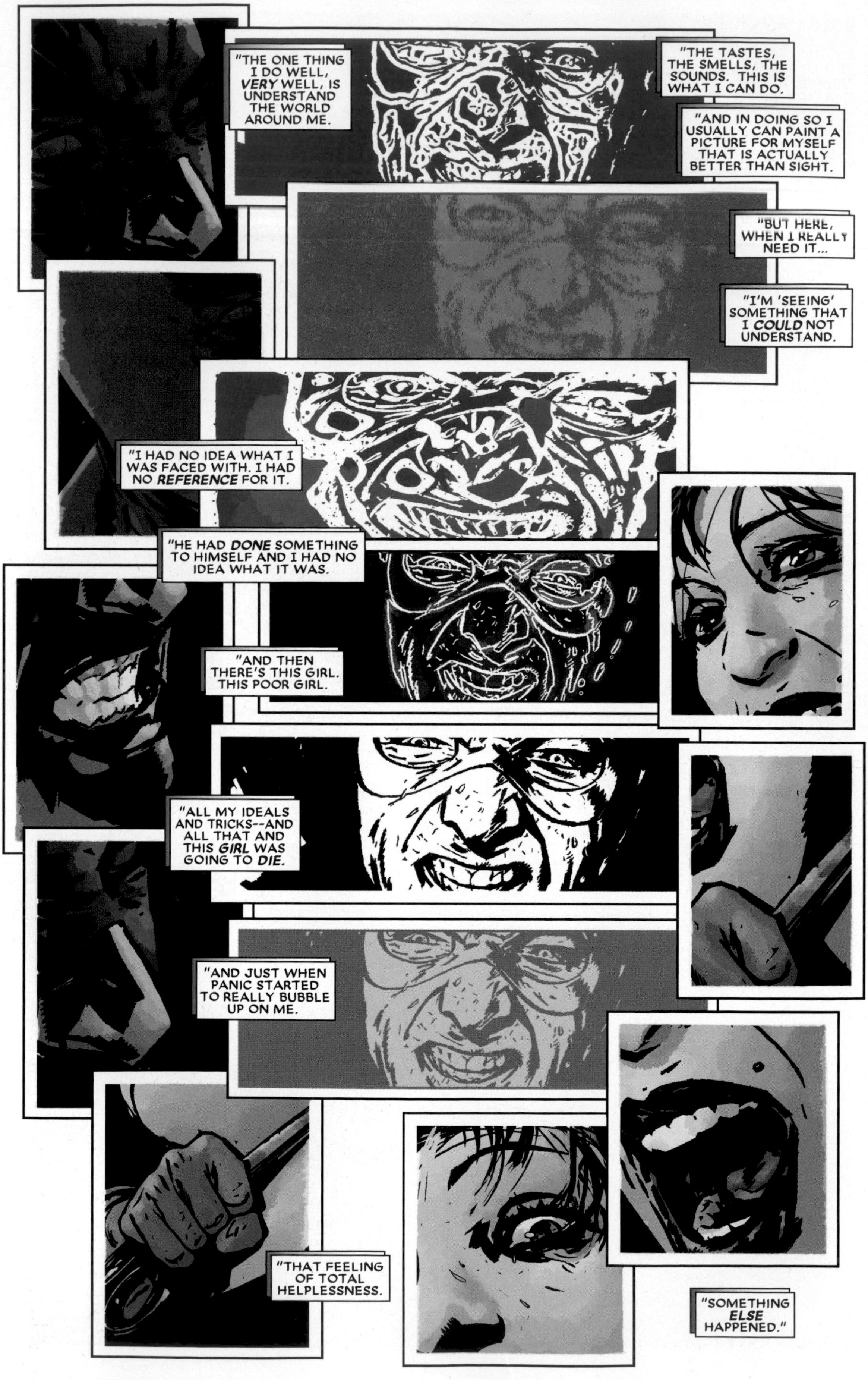
"THE ONE THING I DO WELL, VERY WELL, IS UNDERSTAND THE WORLD AROUND ME.
"THE TASTES, THE SMELLS, THE SOUNDS. THIS IS WHAT I CAN DO.
"AND IN DOING SO I USUALLY CAN PAINT A PICTURE FOR MYSELF THAT IS ACTUALLY BETTER THAN SIGHT.
"BUT HERE, WHEN I REALLY NEED IT...
"I'M 'SEEING' SOMETHING THAT I COULD NOT UNDERSTAND.
"I HAD NO IDEA WHAT I WAS FACED WITH. I HAD NO REFERENCE FOR IT.
"HE HAD DONE SOMETHING TO HIMSELF AND I HAD NO IDEA WHAT IT WAS.
"AND THEN THERE'S THIS GIRL. THIS POOR GIRL.
"ALL MY IDEALS AND TRICKS--AND ALL THAT AND THIS GIRL WAS GOING TO DIE.
"AND JUST WHEN PANIC STARTED TO REALLY BUBBLE UP ON ME.
"THAT FEELING OF TOTAL HELPLESSNESS.
"SOMETHING ELSE HAPPENED."

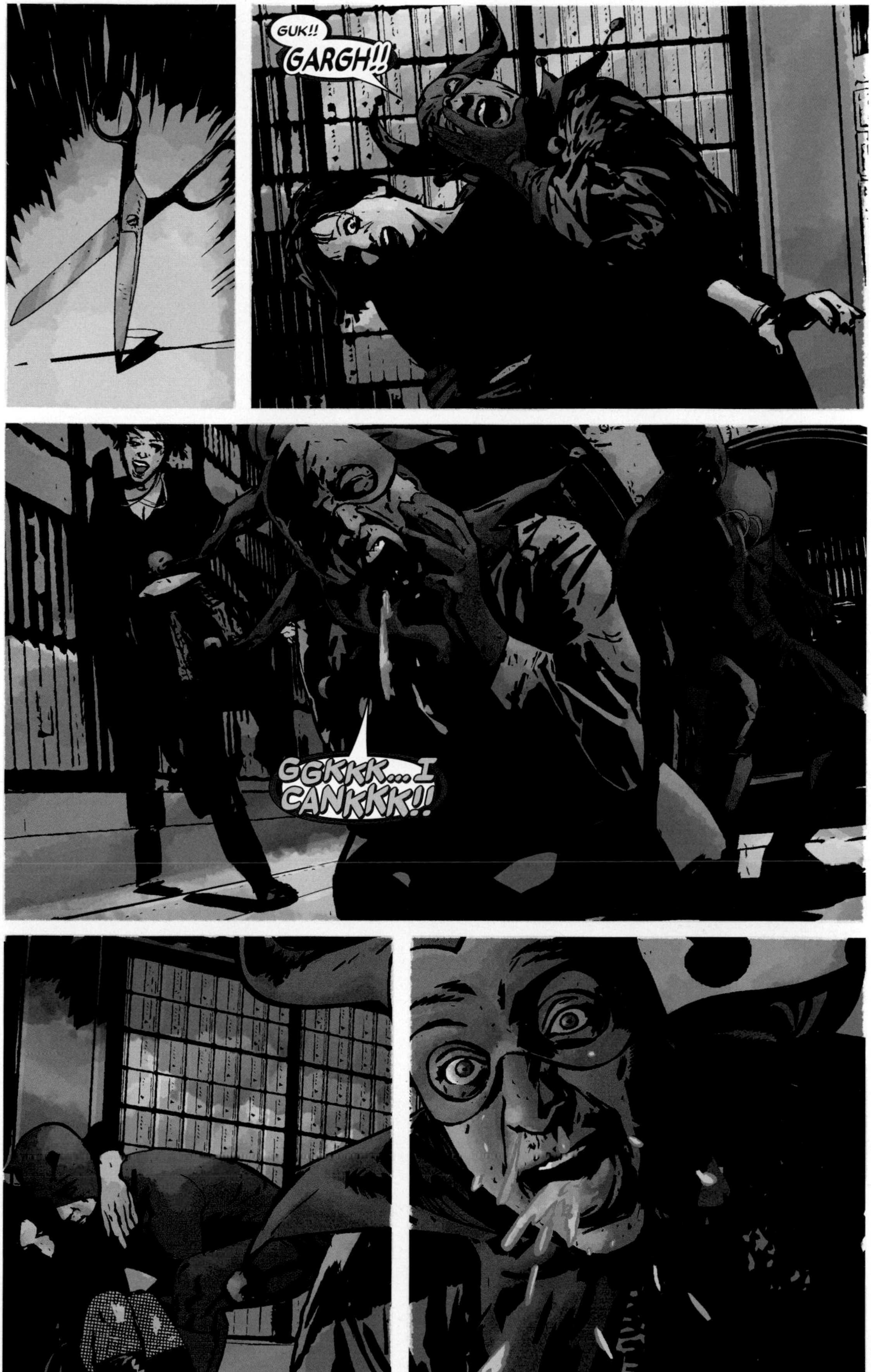
GUK!! GARGH!!
GGKKK... I CANKKK!!

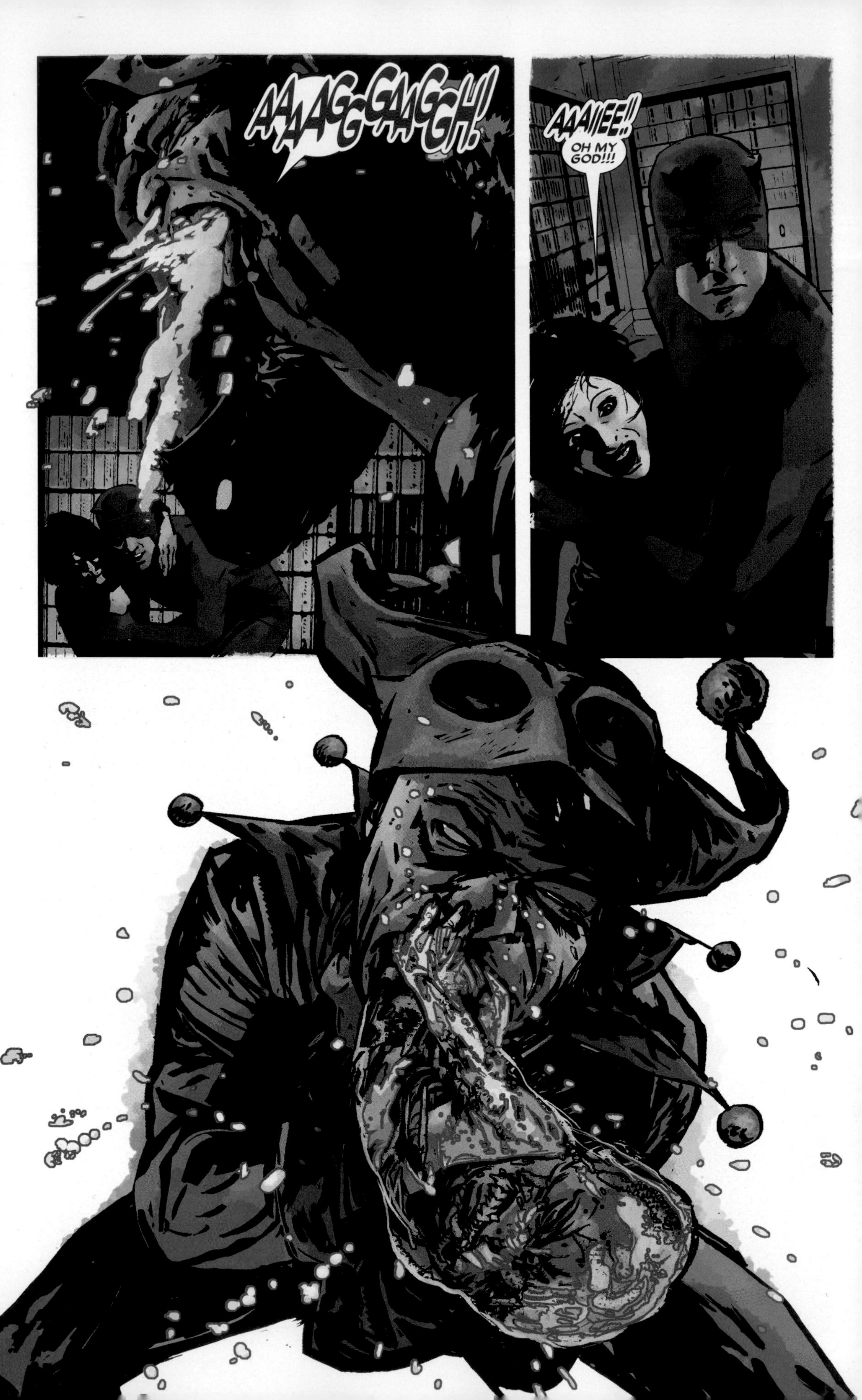
AAAAGG-GAAGGH!!
AAAIIEE!!
OH MY GOD!!!

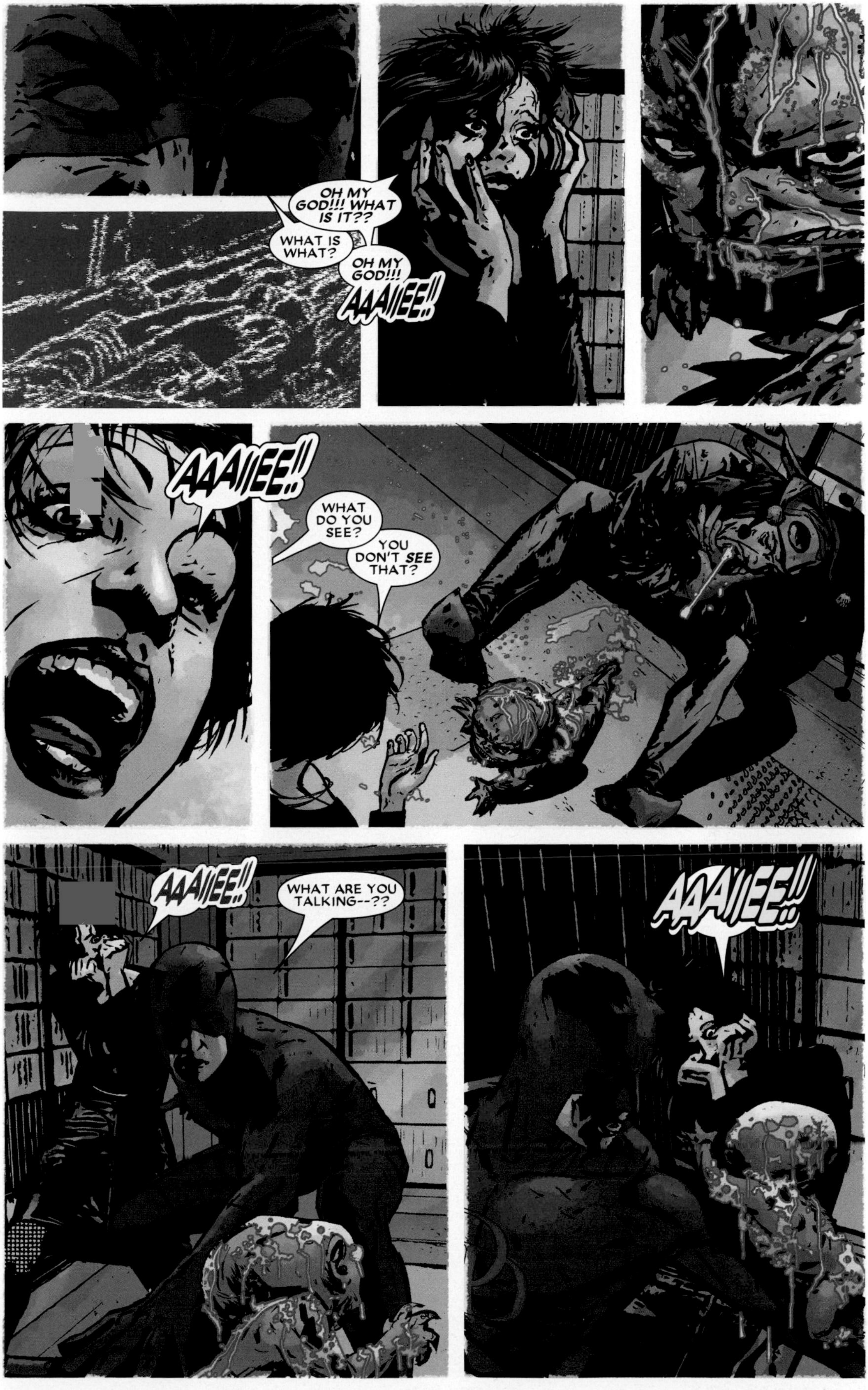
OH MY GOD!!! WHAT IS IT??
WHAT IS WHAT?
OH MY GOD!!!
AAAIIEE!!
AAAIIEE!!
WHAT DO YOU SEE?
YOU DON'T SEE THAT?
AAAIIEE!!
WHAT ARE YOU TALKING--??
AAAIIEE!!!

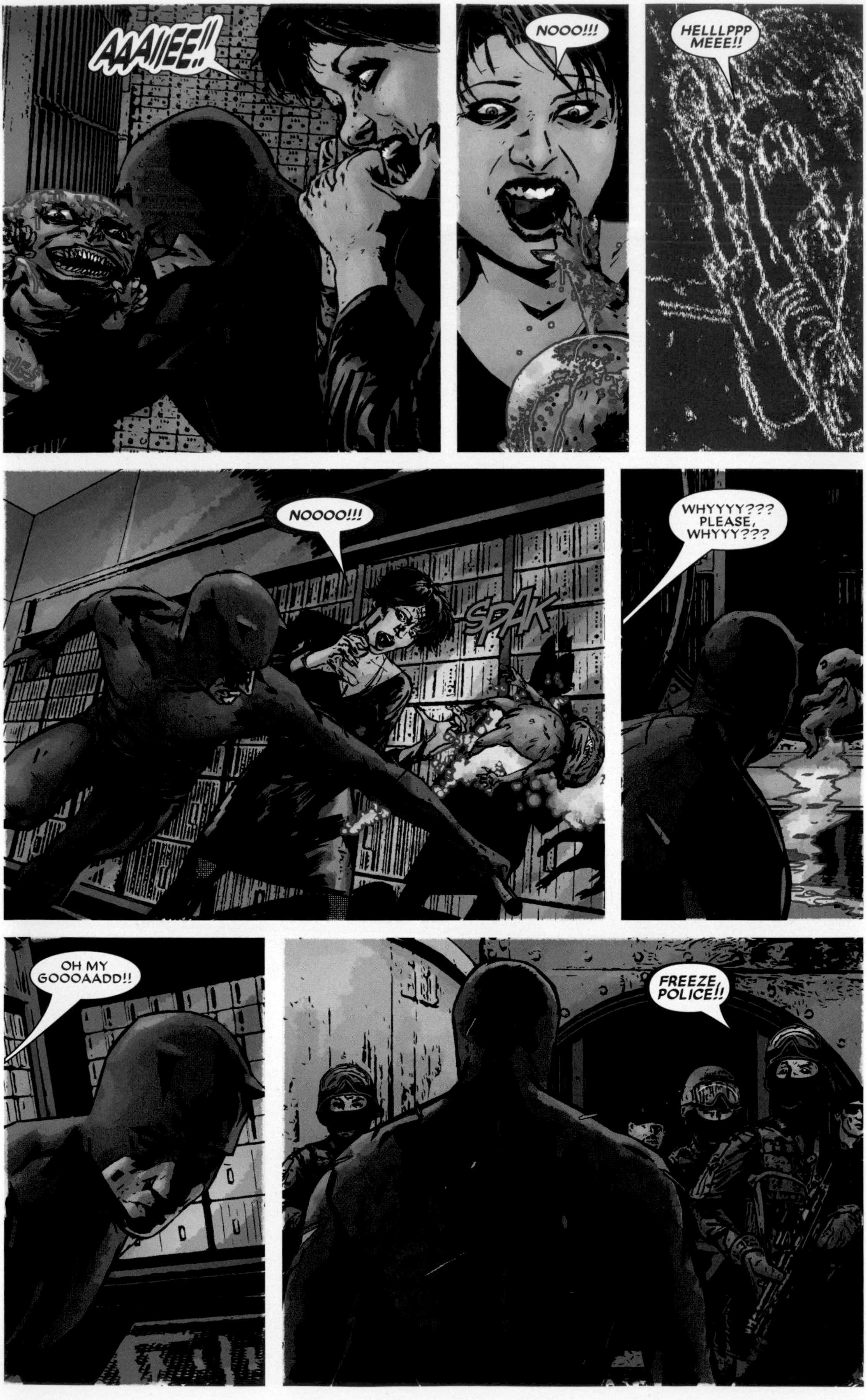
AAAIIEE!!
NOOO!!!
HELLLPPP MEEE!!
NOOOO!!!
SPAK
WHYYYY??? PLEASE, WHYYY???
OH MY GOOOAADD!!
FREEZE, POLICE!!

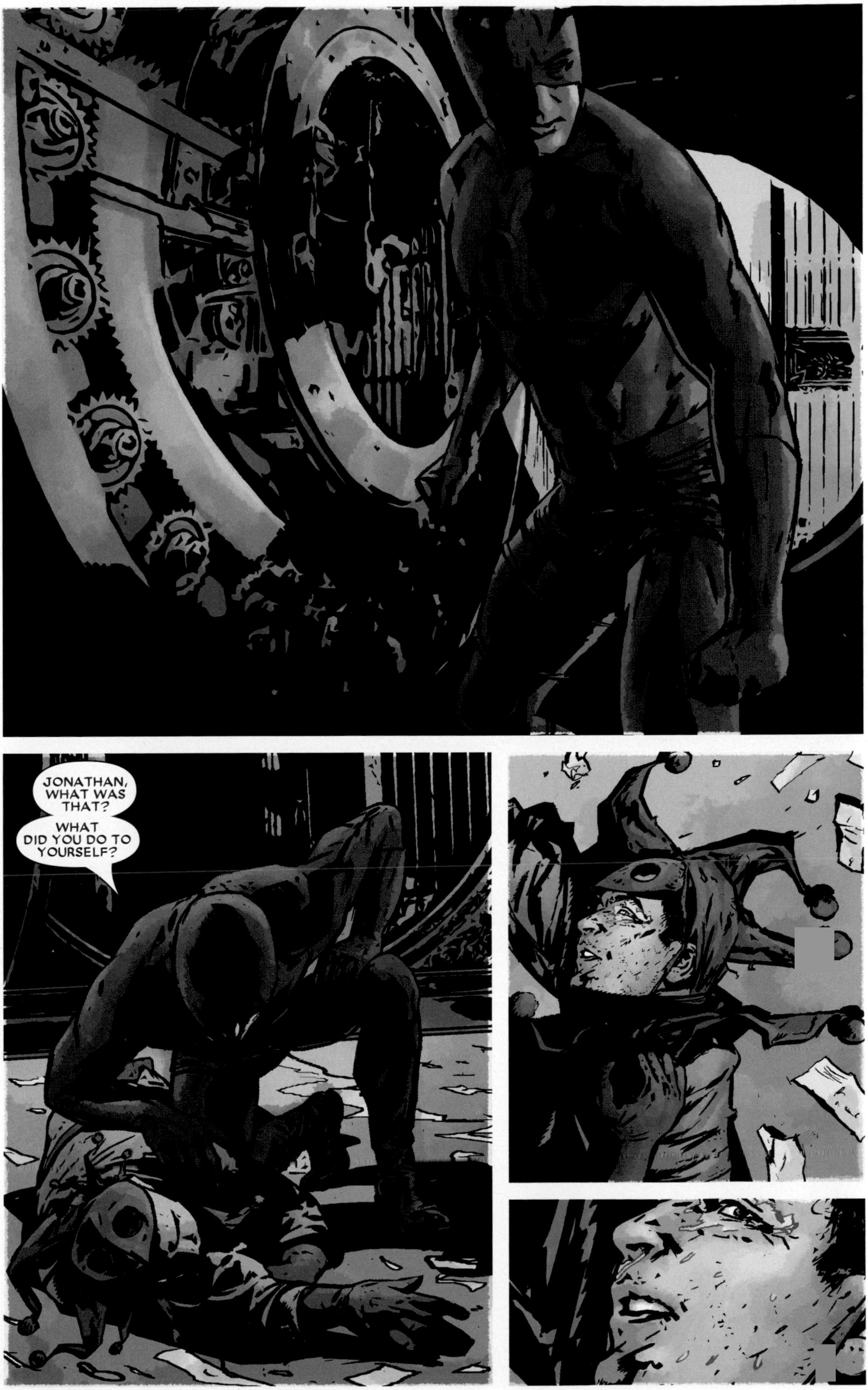
JONATHAN, WHAT WAS THAT?
WHAT DID YOU DO TO YOURSELF?

SNIFF...

AHUHHMMMY BABY!

WHAT— WHAT DID THE JESTER GUY SAY TO YOU?

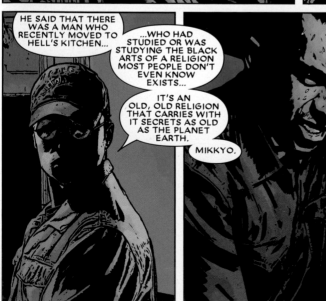

HE SAID THAT THERE WAS A MAN WHO RECENTLY MOVED TO HELL'S KITCHEN...

...WHO HAD STUDIED OR WAS STUDYING THE BLACK ARTS OF A RELIGION MOST PEOPLE DON'T EVEN KNOW EXISTS...

IT'S AN OLD, OLD RELIGION THAT CARRIES WITH IT SECRETS AS OLD AS THE PLANET EARTH.

MIKKYO.

IS THAT—

JAPANESE, YES.

IT LITERALLY MEANS "SECRET TEACHINGS."

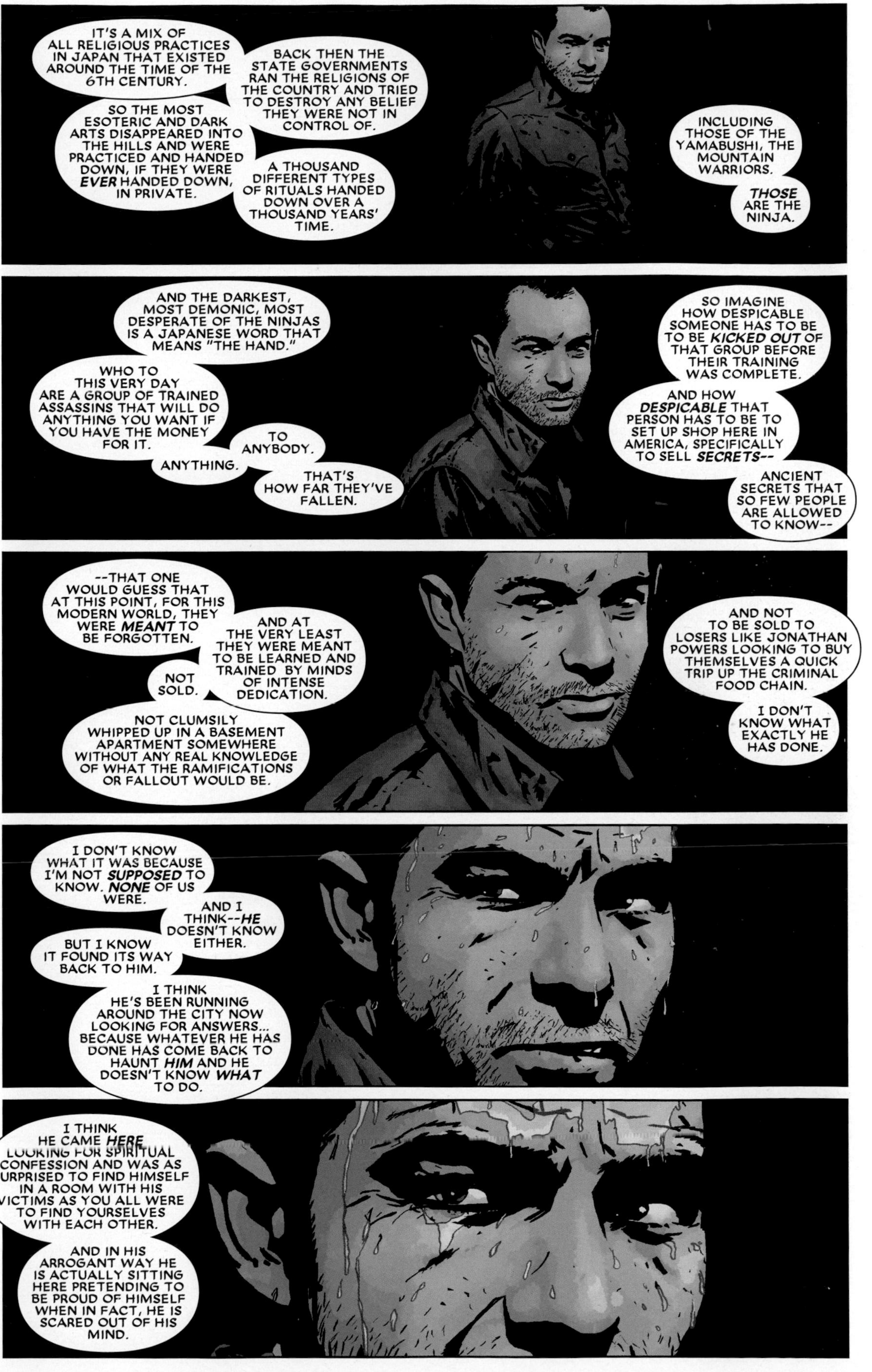
IT'S A MIX OF ALL RELIGIOUS PRACTICES IN JAPAN THAT EXISTED AROUND THE TIME OF THE 6TH CENTURY.
BACK THEN THE STATE GOVERNMENTS RAN THE RELIGIONS OF THE COUNTRY AND TRIED TO DESTROY ANY BELIEF THEY WERE NOT IN CONTROL OF.
SO THE MOST ESOTERIC AND DARK ARTS DISAPPEARED INTO THE HILLS AND WERE PRACTICED AND HANDED DOWN, IF THEY WERE EVER HANDED DOWN, IN PRIVATE.
A THOUSAND DIFFERENT TYPES OF RITUALS HANDED DOWN OVER A THOUSAND YEARS' TIME.
INCLUDING THOSE OF THE YAMABUSHI, THE MOUNTAIN WARRIORS.
THOSE ARE THE NINJA.
AND THE DARKEST, MOST DEMONIC, MOST DESPERATE OF THE NINJAS IS A JAPANESE WORD THAT MEANS "THE HAND."
WHO TO THIS VERY DAY ARE A GROUP OF TRAINED ASSASSINS THAT WILL DO ANYTHING YOU WANT IF YOU HAVE THE MONEY FOR IT.
ANYTHING.
TO ANYBODY.
THAT'S HOW FAR THEY'VE FALLEN.
SO IMAGINE HOW DESPICABLE SOMEONE HAS TO BE TO BE KICKED OUT OF THAT GROUP BEFORE THEIR TRAINING WAS COMPLETE.
AND HOW DESPICABLE THAT PERSON HAS TO BE TO SET UP SHOP HERE IN AMERICA, SPECIFICALLY TO SELL SECRETS--
ANCIENT SECRETS THAT SO FEW PEOPLE ARE ALLOWED TO KNOW--
--THAT ONE WOULD GUESS THAT AT THIS POINT, FOR THIS MODERN WORLD, THEY WERE MEANT TO BE FORGOTTEN.
AND AT THE VERY LEAST THEY WERE MEANT TO BE LEARNED AND TRAINED BY MINDS OF INTENSE DEDICATION.
NOT SOLD.
NOT CLUMSILY WHIPPED UP IN A BASEMENT APARTMENT SOMEWHERE WITHOUT ANY REAL KNOWLEDGE OF WHAT THE RAMIFICATIONS OR FALLOUT WOULD BE.
AND NOT TO BE SOLD TO LOSERS LIKE JONATHAN POWERS LOOKING TO BUY THEMSELVES A QUICK TRIP UP THE CRIMINAL FOOD CHAIN.
I DON'T KNOW WHAT EXACTLY HE HAS DONE.
I DON'T KNOW WHAT IT WAS BECAUSE I'M NOT SUPPOSED TO KNOW. NONE OF US WERE.
AND I THINK--HE DOESN'T KNOW EITHER.
BUT I KNOW IT FOUND ITS WAY BACK TO HIM.
I THINK HE'S BEEN RUNNING AROUND THE CITY NOW LOOKING FOR ANSWERS... BECAUSE WHATEVER HE HAS DONE HAS COME BACK TO HAUNT HIM AND HE DOESN'T KNOW WHAT TO DO.
I THINK HE CAME HERE LOOKING FOR SPIRITUAL CONFESSION AND WAS AS SURPRISED TO FIND HIMSELF IN A ROOM WITH HIS VICTIMS AS YOU ALL WERE TO FIND YOURSELVES WITH EACH OTHER.
AND IN HIS ARROGANT WAY HE IS ACTUALLY SITTING HERE PRETENDING TO BE PROUD OF HIMSELF WHEN IN FACT, HE IS SCARED OUT OF HIS MIND.

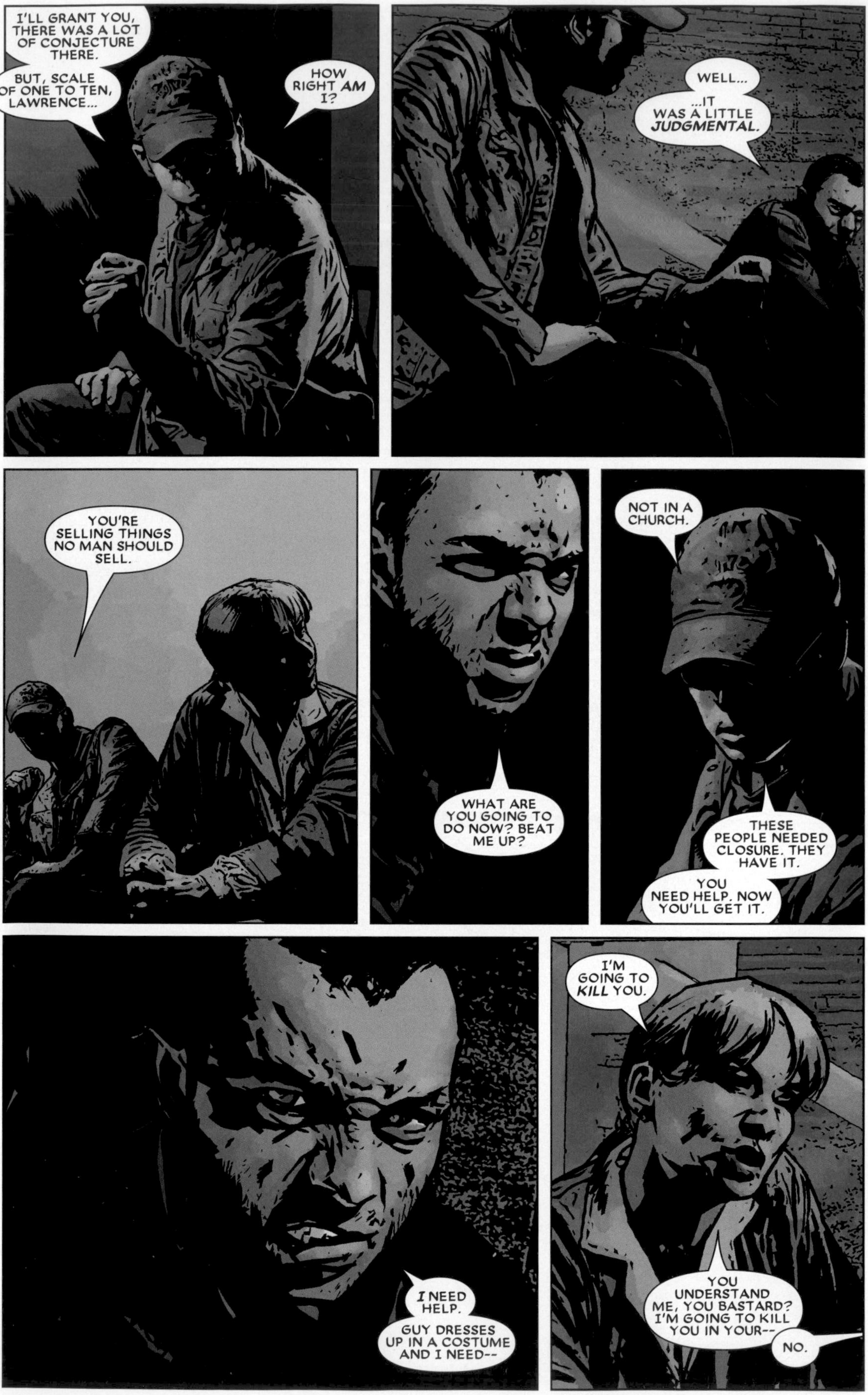
I'LL GRANT YOU, THERE WAS A LOT OF CONJECTURE THERE.
BUT, SCALE OF ONE TO TEN, LAWRENCE...
HOW RIGHT AM I?
WELL...
...IT WAS A LITTLE JUDGMENTAL.
YOU'RE SELLING THINGS NO MAN SHOULD SELL.
WHAT ARE YOU GOING TO DO NOW? BEAT ME UP?
NOT IN A CHURCH.
THESE PEOPLE NEEDED CLOSURE. THEY HAVE IT.
YOU NEED HELP. NOW YOU'LL GET IT.
I NEED HELP.
GUY DRESSES UP IN A COSTUME AND I NEED--
I'M GOING TO KILL YOU.
YOU UNDERSTAND ME, YOU BASTARD? I'M GOING TO KILL YOU IN YOUR--
NO.

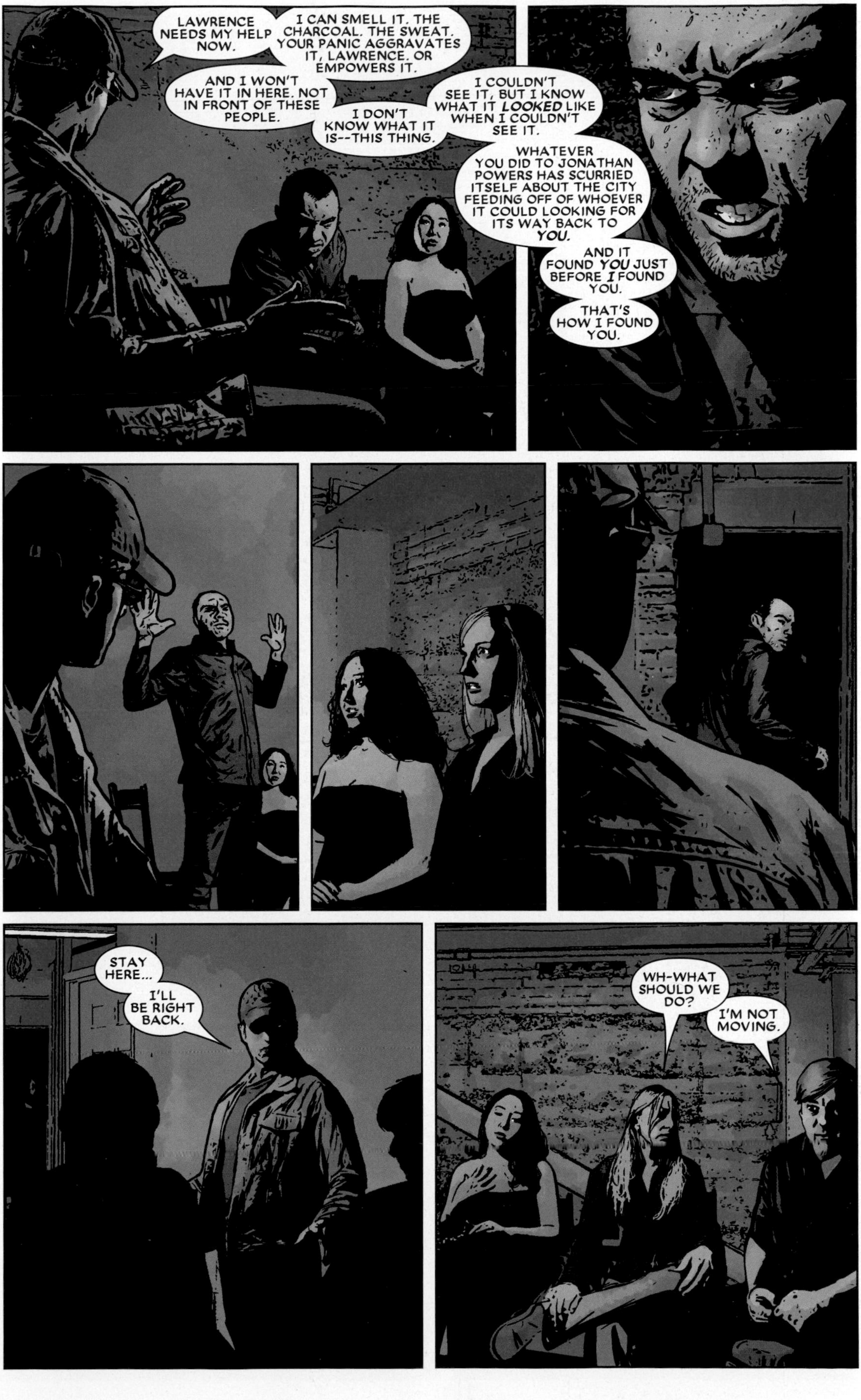
LAWRENCE NEEDS MY HELP NOW.
I CAN SMELL IT. THE CHARCOAL. THE SWEAT. YOUR PANIC AGGRAVATES IT, LAWRENCE. OR EMPOWERS IT.
AND I WON'T HAVE IT IN HERE. NOT IN FRONT OF THESE PEOPLE.
I DON'T KNOW WHAT IT IS--THIS THING.
I COULDN'T SEE IT, BUT I KNOW WHAT IT LOOKED LIKE WHEN I COULDN'T SEE IT.
WHATEVER YOU DID TO JONATHAN POWERS HAS SCURRIED ITSELF ABOUT THE CITY FEEDING OFF OF WHOEVER IT COULD LOOKING FOR ITS WAY BACK TO YOU.
AND IT FOUND YOU JUST BEFORE I FOUND YOU.
THAT'S HOW I FOUND YOU.
STAY HERE...
I'LL BE RIGHT BACK.
WH-WHAT SHOULD WE DO?
I'M NOT MOVING.

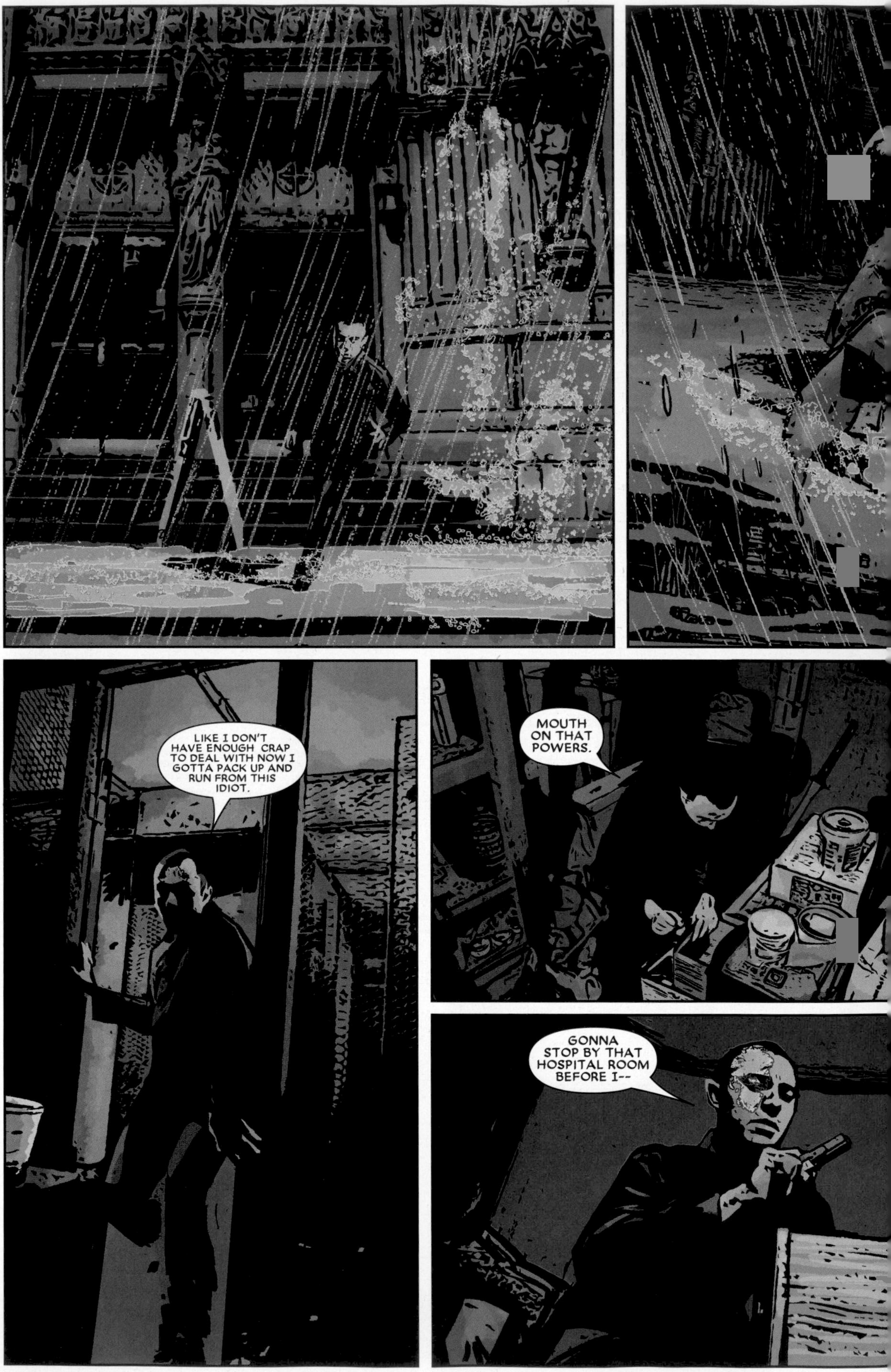
LIKE I DON'T HAVE ENOUGH CRAP TO DEAL WITH NOW I GOTTA PACK UP AND RUN FROM THIS IDIOT.
MOUTH ON THAT POWERS.
GONNA STOP BY THAT HOSPITAL ROOM BEFORE I--

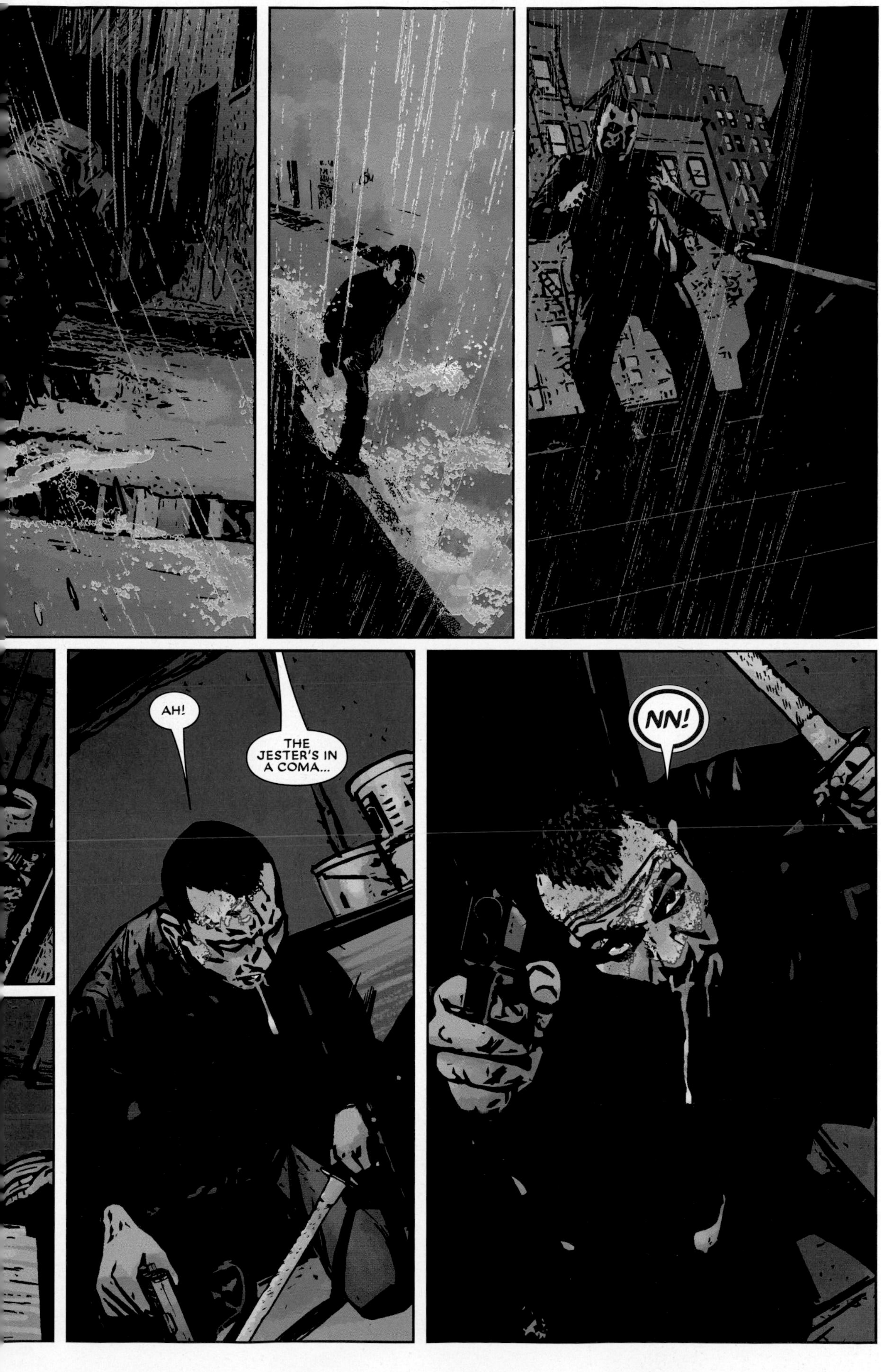
AH!
THE JESTER'S IN A COMA...
NN!

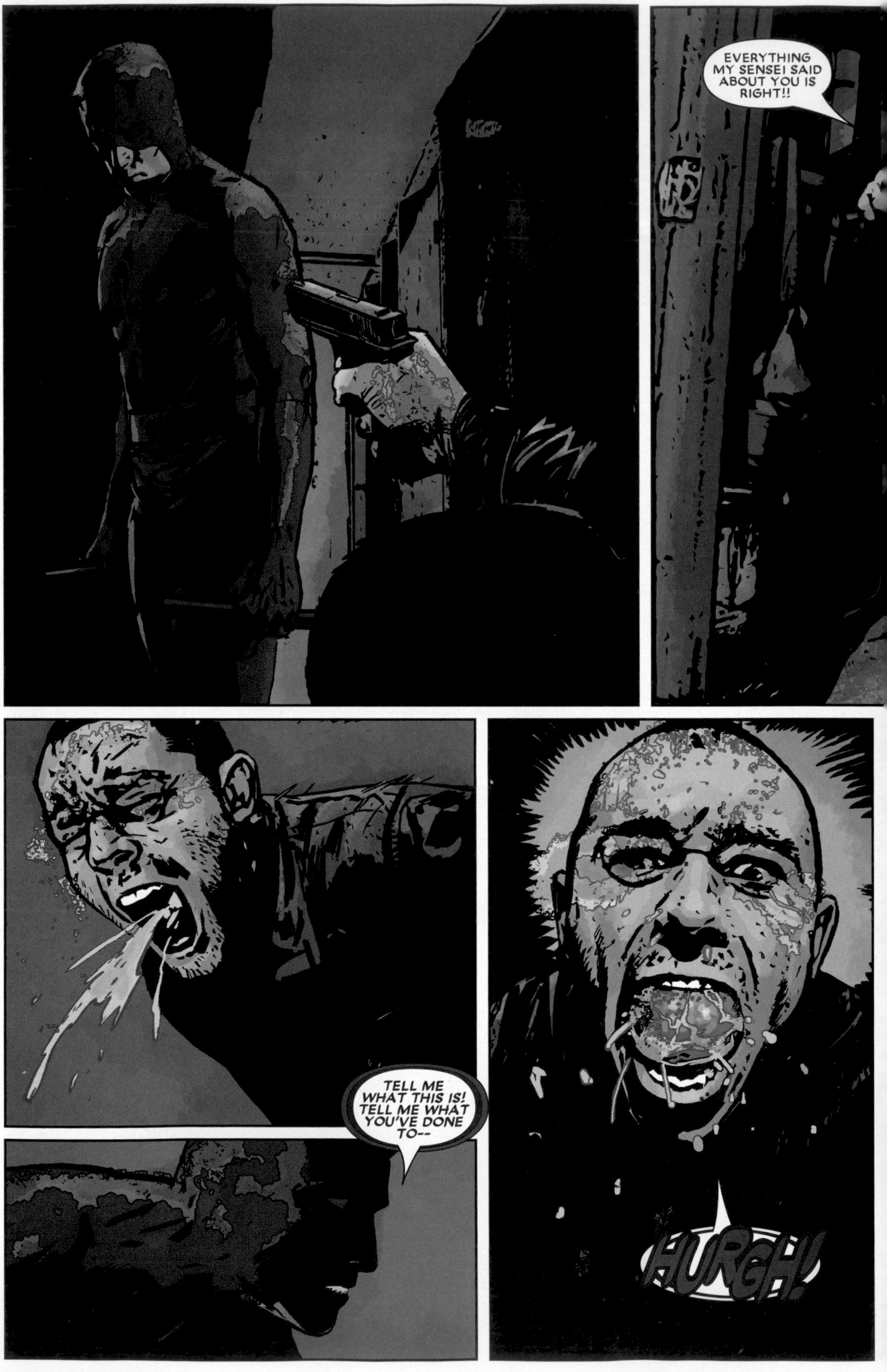
EVERYTHING MY SENSEI SAID ABOUT YOU IS RIGHT!!
TELL ME WHAT THIS IS! TELL ME WHAT YOU'VE DONE TO--
HURGH!

YOU *REEEEALLY* ARE A SELF-RIGHTEOUS #$@%!!

I KNOW PEOPLE MORE SKILLED IN THE DARK ARTS THAN YOU WHO CAN *HELP* YOU WITH THIS.

WHAT HAVE YOU DONE? WHAT'S INSIDE YOU?

URK!

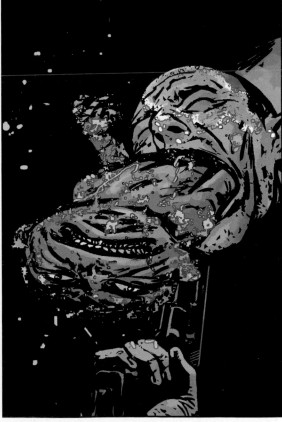

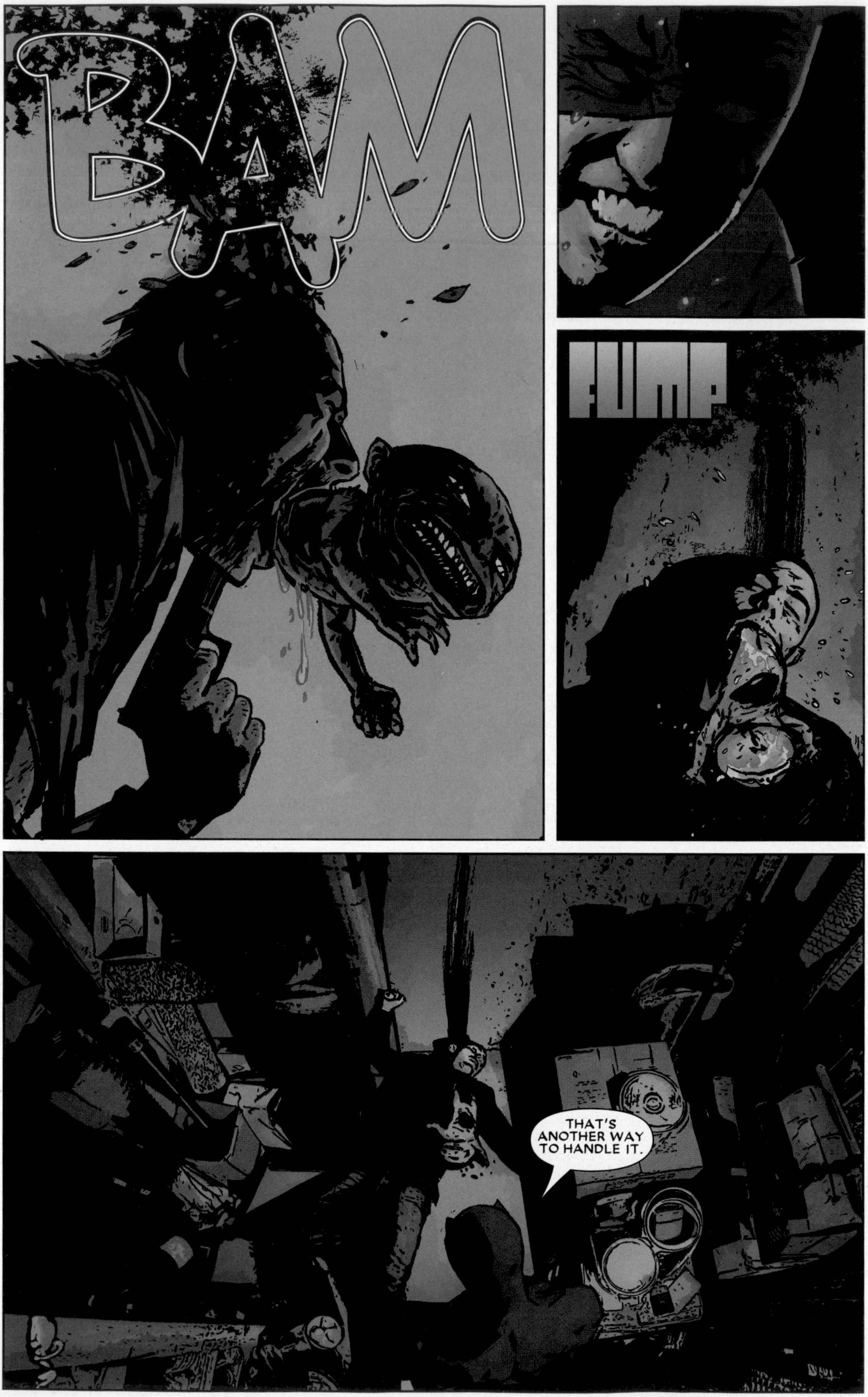
BAM
FUMP
THAT'S ANOTHER WAY TO HANDLE IT.

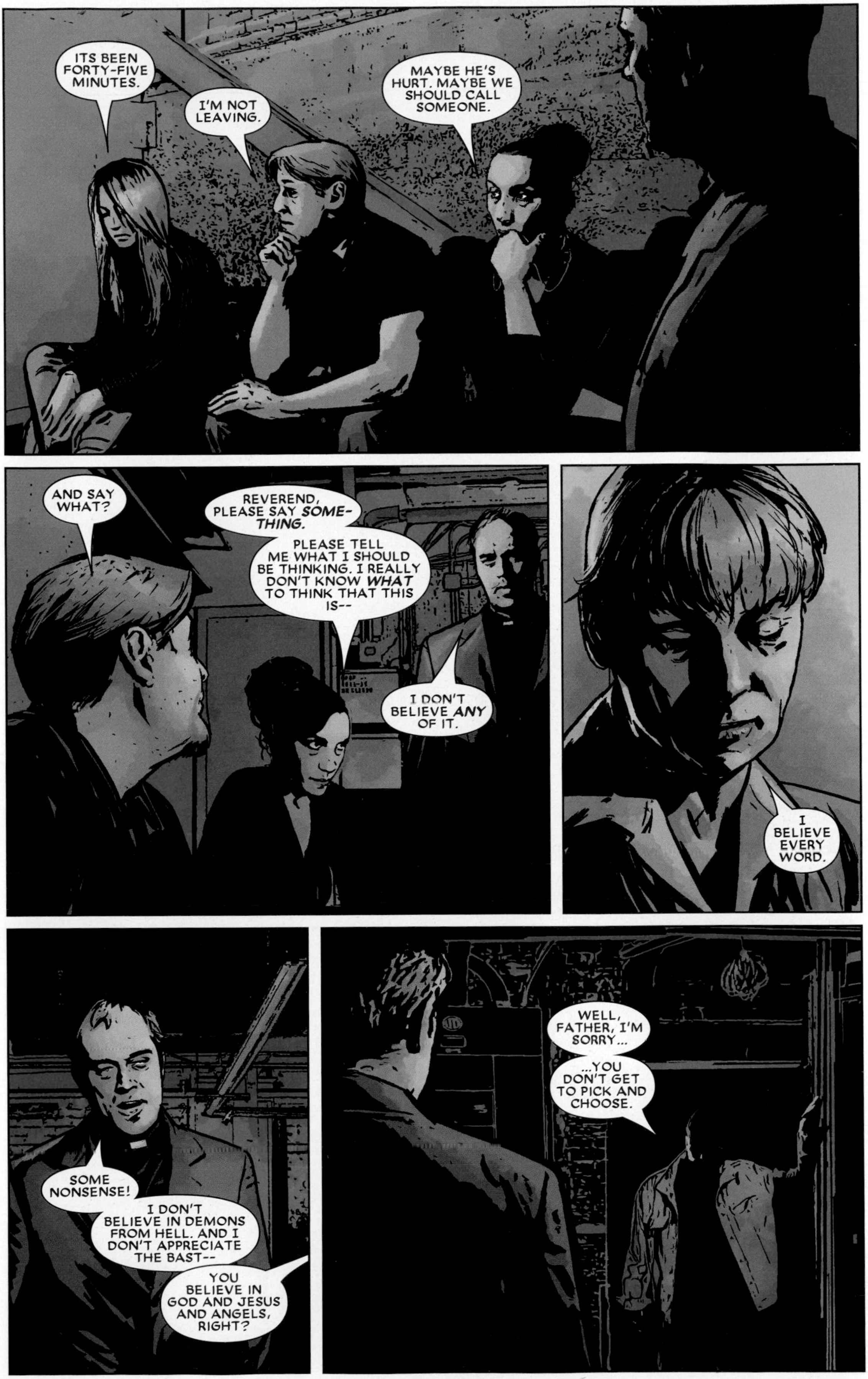
ITS BEEN FORTY-FIVE MINUTES.
I'M NOT LEAVING.
MAYBE HE'S HURT. MAYBE WE SHOULD CALL SOMEONE.
AND SAY WHAT?
REVEREND, PLEASE SAY *SOMETHING.*
PLEASE TELL ME WHAT I SHOULD BE THINKING. I REALLY DON'T KNOW *WHAT* TO THINK THAT THIS IS--
I DON'T BELIEVE *ANY* OF IT.
I BELIEVE EVERY WORD.
SOME NONSENSE!
I DON'T BELIEVE IN DEMONS FROM HELL. AND I DON'T APPRECIATE THE BAST--
YOU BELIEVE IN GOD AND JESUS AND ANGELS, RIGHT?
WELL, FATHER, I'M SORRY...
...YOU DON'T GET TO PICK AND CHOOSE.

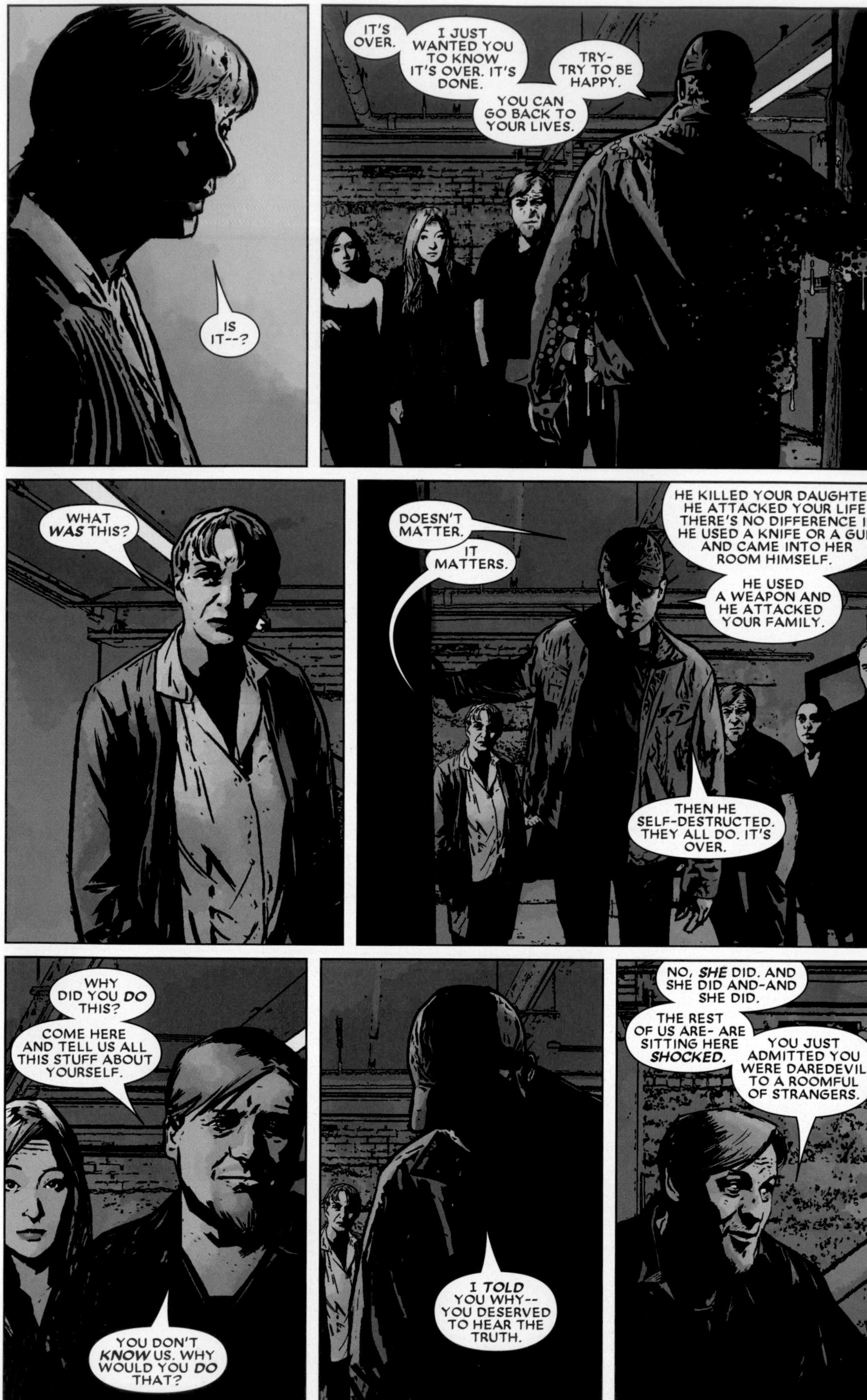
IS IT--?
IT'S OVER.
I JUST WANTED YOU TO KNOW IT'S OVER. IT'S DONE.
YOU CAN GO BACK TO YOUR LIVES.
TRY- TRY TO BE HAPPY.
WHAT *WAS* THIS?
DOESN'T MATTER.
IT MATTERS.
HE KILLED YOUR DAUGHTER. HE ATTACKED YOUR LIFE. THERE'S NO DIFFERENCE IF HE USED A KNIFE OR A GUN AND CAME INTO HER ROOM HIMSELF.
HE USED A WEAPON AND HE ATTACKED YOUR FAMILY.
THEN HE SELF-DESTRUCTED. THEY ALL DO. IT'S OVER.
WHY DID YOU *DO* THIS?
COME HERE AND TELL US ALL THIS STUFF ABOUT YOURSELF.
YOU DON'T *KNOW* US. WHY WOULD YOU *DO* THAT?
I *TOLD* YOU WHY-- YOU DESERVED TO HEAR THE TRUTH.
NO, *SHE* DID. AND SHE DID AND-AND SHE DID.
THE REST OF US ARE- ARE SITTING HERE *SHOCKED.*
YOU JUST ADMITTED YOU WERE DAREDEVIL TO A ROOMFUL OF STRANGERS.

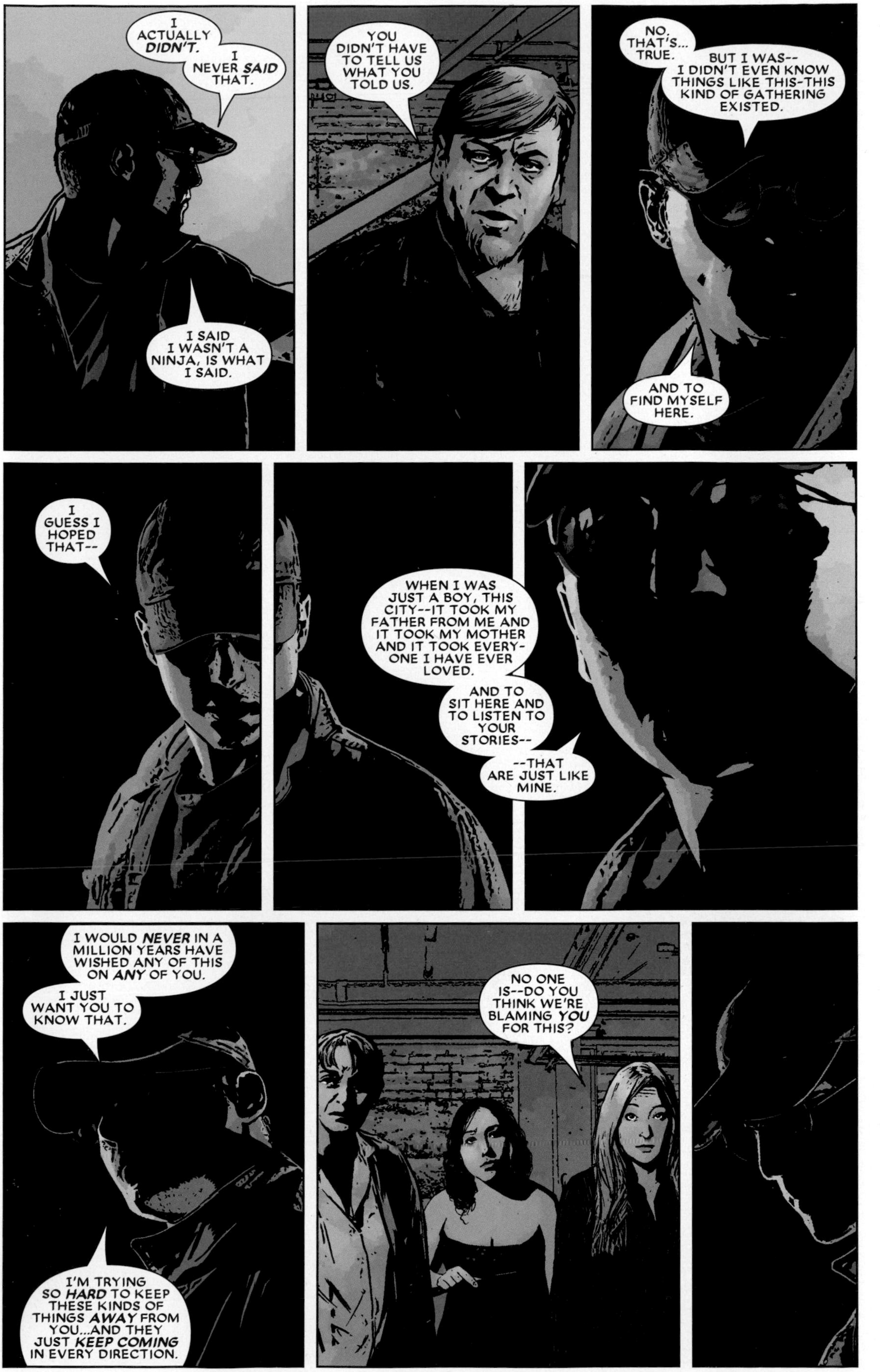

I ACTUALLY DIDN'T.
I NEVER SAID THAT.
I SAID I WASN'T A NINJA, IS WHAT I SAID.
YOU DIDN'T HAVE TO TELL US WHAT YOU TOLD US.
NO. THAT'S... TRUE.
BUT I WAS-- I DIDN'T EVEN KNOW THINGS LIKE THIS-THIS KIND OF GATHERING EXISTED.
AND TO FIND MYSELF HERE.
I GUESS I HOPED THAT--
WHEN I WAS JUST A BOY, THIS CITY--IT TOOK MY FATHER FROM ME AND IT TOOK MY MOTHER AND IT TOOK EVERY-ONE I HAVE EVER LOVED.
AND TO SIT HERE AND TO LISTEN TO YOUR STORIES--
--THAT ARE JUST LIKE MINE.
I WOULD NEVER IN A MILLION YEARS HAVE WISHED ANY OF THIS ON ANY OF YOU.
I JUST WANT YOU TO KNOW THAT.
I'M TRYING SO HARD TO KEEP THESE KINDS OF THINGS AWAY FROM YOU...AND THEY JUST KEEP COMING IN EVERY DIRECTION.
NO ONE IS--DO YOU THINK WE'RE BLAMING YOU FOR THIS?

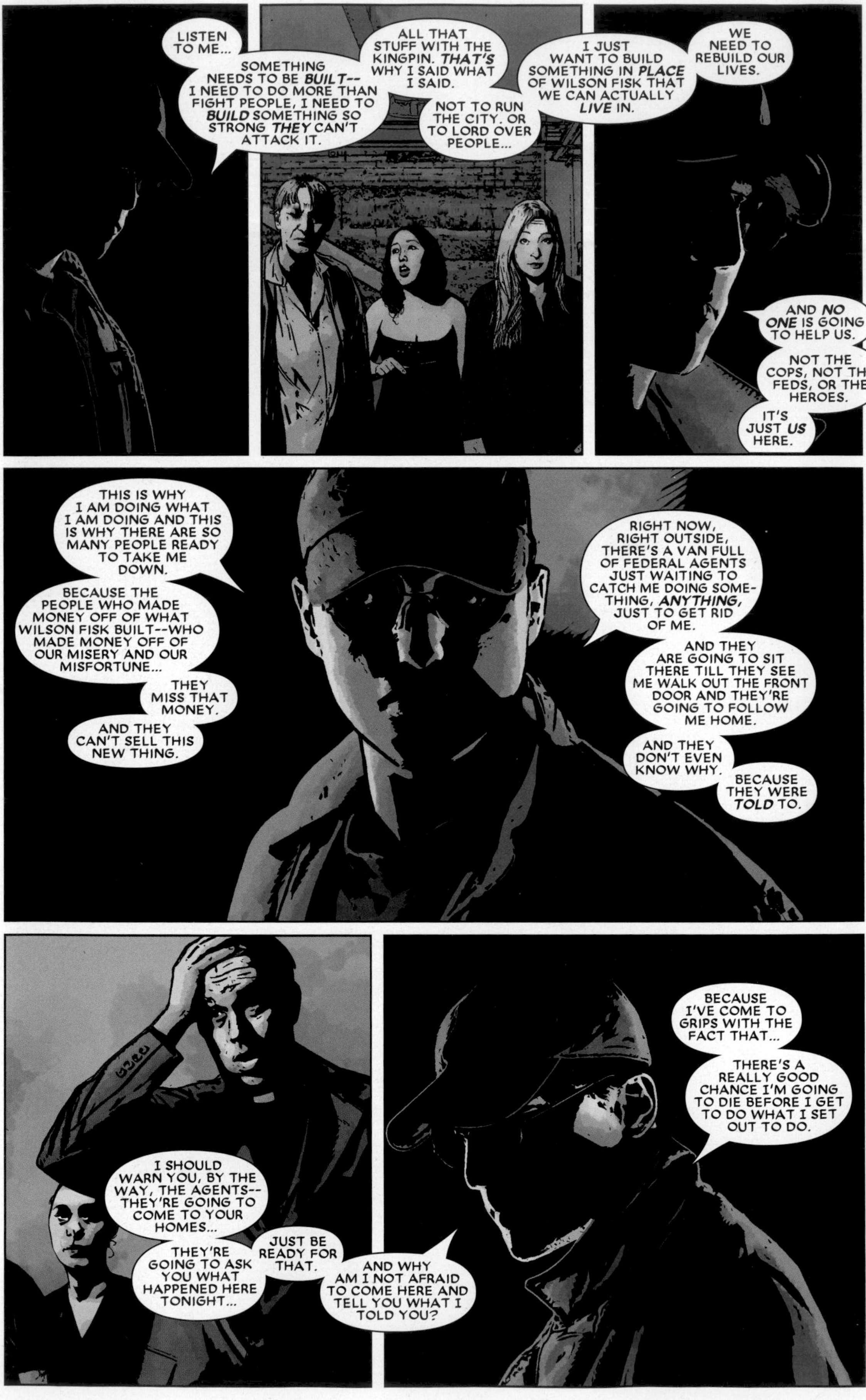

LISTEN TO ME...
SOMETHING NEEDS TO BE BUILT-- I NEED TO DO MORE THAN FIGHT PEOPLE, I NEED TO BUILD SOMETHING SO STRONG THEY CAN'T ATTACK IT.
ALL THAT STUFF WITH THE KINGPIN. THAT'S WHY I SAID WHAT I SAID.
NOT TO RUN THE CITY. OR TO LORD OVER PEOPLE...
I JUST WANT TO BUILD SOMETHING IN PLACE OF WILSON FISK THAT WE CAN ACTUALLY LIVE IN.
WE NEED TO REBUILD OUR LIVES.
AND NO ONE IS GOING TO HELP US.
NOT THE COPS, NOT THE FEDS, OR THE HEROES.
IT'S JUST US HERE.
THIS IS WHY I AM DOING WHAT I AM DOING AND THIS IS WHY THERE ARE SO MANY PEOPLE READY TO TAKE ME DOWN.
BECAUSE THE PEOPLE WHO MADE MONEY OFF OF WHAT WILSON FISK BUILT--WHO MADE MONEY OFF OF OUR MISERY AND OUR MISFORTUNE...
THEY MISS THAT MONEY.
AND THEY CAN'T SELL THIS NEW THING.
RIGHT NOW, RIGHT OUTSIDE, THERE'S A VAN FULL OF FEDERAL AGENTS JUST WAITING TO CATCH ME DOING SOME-THING, ANYTHING, JUST TO GET RID OF ME.
AND THEY ARE GOING TO SIT THERE TILL THEY SEE ME WALK OUT THE FRONT DOOR AND THEY'RE GOING TO FOLLOW ME HOME.
AND THEY DON'T EVEN KNOW WHY.
BECAUSE THEY WERE TOLD TO.
I SHOULD WARN YOU, BY THE WAY, THE AGENTS-- THEY'RE GOING TO COME TO YOUR HOMES...
THEY'RE GOING TO ASK YOU WHAT HAPPENED HERE TONIGHT...
JUST BE READY FOR THAT.
AND WHY AM I NOT AFRAID TO COME HERE AND TELL YOU WHAT I TOLD YOU?
BECAUSE I'VE COME TO GRIPS WITH THE FACT THAT...
THERE'S A REALLY GOOD CHANCE I'M GOING TO DIE BEFORE I GET TO DO WHAT I SET OUT TO DO.

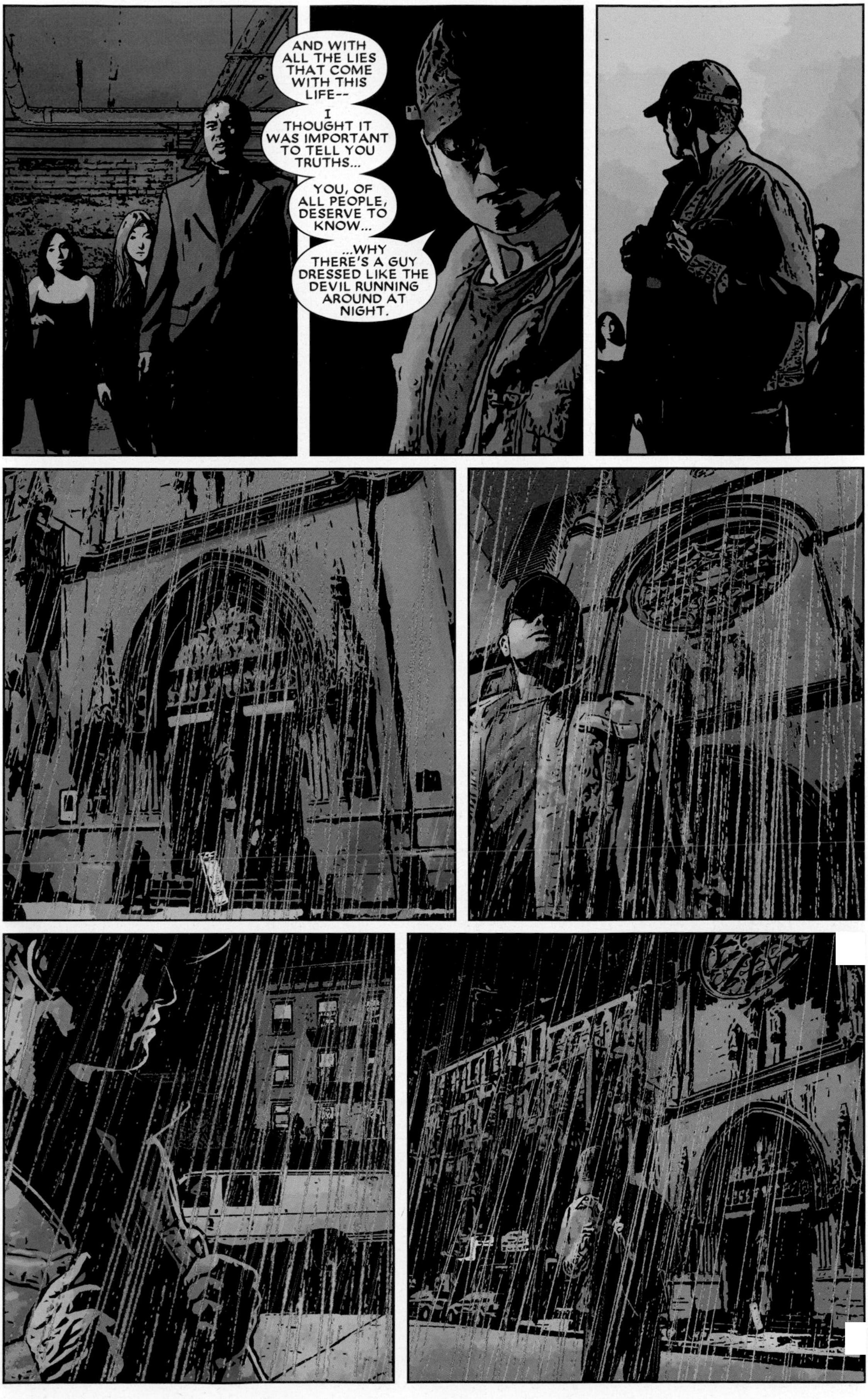
AND WITH ALL THE LIES THAT COME WITH THIS LIFE--
I THOUGHT IT WAS IMPORTANT TO TELL YOU TRUTHS...
YOU, OF ALL PEOPLE, DESERVE TO KNOW...
...WHY THERE'S A GUY DRESSED LIKE THE DEVIL RUNNING AROUND AT NIGHT.

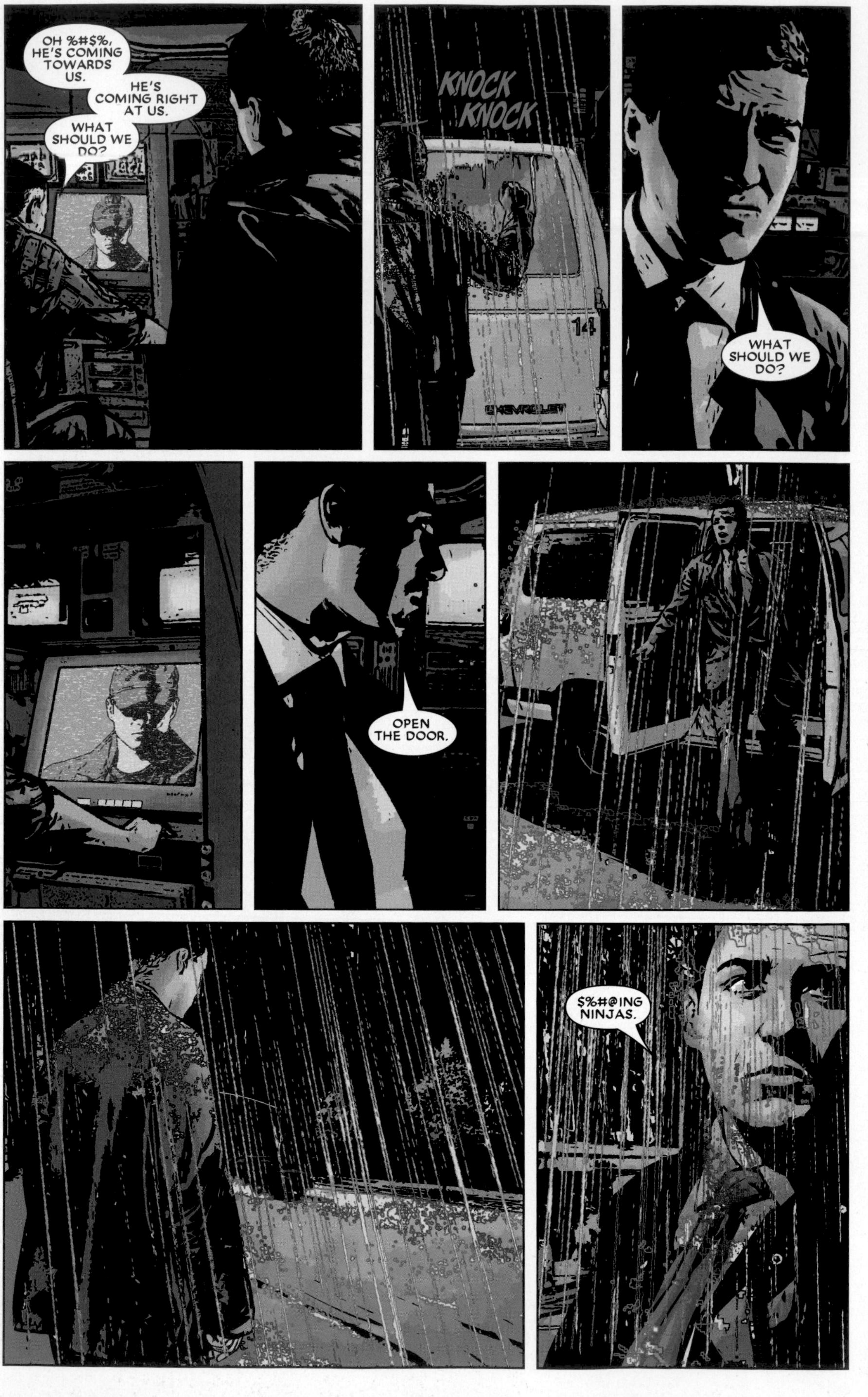
OH %#$%, HE'S COMING TOWARDS US.
HE'S COMING RIGHT AT US.
WHAT SHOULD WE DO?
KNOCK KNOCK
WHAT SHOULD WE DO?
OPEN THE DOOR.
$%#@ING NINJAS.

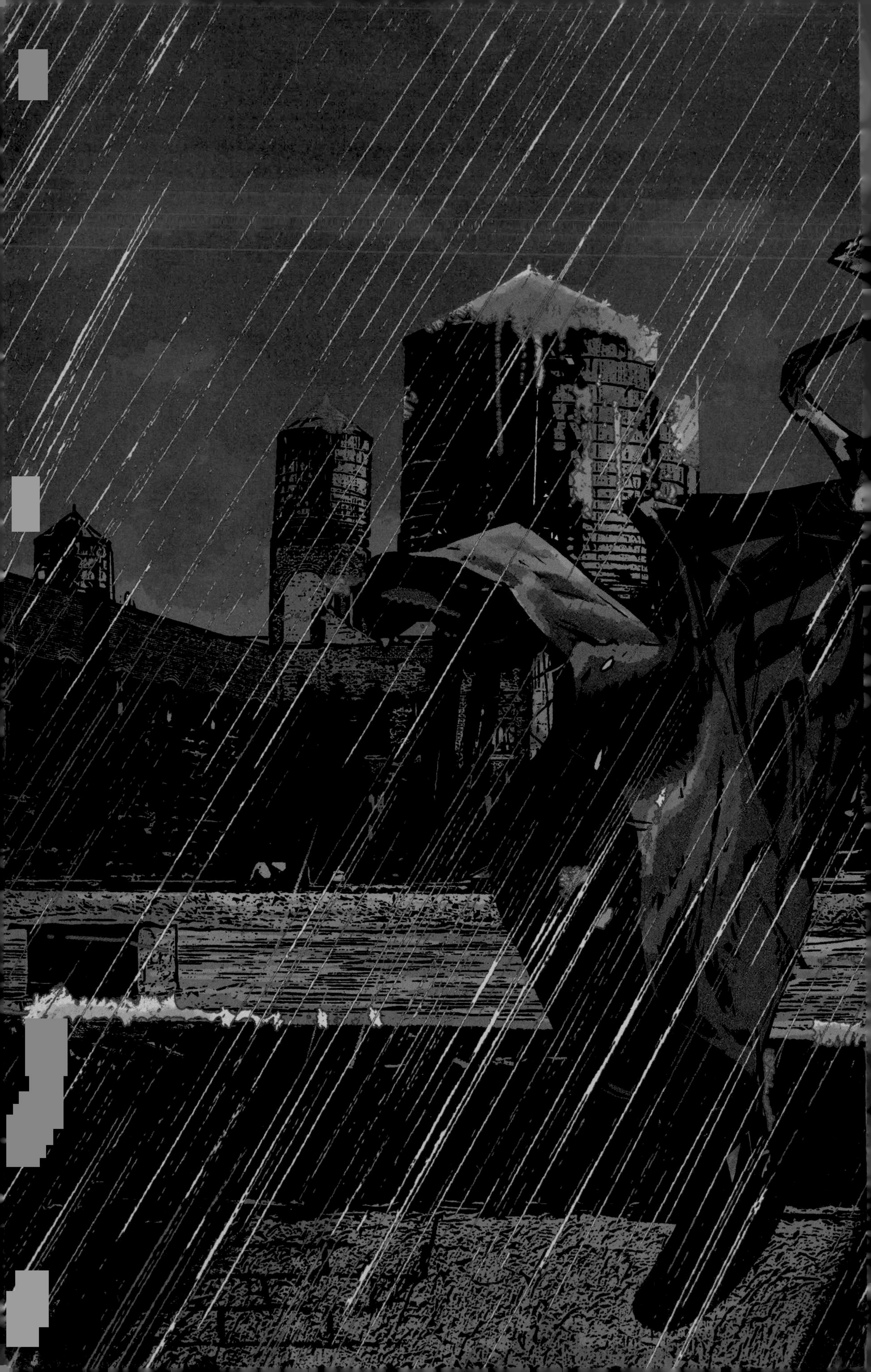

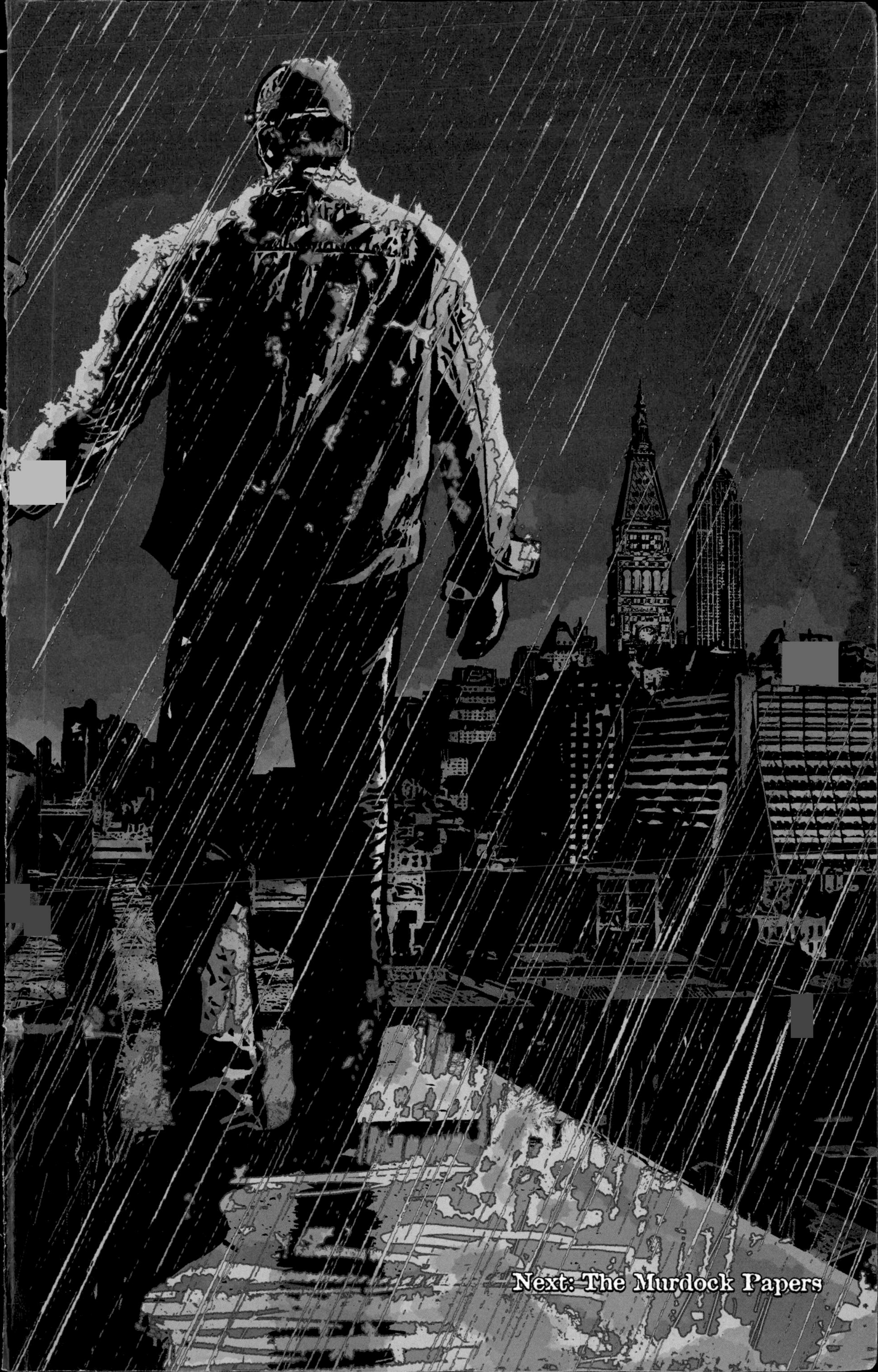
Next: The Murdock Papers